Junior Great Books®

Series 3   Book Two

Leader's Edition

The interpretive discussion program that moves
students toward excellence in reading comprehension,
critical thinking, and writing

Junior Great Books®

Series 3   Book Two

Leader's Edition

THE GREAT BOOKS FOUNDATION

A nonprofit educational organization

Copyright © 2006 by The Great Books Foundation
Chicago, Illinois
All rights reserved
ISBN 1-933147-19-9

First Printing
9 8 7 6 5 4 3 2 1
Printed in China

Published and distributed by

THE GREAT BOOKS FOUNDATION
A nonprofit educational organization
35 East Wacker Drive, Suite 2300
Chicago, IL 60601-2205

www.greatbooks.org

Contents

PROGRAM OVERVIEW

UNITS

APPENDIXES

About Junior Great Books

Welcome! This edition of Junior Great Books preserves the features that have made the program unique and exciting—a focus on high-quality literature and student-centered discussion—while providing additional support for the discussion leader and tools for teaching specific language arts skills. Whether you and your students are familiar with Junior Great Books or are new to the program, you will find that it provides a superb framework for teaching reading comprehension, critical thinking, and writing, all in the context of students sharing ideas about great literature.

THE JUNIOR GREAT BOOKS METHOD OF LEARNING

The Junior Great Books program employs a method of interpretive reading and discussion known as Shared Inquiry.™ This distinctive approach to learning enables leaders—the teachers, parent volunteers, and other adults who lead Junior Great Books programs—to foster a vibrant environment in which students acquire the habits and strategies of self-reliant thinkers, readers, and learners. Through their own curiosity and attentive questioning, leaders serve as partners in inquiry with their students, helping the group work together to discover meaning in a selection and to build interpretations. The process reaches its fullest expression in Shared Inquiry discussion, where leaders and students think and talk about an interpretive question that arises from a particular story.

Junior Great Books has been widely recognized as an exemplary program by numerous independent educational organizations for its research base and positive effect on student achievement and interest level in reading. Research demonstrates that regular, sustained use of the program improves student achievement. Reading and critical-thinking skills were measurably improved for students across the academic spectrum—from at-risk to highly capable—as both strong and struggling readers engaged in an inquiry process that unlocks even the most challenging texts.

JUNIOR GREAT BOOKS FEATURES

HIGH-QUALITY LITERATURE. Junior Great Books includes outstanding works of literature by award-winning authors. The stories are specially selected for their engaging, vivid writing and their ability to support multiple interpretations.

IN-DEPTH READING, CRITICAL-THINKING, AND WRITING ACTIVITIES. In the course of a semester, students will read ten stories, exploring each through a sequence of activities that includes two readings, directed note taking, Shared Inquiry discussion, and writing. Junior Great Books activities have language arts objectives, stated in clear, standards-based language, in reading comprehension, critical thinking, and writing (see pages xi–xiv for more about the program's focus on these key learning strands).

FURTHER SUPPORT FOR THE WRITING PROCESS. Expository and creative writing activities in each unit emphasize the writing process and the exploration of writing forms. Student writing is guided by graphic organizers, prompts, and other tools.

TEACHING AND LEARNING IN STAGES. Objectives in the three learning strands—reading comprehension, critical thinking, and writing—advance in difficulty and sophistication over three stages in the course of a semester, ensuring that students achieve success early and develop mastery over time. Each stage begins with a summary of learning goals and key features. At the end of each stage, activities are provided to help students review concepts, compare ideas across stories, and integrate their skills. Book Two introduces strategies and objectives that extend the learning begun in Book One.

LEADER LEARNING. Through activity instructions, marginal notes, and boxed features, this Leader's Edition provides regular opportunities to develop your questioning skills and support for your development as a Shared Inquiry leader. The Great Books Foundation also offers a series of professional development workshops, on-site consultation days, and planning sessions designed to introduce leaders to Shared Inquiry and to provide continuing support.

INFORMAL AND FORMAL ASSESSMENTS. Student learning mini-rubrics in each unit help you make quick, informal assessments of your students' levels of success in meeting an activity's main objective. Story comprehension tests, instructions for grading discussion participation and writing, and leader reflection guidelines help you assess your students' progress as well as your own.

JUNIOR GREAT BOOKS MATERIALS

THE STUDENT ANTHOLOGY. Praised for their rich language and international range, and chosen carefully for their ability to support multiple interpretations, the stories in Junior Great Books capture students' attention and imagination and engage the best of their thinking. Progressing in reading level, conceptual complexity, and length throughout the series, the stories are the foundation for a thoughtful process of reading, discussion, and writing.

READER'S JOURNAL. The Reader's Journal gives students a convenient and enjoyable way to collect their thoughts and ideas about each story. Students draw or write in response to the story, practice specific reading comprehension skills, and respond to discussion. The Reader's Journal also contains organizational tools for prewriting and drafting, a glossary of challenging words found in the student anthology, and a Writing Notebook section for students' revised written material.

CDs. These professionally recorded audio versions of each selection give students another chance to listen to the story as it is read aloud with fluency, and help less-proficient readers increase their comprehension of the story.

LEADER'S EDITION. Each Leader's Edition contains the full text of the student anthology, with marginal notes and definitions for selected vocabulary; detailed support for a full complement of activities for each story; preparation suggestions for Shared Inquiry discussion; and assessment tools and rubrics. The ten units and three review sections constitute a progressive program of both instruction and learning, enabling you to teach reading comprehension, critical-thinking, and writing skills in a systematic way.

A SAMPLE PAGE FROM THE LEADER'S EDITION

Each Junior Great Books unit contains activities that provide systematic instruction and practice in reading comprehension strategies, critical thinking, and writing—all in the context of discussing high-quality literature. Each activity is clearly presented on its own page or pages for the leader's easy use.

A student learning objective is clearly defined at the start of each activity.

The student learning mini-rubric allows for a quick, informal assessment of student understanding while you conduct activities.

Tips, teaching notes, and activity rationales in the margins provide a context for conducting the activity.

This icon alerts you when an activity calls for students' Reader's Journals.

The amount of time needed for each activity is clearly marked to aid in planning.

Concise descriptions give you an overview of what you and your students will be doing in the activity.

Clear, detailed instructions guide you step by step through each activity.

SESSION 4

Shared Inquiry Discussion (45 minutes)

Students discover meaning in the story by discussing an interpretive question.

STUDENT LEARNING OBJECTIVE

CRITICAL THINKING: To answer an interpretive question with clear and specific ideas

LOOK FOR STUDENTS TO

Offer a thoughtful answer to an interpretive question

Explain their answer to an interpretive question

Elaborate on their ideas about an interpretive question

MODELING CURIOSITY

During the discussion, take advantage of the chance to be yourself. Allow your students' ideas to delight, overwhelm, confuse, or enlighten you. You are providing them with a model of an active, curious mind, eager to learn alongside them as everyone works together to figure out the story's meaning. Asking follow-up questions not only challenges your students to do their own thinking—it lets them know that you take their ideas seriously.

Use the Leader Discussion Planner on the facing page to prepare yourself for Shared Inquiry discussion. To prepare your group, have everyone sit in a circle or a square; remind them of the five discussion guidelines and any behavioral guidelines you want to share. Then follow these steps to conduct the discussion:

1. Write the focus question on the board and have students copy it on the Building Your Answer page of the Reader's Journal (page 40).

2. Give students a few minutes to review the story and to write down an answer.

3. Begin the discussion by asking the focus question. On your seating chart, keep track of students' participation and ideas.

4. Lead the discussion by asking follow-up questions to help students explain their ideas (see sample questions in your Leader Discussion Planner, page 133), provide evidence, and respond to one another. Aim to have the discussion last 20 to 30 minutes.

5. As the discussion winds down, have students finish the Building Your Answer page. Then ask volunteers to share what they wrote.

6. Spend a few minutes talking about the discussion. Ask students what they liked about it, what was hard about it, what they think makes a good discussion, and what might go better next time.

132   STAGE 5 · UNIT 4

Junior Great Books Activities

Each semester of Junior Great Books is composed of ten story units. Work on a unit consists of two readings of the story, questioning and note-taking activities, Shared Inquiry discussion, and writing activities or further related reading. Following is a typical schedule for a unit's work. Activities are grouped into **sessions** to indicate those activities that we recommend be done together. A session is generally 45 to 50 minutes, about the length of a traditional class period.

In this book, some sessions will need to be lengthened, as they feature longer stories or more advanced exploration of interpretive questions. Suggested time allotments and tips on how to handle longer sessions appear in those particular activities.

SESSION 1
- Prereading
- First reading
- Sharing questions

SESSION 2
- Second reading with directed notes

SESSION 3
- Vocabulary

SESSION 4
- Shared Inquiry discussion

SESSION 5 OPTIONS
- Expository writing
- Creative writing
- Curriculum Connections

Additional implementation options and information about pacing is found on pages xx–xxii of this overview. In each unit, students explore a single story through the sequence of activities detailed on the next page.

Think-Alouds in the margins of the Leader's Edition story help you model reading comprehension strategies as you read the story aloud to the students for the first time.

Second reading activities in some units include **reader's theater** sidebars, which provide basic techniques to help students dramatize parts of the story.

In the Shared Inquiry discussion activity, **Overheard in the Classroom** offers examples of dialogues between students and leaders that are characteristic of Shared Inquiry discussions. Overheard in the Classroom also appears in the vocabulary activity to illustrate target words.

The **prereading** activity engages students in a brief discussion of a topic related to the story, or invites them to preview features of the story they are about to read.

In the **first reading**, you read the story aloud while students take simple notes related to a featured reading comprehension strategy.

The **sharing questions** activity encourages students to ask questions that reflect their curiosity—or struggles—after a first reading of the story, and to write down a question that particularly intrigues or confuses them (their "keeper question"). In Book Two of Series 3, students concentrate on identifying and exploring interpretive questions. Students' keeper questions are also explored in greater depth, as students discuss the elements of a good keeper question and locate relevant evidence in the story.

The **second reading with directed notes** gives students an opportunity to read or listen to the story a second time. Students take notes in response to an issue or element in the story. After the reading, students explore their notes in pairs, small groups, or with the whole class.

In Stage 6 of Book Two, the leader can choose from among two note-taking options, tailoring the activity to the needs and interests of students. Eventually, if the leader wishes, students can help choose the note-taking activity.

The **vocabulary** activity, based on *Bringing Words to Life: Robust Vocabulary Instruction* by I. L. Beck, M. G. McKeown, and L. Kucan (New York: The Guilford Press, 2002), features three words from each story that are valuable to understanding the story and appropriate for grade-level vocabulary development. Students investigate the meaning of these words by drawing on their own knowledge and the story context to hear and use them in a variety of ways.

Each **Shared Inquiry discussion** begins with independent thought: students write their own answers to an interpretive question that you pose as the focus question for discussion. Guided by your follow-up questions, students then discuss and develop their ideas, supporting them with evidence from the story. As the discussion comes to a close, students individually record their conclusions in writing.

In the **expository** and **creative writing** activities, students are given a writing assignment to extend and express their thinking about a story. Building on the explicit strategies for prewriting and drafting that they learned in Book One, students are now introduced to literary terms and concepts that enrich their writing and further illuminate story themes and ideas. Students also explore a variety of writing forms including essays, letters, poems, and stories.

The **Curriculum Connections** pages, at the end of each unit, list other works by the story's author and resources that link the story to other subjects in your curriculum.

Three or four units compose a stage of learning in the Junior Great Books program; there are three stages per semester. At the end of each stage, **Reflect and Connect** gives your students a chance to review the reading, writing, and discussion activities they have completed so far. The Reflect and Connect section also allows you to examine students' progress in meeting the learning objectives for that particular stage. Specific topics for student and leader reflection include: reading comprehension strategies, Shared Inquiry discussion, story-to-story comparisons, and writing revision. Reflect and Connect also directs you to the assessment kit (for more information about assessment, see page xvi).

Junior Great Books and Learning Strands

Each unit in Junior Great Books presents an engaging sequence of activities that clearly and consistently develop students' reading comprehension, critical thinking, and writing. Most activities in the sequence involve two or even all three of these learning strands, but for ease of planning and assessment, only one strand is explicitly highlighted in each activity's student learning objective box. Shaded diamonds (♦) below indicate which learning strand is highlighted as an objective in each activity. Open diamonds (◇) indicate which of the other learning strands play a significant role in the activity.

		LEARNING STRANDS BY ACTIVITY		
SESSION	ACTIVITIES	READING COMPREHENSION	CRITICAL THINKING	WRITING
1	Prereading	♦		
	First reading	♦	◇	◇
	Sharing questions	♦	◇	◇
2	Second reading with directed notes	♦	◇	◇
3	Vocabulary	♦		
4	Shared Inquiry discussion	◇	♦	◇
5	Writing	◇	◇	♦

It is important to remember that, while only three language arts learning strands are featured as objectives, listening and speaking skills are integral to the Junior Great Books program. For a broader look at the progression across strands, see the Series 3 Learning Goals chart (appendix B, page 421).

READING COMPREHENSION

Students develop effective reading comprehension strategies by having repeated opportunities to practice them for different purposes across a wide variety of activities. The first five activities in each unit (Sessions 1–3) have a strong focus on reading comprehension.

◆ The **prereading** activity sets the stage for students to begin to construct meaning in a story. Students explore their knowledge of story concepts or become familiar with a concept that may be new to them.

◆ The **first reading** provides explicit instruction in essential reading comprehension strategies. A different strategy is featured at each stage of the program.

READING COMPREHENSION STRATEGIES

BOOK TWO

Stage 4: Making inferences

Stage 5: Determining important ideas

Stage 6: Synthesizing

◆ During the **sharing questions** activity, students pose questions about things they find puzzling or curious after the first reading. Asking questions keeps students closely engaged with the story and clears up any confusion.

◆ When students read or listen to the story again in the **second reading with directed notes**, they mark passages related to specific issues or elements in the story. Rereading with a purpose and taking notes helps students practice finding evidence and explaining how it supports a conclusion about the story—key steps to becoming strong readers. While the highlighted objective involves reading comprehension, this activity incorporates many of the elements of critical thinking featured in the Shared Inquiry discussion.

◆ The **vocabulary** activity focuses on selected words that are especially important to comprehension of the story. The activity encourages students' active engagement in constructing the meaning of words, using their own experience and the story context.

While reading comprehension is not the highlighted objective in Shared Inquiry discussion and the writing activities, it is an important component of both. When engaged in Shared Inquiry discussion, students must consistently return to the story to support their ideas, gaining understanding through multiple readings of key passages. Students also practice comprehension strategies through the writing activities, closely examining elements of a story, or their own interpretations of it, as they take prewriting notes and develop drafts.

CRITICAL THINKING

The Junior Great Books program identifies three basic elements of critical thinking about a story:

IDEA—generating and clarifying ideas about a story's meaning

EVIDENCE—supporting and checking these ideas, based on what is in the story

RESPONSE—considering alternative ideas and adjusting an interpretation

Each unit focuses on one of these elements, rotating this focus from unit to unit within each stage. Thus, in each stage of the program, your students practice all three elements of critical thinking—most explicitly through Shared Inquiry discussion, but during other activities as well.

At the heart of the Junior Great Books program is **Shared Inquiry discussion**, where students explore and discuss their own answers to questions about a story—questions that have more than one reasonable answer, thus reflecting multiple meanings in a story. By focusing on such questions, students are encouraged to think critically and deeply about the meaning of what they read, and to use evidence from the story to support their ideas.

By participating in Shared Inquiry discussion, students engage naturally and consistently in critical thinking. As they learn to build their answer to an interpretive question, students form a model for exploring a story's meaning that can guide their individual reading later on. Furthermore, by collaborating with classmates during discussions, students experience a model of productive and respectful public discourse—an experience that can guide, inform, and enrich their thinking in school and in life.

The sharing questions, second reading with directed notes, and writing activities also contribute strongly to critical thinking. While sharing questions, students progress from recognizing different types of questions to concentrating on those that address interpretive issues; this progression reflects sophisticated critical thinking. Each note-taking assignment during the second reading is based on an important issue or element in the story. Sharing notes with classmates, aided by your questions, makes students aware that there is more than one way to understand a story.

The second reading's Spotlight on Follow-Up Questions and the student learning mini-rubrics also address the three basic elements of critical thinking to help you encourage and assess your students' progress. The expository and creative writing assignments allow students to render their interpretations of a story in writing.

WRITING

Writing is an integral part of the Junior Great Books program. At the end of each unit, options for **expository writing** (Writing to Explain in the Reader's Journal) and **creative writing** (Writing to Explore in the Reader's Journal) complement reading and critical thinking by helping students extend or consolidate their ideas into more complete interpretations.

The writing activities in Book Two, as in Book One, encourage students to draw upon the thoughtful understanding of the story they gained from Shared Inquiry discussion, but unlike the activities in Book One, students do not always work closely with the focus question to develop written drafts. Instead, students are asked to integrate their understanding of the story with something new—an important literary concept pertinent to the story.

In the expository writing activities, work with these literary elements advances in sophistication. Eventually, students are asked to explain how and why particular literary elements contribute to their interpretations of the story. Creative writing activities allow students to experiment with figurative language, as well as different writing structures (descriptive paragraphs, sets of instructions, letters, poems, and folktales). In all writing activities, students continue to practice the prewriting and drafting strategies they learned in Book One, with increasing independence. You can choose which activity best complements your students' work on a particular unit, and use either or both at your discretion. Because the activities are largely process oriented, you may choose to focus on one portion of an activity if your students are struggling with writing.

Writing prompts, graphic organizers, and partnered writing activities in the Reader's Journal give students consistent, structured writing practice that supports their learning in reading comprehension and critical thinking. Students use the journal to record a body of questions and responses to the story. This accumulated material provides the foundation and inspiration for the prewriting and writing assignments at the end of each unit. At the end of each stage, students may revise their work as part of Reflect and Connect and collect those drafts in the Writing Notebook section of the Reader's Journal.

In addition, the Reader's Journal includes **Curious Words**, a section for students to create their own glossary of words that surprise or delight them.

Your Role in Shared Inquiry

As a Shared Inquiry leader, you create an effective environment for learning by consistently asking questions in response to your students' ideas. As you continue to gain experience conducting discussions, asking questions will become natural and comfortable for you and your students.

Your role as a leader of learners will be most pronounced in Shared Inquiry discussion. Below are the five guidelines for Shared Inquiry discussion. These guidelines, observed by Great Books discussion participants of all ages, will help you and your students contribute to focused and lively conversations about the story.

1. **READ THE STORY CAREFULLY BEFORE PARTICIPATING IN THE DISCUSSION.** If participants have not read the story, they cannot support their opinions with evidence from the story or respond to other participants' ideas about the story.

2. **DISCUSS ONLY THE STORY EVERYONE HAS READ.** This will give everyone an equal chance to contribute, as all participants in the discussion will be familiar with the discussion topic. By keeping the focus on the story, no one is excluded and the discussion does not drift off on tangents about personal experiences or film versions of stories.

3. **SUPPORT YOUR IDEAS WITH EVIDENCE FROM THE STORY.** Discussion improves reading comprehension and critical-thinking skills when students analyze the story carefully. The Shared Inquiry method helps students learn to go beyond just agreeing with a classmate or discussion leader as they explain their reasoning and link it to evidence in the story.

4. **LISTEN TO OTHER PARTICIPANTS AND RESPOND TO THEM DIRECTLY.** Shared Inquiry discussion is about the give-and-take of ideas, a willingness to listen to others and to talk to them respectfully. By directing comments and questions to other group members, and not always to the leader, students will find the discussion more spirited and dynamic.

5. **EXPECT THE LEADER TO ONLY ASK QUESTIONS.** It may feel strange not to tell students what the story means; however, readers must learn to develop their own ideas about meaning. Asking questions also helps show students that you, too, wonder about the story's meaning—that you do not have a specific answer that you are waiting to hear. Additionally, avoid offering judgments, positive or negative, about participants' ideas. Even praising an early response may inadvertently discourage other students from disagreeing with that idea. Students need to feel that when they try new ways of thinking, their ideas are being listened to and supported without being evaluated.

Your own intellectual curiosity about your students' ideas and about the literature itself is the foundation for leading a strong discussion. Posing interpretive questions about which you have genuine interest or uncertainty will make you a model of a thoughtful reader to your students; listening and responding to your students with true enthusiasm will encourage them to participate in discussion.

HOW TO USE QUESTIONING STRATEGIES

To support you as you develop your own questioning skills, each unit includes a Spotlight on Follow-Up Questions—a brief explanation and sample questions that illustrate a particular strategy you can practice to follow up on your students' comments. In Book Two, the spotlights continue to change from unit to unit, allowing you to practice questioning strategies introduced in Book One while expanding your repertoire of follow-up questions that support the critical-thinking elements of idea, evidence, and response. The questioning strategies build on each other logically from stage to stage, and those you learn first will continue to be valuable parts of your leadership throughout the program. In Stage 6, you are encouraged to target your follow-up questions to a critical-thinking element of your own choice, based on your students' needs and interests. A list of all sample follow-up questions in Book Two can be found on page 434 of appendix C.

The Spotlight on Follow-Up Questions appears in the second reading activity in each unit. Additional sample follow-up questions also appear in the Shared Inquiry discussion activity of each unit.

It takes time and practice to become a skilled Shared Inquiry leader, but the rewards are significant. This Leader's Edition offers structure and support to help leaders scale the learning curve. You can find further support through the Great Books Foundation's professional development offerings. Customized workshops and on-site consultations are designed to help you learn, practice, and then master the Shared Inquiry approach.

Assessment

Junior Great Books program calls for distinctive assessment strategies. The program defines three kinds of assessment to enable you to judge how well activities are going for your class, to evaluate each student's individual progress, and to allow your students to reflect on their learning and you to reflect on your own learning.

INFORMAL STUDENT AND CLASSROOM ASSESSMENT

You perform informal assessments when you ask yourself, "How is this going?" and look for signs that your students are learning as you think they should. This Leader's Edition orients you to the kinds of classroom behaviors and actions that signify increasing success as you and your students progress from story to story.

◆ The stage introduction previews general levels of student response.

◆ Each activity states a student learning objective in concrete terms.

◆ Each core activity (except the first reading) includes a student learning mini-rubric showing levels of performance for that activity.

The more you use these tools, the better you will be able to gauge your students' reactions and guide their progress in Junior Great Books.

GRADING INDIVIDUAL STUDENT WORK

We recommend that you use several different assessments to get a true picture of how students are doing. Ideally, some assessments should focus on revised, fully completed work and others should be adapted for students' work in progress.

The assessment kit (page 393) includes the following ways for you to assess each student's achievement and progress in the program:

- **STORY COMPREHENSION TESTS**—three multiple-choice comprehension tests, each based on one story from each stage of the program

- A **CRITICAL-THINKING RUBRIC** describing three traits for assessing students' achievement in Shared Inquiry discussion

- A **WRITING RUBRIC** to use in grading students' expository writing assignments

- A guide for **ACTIVITY SCORES** to track students' participation in each activity using the student learning mini-rubrics

- A **PORTFOLIO ASSESSMENT**, suggestions for using activity pages from the Reader's Journal to monitor students' progress

Each assessment is accompanied by comprehensive instructions for evaluating student learning. The assessment kit also provides suggestions for planning a multifaceted student assessment based on your learning objectives for Junior Great Books, and offers ideas on assessment scheduling.

> **Shared Inquiry** is a perfect laboratory for students to experiment with ideas. Many students respond more freely and think more imaginatively when they see that their oral participation, their note taking, and even their prewriting responses are treated as works in progress.

STUDENT AND LEADER REFLECTION

Reflection, or self-assessment, is a powerful learning tool for both students and leaders. As you and your students think over, discuss, and write about your experiences with the stories, you will become more aware of how these experiences help you learn.

At the end of each stage, in Reflect and Connect, students review what they learned during reading and discussion and apply it in new ways. The Reflect and Connect activities will help deepen students' recollections and understanding of both the stories themselves and the various elements of Shared Inquiry learning.

The assessment kit includes a leader reflection form for each stage to help you consider your students' progress, evaluate your own implementation of stage-specific strategies, and set your goals for the next stage. The leader reflection increases your insight into your students' needs and how to meet them.

You will also find a form labeled Our Collaboration in appendix C (page 427). You may wish to give a copy to students at the end of each stage to help them reflect on their participation and progress in Shared Inquiry discussions.

Junior Great Books Objectives   SERIES 3, BOOK TWO

Book Two (Stages 4–6) builds on Book One, providing students with more opportunities to practice metacognitive thinking and independent learning.

READING COMPREHENSION	CRITICAL THINKING	WRITING	LEADER LEARNING (SPOTLIGHT ON FOLLOW-UP QUESTIONS)
STAGE 4: Considering Interpretations Students begin to explore multiple interpretations of a story and to consider their classmates' ideas as they develop their own conclusions.			
UNIT 1 The Dream Weaver • To preview text features before reading the story • To recall experience with and knowledge about a concept in the story • To become familiar with a concept in the story • To recognize and make inferences while reading • To ask questions about the story, identifying those that are interpretive • To understand and use new words in a variety of contexts • To reread with a purpose and articulate ideas about the story	**Idea:** To clarify ideas in response to an interpretive question	• To use a graphic organizer to record ideas about character traits • To use vivid language to capture personal experiences	To ask follow-up questions to help students clarify their ideas
UNIT 2 Jean Labadie's Big Black Dog	**Evidence:** To provide evidence that supports an answer to an interpretive question	• To use a graphic organizer to record problems and solutions in the story • To use expressive language in vivid description	To ask follow-up questions to help students become aware that evidence can support more than one conclusion
UNIT 3 Caporushes	**Response:** To refer to other students' ideas when responding to an interpretive question	• To use similes in a narrative retelling • To use similes to describe a character	To ask follow-up questions to help students reflect and comment on their classmates' ideas
REFLECT AND CONNECT Reading and discussion review, story-to-story comparison, and writing revision			

READING COMPREHENSION	CRITICAL THINKING	WRITING	LEADER LEARNING (SPOTLIGHT ON FOLLOW-UP QUESTIONS)
STAGE 5: Exploring Ideas Students support their answers to interpretive questions with evidence from the story and consider their classmates' ideas.			
UNIT 4 The Upside-Down Boy • To recall experience with and knowledge about a concept in the story • To determine important ideas in the story • To identify interpretive questions that address important issues in the story • To understand and use new words in a variety of contexts • To reread with a purpose and articulate ideas about the story	**Idea:** To answer an interpretive question with clear and specific ideas	• To write an essay about imagery in the story • To use metaphor in a poem	To ask follow-up questions to help students explain their ideas
UNIT 5 The Green Man	**Evidence:** To answer an interpretive question with specific evidence from the story	• To demonstrate understanding of setting and character in an essay • To develop a set of instructions	To ask follow-up questions to help students provide more precise evidence to support their ideas
UNIT 6 The Ugly Duckling	**Response:** To consider other students' ideas when answering an interpretive question	• To retell story events in writing in the correct sequence • To write and respond to letters	To ask follow-up questions to highlight connections between different students' ideas
REFLECT AND CONNECT Reading and discussion review, story-to-story comparison, and writing revision			

	READING COMPREHENSION	CRITICAL THINKING	WRITING	LEADER LEARNING (SPOTLIGHT ON FOLLOW-UP QUESTIONS)
STAGE 6:	**Putting the Puzzle Together** Students explore interpretations of a story thoroughly and specifically, establishing discussion and independent thinking skills.			
UNIT 7 White Wave	• To recall experience with and knowledge about a concept in the story • To become familiar with a concept in the story • To begin to synthesize by summarizing and responding to parts of the story	**Idea/Evidence/Response:** To answer an interpretive question using evidence from the story and considering other students' ideas	• To summarize the story with an understanding of plot as a literary element • To develop an oral description and then convey it in writing	To ask follow-up questions to help students add depth to reasoning
UNIT 8 The Mousewife	• To explore interpretive questions about the story • To understand and use new words in a variety of contexts • To reread with a purpose and articulate ideas about the story		• To identify and explain a story's theme in an essay • To write with an awareness of setting	To choose a target area for follow-up questions
UNIT 9 How the Tortoise Became			• To identify and explain a story's theme in an essay • To write a narrative with a beginning, middle, and end	
UNIT 10 Two Wise Children			• To write an essay demonstrating a knowledge of theme and other story elements • To write a vivid, persuasive narrative	
REFLECT AND CONNECT	Reading and discussion review, story-to-story comparison, and writing revision			

LOOKING BACK AT BOOK ONE

Since Book Two of this series builds on the learning progression in Book One, it is strongly recommended that you complete Book One before introducing students to Book Two. This Leader's Edition provides guideposts to refresh your memory about concepts covered in Book One and to help you navigate Book Two if you are still new to the Junior Great Books program:

♦ Easily identifiable **light blue sidebars** in certain activities briefly review concepts learned in Book One. These sidebars are found primarily in the Stage 4 units. Page references direct the leader to sections or pages in Book One where these concepts are first introduced.

♦ A step-by-step review of the different question types introduced in Book One is provided in the sharing questions activity of Unit I, page 10.

♦ Key reading, critical-thinking, and writing strategies developed in Book One are revisited, shored up, and then expanded upon in this volume.

Depending on students' familiarity with (or retention of) Book One concepts, leaders can decide how to best introduce, review, or summarize Book One material before continuing with a Book Two activity. In all cases, if you or your students are unfamiliar with a particular concept or strategy in Book Two, it is recommended that you return to Book One for guidance.

Implementation Planning

Junior Great Books can be implemented in a wide variety of ways, from after-school, parent-led enrichment classes to intensive schoolwide reform projects. On page xxii is a small selection of implementation possibilities. For teachers of English-language learners or struggling students, we recommend plan A or B, with extra sessions of reading allotted to ensure thorough understanding. For teachers with parent volunteers, there are many opportunities to involve parents even if they are not trained as Shared Inquiry discussion leaders, such as having them read to students who were absent during your class reading. The activities you choose and the amount of class time you devote to the program will depend on your students' needs and the instructional objectives most important to you. We recommend that you leave two to three days at the end of each stage for some or all of the Reflect and Connect activities and for assessment.

PACING

A challenge in any school environment is to leave sufficient time for a new program, such as Junior Great Books, to be effective without compromising other classroom activities and requirements. Since the program's stories and activities progress in complexity throughout this series, units ideally should be completed at regular intervals without any omissions. However, Junior Great Books can be worked into a variety of school schedules and classroom setups. The key is to maintain consistency and some level of frequency—to build your comfort with Shared Inquiry and your students' habits of reading and thinking.

A unit can generally be completed in a week's time, or five 45- to 50-minute sessions. Since this book contains some lengthy selections and activities, occasionally you may find it necessary to take one or more additional days for some sessions (especially Session 1), thus moving into the following week to finish a unit. Since the activities in each unit build upon one another, sessions should take place on consecutive days when possible; conducting one session per week for five weeks in a row will not yield effective results.

Series 3 (Book One and Book Two) contains twenty units plus Reflect and Connect and assessment options—enough material to carry you through an entire school year of daily Junior Great Books activities. However, if limited time is available, we recommend undertaking several consecutive units in depth rather than skimming the entire series. Since the program has already been divided into stages, this strategy is easy to adopt.

The program's staged approach also makes it ideally suited to sharing a time slot with another language arts program. You might plan a block of the units from one stage so that the class can gain experience and achieve consistency, and then switch to a block of the other program.

IMPLEMENTATION OPTIONS

RELATION TO CURRICULUM AND PROGRAM OBJECTIVES	GROUP SIZE OR CONFIGURATION	NUMBER OF UNITS PER SEMESTER	NUMBER OF SESSIONS NEEDED PER UNIT	PREREADING	FIRST READING AND SHARING QUESTIONS	SECOND READING	VOCABULARY	SHARED INQUIRY DISCUSSION	EXPOSITORY OR CREATIVE WRITING
				SESSION 1		SESSION 2	SESSION 3	SESSION 4	SESSION 5
A. **Full program:** Reading comprehension, critical thinking, and writing*	Whole class	8–10	5	✓	✓	✓	✓	✓	✓
B. **Targeted program:** Reading comprehension and critical thinking	Whole class or selected groups	5–8	4	✓	✓	✓	✓	✓	occasional
C. **Targeted program:** Critical thinking and writing	Whole class or selected groups	4–8	4	occasional	✓	✓	occasional	✓	✓
D. **Enrichment:** Reading comprehension and critical thinking**	Whole class or selected groups	3–6	1–3		✓	✓		✓	occasional
E. **Extracurricular:** Shared Inquiry discussions only, weekly, parent-led †	Selected groups, usually stronger readers or gifted/talented students	5–10	1					✓	

* Junior Great Books activities within each unit support and reinforce one another. This implementation model provides the greatest support for the full range of program goals in reading comprehension, critical thinking, and writing. In this model, Junior Great Books is fully incorporated into the school's language arts curriculum. Some schools use the program in addition to a basal program; others use the basal as a supplement. This type of implementation is often supported by a formal plan for ongoing professional development and consulting.

** An enrichment program focused only on critical thinking can be implemented by conducting just the Shared Inquiry discussion during the school day. For groups that meet one day per unit, students do all readings independently. This model is recommended for stronger readers, but can be used with the entire class where appropriate.

† Extracurricular programs are often good opportunities to involve parents as volunteer leaders in a substantive educational activity. Some programs meet before or after school or at lunch, and others are arranged as pullout programs. Students volunteer for participation or are recommended by teachers, and are expected to read the stories at home.

About the Great Books Foundation

The Great Books Foundation is an independent, nonprofit educational organization whose mission is to help people learn to think and share ideas. Toward this end, the Foundation offers workshops in the Shared Inquiry method and publishes collections of classic and modern texts for both children and adults.

The Great Books Foundation was established in 1947 to promote liberal education for the general public. In 1962, the Foundation extended its mission to children with the introduction of Junior Great Books. Since its inception, the Foundation has helped thousands of people throughout the United States and in other countries begin their own discussion groups in schools, libraries, and community centers. Today, Foundation instructors conduct hundreds of workshops each year, in which educators and parents learn to lead Shared Inquiry discussion.

The Great Books Foundation offers workshops in Shared Inquiry to help people get the most from discussion. Participants learn how to read actively, pose fruitful questions, and listen and respond to others effectively in discussion. All participants also practice leading a discussion and have an opportunity to reflect on the process with others. For more information about Great Books materials or workshops, call the Great Books Foundation at **1-800-222-5870** or visit our Web site at **www.greatbooks.org**.

The Dream Weaver

Concha Castroviejo

Rogelia's daydreaming seems to get in the way of everything she does until she meets Gosvinda, who teaches her the art of weaving dreams.

Jean Labadie's Big Black Dog

French-Canadian folktale as told by Natalie Savage Carlson

Jean Labadie makes up a story about having a ferocious dog to keep his neighbor André from stealing his chickens, but André and the entire village have their own stories about Jean's imaginary dog.

Caporushes

English folktale as told by Flora Annie Steel

Banished from her father's home, clever Caporushes survives as a maid in a nearby manor and wins the heart of the young master before reconciling with her father.

STAGE 4: CONSIDERING INTERPRETATIONS

By Stage 4, students have learned that interpretive questions can have more than one possible answer. Here, they begin to explore these multiple interpretations of a story—selecting, clarifying, and explaining those ideas that will best support their conclusions, and reflecting on their classmates' responses in order to broaden and improve on their own ideas. Throughout Stage 4, numerous concepts introduced in Book One are briefly reviewed in sidebars. Due to longer stories and more advanced activities, some sessions require more time than a traditional class period. Suggested time allotments and tips on how to handle longer sessions appear in the relevant activities.

	Student Learning Objectives			Leader Learning Objectives
	READING COMPREHENSION	**CRITICAL THINKING**	**EXPOSITORY AND CREATIVE WRITING**	**SPOTLIGHT ON FOLLOW-UP QUESTIONS**
STAGE 4: CONSIDERING INTERPRETATIONS	• To recognize and make inferences while reading • To reread with a purpose and articulate ideas about the story • To identify different types of questions about the story	To recognize multiple interpretations of the story	• To practice prewriting strategies and drafting methods • To integrate literary terms and concepts into writing	To ask follow-up questions that help students recognize differing ideas
STAGE 5: EXPLORING IDEAS	• To determine important ideas in the story • To reread with a purpose and articulate ideas about the story • To identify interpretive questions about important issues in the story	To consider multiple interpretations of the story	• To develop prewriting strategies and drafting methods • To integrate literary terms and concepts into writing	To ask questions that help students explore ideas
STAGE 6: PUTTING THE PUZZLE TOGETHER	• To begin to synthesize information in the story • To reread with a purpose and articulate ideas about a story • To explore interpretive questions about the story	To discuss multiple interpretations of the story	• To hone drafting methods • To integrate literary terms and concepts into writing	• To ask questions that help students add depth to their reasoning • To choose a target area for follow-up questions

Reading Comprehension

In Stage 4, students learn to recognize and make inferences while reading, a strategy you model during the first reading. The sharing questions activity in Unit 1 provides a review of the different types of questions that may emerge after the first reading. In subsequent units, students practice identifying interpretive questions. Note-taking activities during the second reading help students locate evidence in the story and explain how it supports their ideas about a particular concept in the story.

Critical Thinking

The critical-thinking objectives in Stage 4 focus on recognizing that there can be multiple interpretations of a story. In Shared Inquiry discussion, you will help students clarify their own ideas, support their ideas with specific evidence from the story, and refer to other students' ideas when formulating a response.

Expository and Creative Writing

Stage 4 expository writing activities focus on the use of various graphic organizers as prewriting tools. Students record ideas about character traits, learn to sequence a character's problems and solutions, and practice creating and using similes. Creative writing activities give students opportunities to use vivid descriptive language and similes in their writing.

Spotlight on Follow-Up Questions

Located in the second reading with directed notes, each Spotlight on Follow-Up Questions in Stage 4 provides explicit instruction to help you develop your follow-up questioning skills in a systematic way. Each unit features follow-up questions targeted to the reading comprehension and critical-thinking objectives for that unit. Your follow-up questions will help students with these elements of critical thinking:

- Idea—Clarifying their ideas about the story
- Evidence—Becoming aware that evidence can support more than one conclusion
- Response—Reflecting and commenting on classmates' ideas

You can practice each questioning strategy during the second reading activity as well as later on, in Shared Inquiry discussion.

Curriculum Connections

Use Curriculum Connections to find books by the authors of the Stage 4 stories, as well as resources linking the stories to art, folklore, science, social studies, and other subjects. Icons indicate whether books are appropriate for classroom read-alouds or independent reading, according to the books' reading and interest levels.

Reflect and Connect

Reflect and Connect allows your students to compare concepts across stories and reinforces what they have learned in Stage 4. It also contains guidelines to help you evaluate your students' progress in meeting the learning objectives thus far.

The Dream Weaver

Concha Castroviejo

STORY LENGTH: 14 pages   READ-ALOUD TIME: About 15 minutes

◆ ABOUT THE STORY

Rogelia is considered a good-for-nothing by her family because she daydreams and does her chores clumsily. One day she meets an old woman named Gosvinda, who says that she is a weaver of dreams. Rogelia runs away to Gosvinda's house in the forest and becomes an accomplished dream weaver. But Gosvinda tells Rogelia that she must return to her family and work for a time in order to discover if dream weaving is her destiny.

◆ ABOUT THE AUTHOR

Concha Castroviejo was born in Spain in 1915. She published her first short stories in the local newspaper of her hometown, Santiago de Compostela. In 1961, Castroviejo was awarded the Doncel Prize for her book *El jardin de las siete puertas* (*The Garden of the Seven Doors*), from which "The Dream Weaver" is taken. She died in 1995.

The story starts on page 25 of the Leader's Edition, and on page 9 of the student anthology.

Unit Overview

❖ May require two class periods

☆ Core activity

Prereading (5–10 minutes)

Students prepare to read by briefly previewing the story.

1. Tell students that you are going to read a new story. Explain that strong readers often get a sense of what to expect by taking a look at the story's title, pictures, and other features before reading.

2. Have students read the title and look at the pictures in the story. If students are not sure about the meaning of the word *weaver*, share this definition with them:

   A **weaver** is a person who joins or laces threads together in a pattern to make something, such as cloth.

3. Ask students to suggest what they think the story might be about. Help them by asking questions such as:
   - Which character do you think is the dream weaver? Why?
   - What do you think a dream weaver might do? Why do you think so?
   - Will the story be about something magical or about something from real life? Why do you think so?
   - Does anyone have another idea?

4. Optional: Have students look more closely at one illustration and consider what it might show about the story. Prompt them by asking:
   - What do you think is happening in the picture?
   - What might this have to do with a dream weaver?
   - Does anyone have another idea about the picture?

Sharing Questions (20–40 minutes)

Students share different types of questions about the story.

REVIEWING QUESTION TYPES

Customize this activity to suit your classroom. If you started Book Two immediately after having completed Book One, your students may not need a review of the various question types. On the other hand, if there has been a significant break between completing Book One and beginning this volume, they may need additional time to review. More information about each of the question types can be found in your professional development materials and on the following pages in your Book One Leader's Edition:

◆ Turning statements into questions, page 11

◆ Factual questions, page 44

◆ Vocabulary questions, page 76

◆ Background questions, page 118

◆ Speculative questions, page 146

◆ Evaluative questions, page 220

If you wish to split this session into two class periods, be sure to collect students' questions on the same day you read the story, while their curiosity is still fresh.

STUDENT LEARNING OBJECTIVE

READING COMPREHENSION: To ask questions about the story, identifying those that are interpretive

LOOK FOR STUDENTS TO

Mention puzzling, confusing, or interesting aspects of the story

Ask questions about the story

Recognize interpretive questions about the story

1. Record questions on the board with students' names, or have students write their questions on strips of paper to post around the room.

2. Remind students that factual questions are questions that can be resolved after the first reading because the story presents only one definite answer. Encourage students to identify and answer factual and vocabulary questions on their own, using the text, the Reader's Journal glossary, a dictionary, or classmates for help.

3. Remind students that in Book One, they learned to identify evaluative, speculative, and background questions. Briefly review these types of questions by looking at one example of each. Choose from among students' questions or use these examples:

   ◆ Background question: *What does it mean when Rogelia says her bonnet is for "feast days"? What is a feast day?*

   ◆ Speculative question: *Does Rogelia talk about her family with Gosvinda?*

   ◆ Evaluative question: *Should Rogelia's sisters apologize to her for calling her clumsy and stupid?*

   Help the class revise, answer, or skip them, as appropriate.

4. Point to a remaining question that you think might be interpretive.

5. Test the question by asking students to offer possible answers that can be supported with evidence from the story.

6. If students are able to find support for two different answers, do not explore the question in detail. Tell students that they have identified an interpretive question—the kind of question you want them to keep in mind as they reread the story.

7. Repeat the process for as many questions as time allows.

8. Tell students that they are ready to choose their keeper question and that any of the interpretive questions they have identified would be a good choice. Have them write the keeper question on page 2 of the Reader's Journal, and encourage them to think about it as they read the story again.

9. Use your Leader Discussion Planner (page 17) to jot down posted questions that you will want to remember later for Shared Inquiry discussion.

10. Have students turn to page 3 in the Reader's Journal to practice making inferences as a reading strategy. This can also serve as homework.

REVIEW

KEEPER QUESTION

Choosing a question to think about during the second reading helps students sustain interest in the story and encourages their curiosity. Students need not dwell on the question, nor do they need to answer it. However, the question can help students focus during the second reading, and it can help shape their understanding of the story. While we suggest that students work toward choosing interpretive questions, it is not important which kind of question they choose, as long as they are genuinely interested in thinking about it further (as opposed to choosing a question they can already answer).

Second Reading with Directed Notes (45 minutes)

Students mark passages to note contrasting ideas in the story.

STUDENT LEARNING OBJECTIVE

READING COMPREHENSION: To reread with a purpose and articulate ideas about the story

LOOK FOR STUDENTS TO

Offer a literal explanation or paraphrase of the passage

Infer motives and causes from the passage

Offer a detailed explanation of the passage

REVIEW

INDICATIONS OF SUCCESS

As in Book One, the student learning mini-rubric (with the heading Look for Students to) shows three levels of performance to help you assess and guide your students' learning during the second reading activity. Student learning mini-rubrics also appear in the sharing questions activity and in Shared Inquiry discussion. For more about assessing student progress in Junior Great Books, see appendix A.

SPOTLIGHT on Follow-Up Questions

For this unit, the spotlight is on **asking follow-up questions to help students clarify their ideas.** Listen for times when students do not say exactly what they mean, or when you do not quite understand words or phrases they are using. Asking questions for clarification can also help you identify and explore similarities and differences in students' answers. In some cases, students may see a request for more information as an implication that an initial answer is not correct. You can assure students by your tone and body language that you are genuinely interested in their answers and simply want to guide their attention to specific parts of their comments.

FOLLOW-UP QUESTIONS: CLARIFYING IDEAS

◆ How does this passage show you that?

◆ Who has a different idea about the passage?

◆ When you say Rogelia is being bad, what do you mean by "bad"?

BEFORE READING

1. Explain to students that during the second reading they will be taking notes. Write the following on the board:

   W = Rogelia **wants** to do something.

   H = Rogelia **has** to do something.

2. Tell students that as they reread the story, they should mark with a **W** places where Rogelia **wants** to do something, and mark with an **H** places where she **has** to do something.

3. Ask students to think about why they are choosing those places, as they make their notes.

DURING READING

4. Tell students to read the story on their own or with a partner, or have them listen to the story read aloud (by you or on the CD), making notes as they go.

AFTER READING

5. Have students read aloud passages they marked with a **W** or an **H**, and ask them to explain why they chose those passages.

6. Ask follow-up questions to help students clarify or elaborate on their ideas. Remember to ask if anyone sees a passage differently. Examine as many passages and notations as time allows.

7. Use your Leader Discussion Planner (page 17) to jot down questions or ideas to explore later.

8. Have students turn to Head in the Clouds on page 4 of the Reader's Journal and choose a topic for writing or drawing.

FLUENCY TIP

Before students share their notes with the class, have them practice reading aloud with appropriate pacing. Tell them to underline the punctuation in their passage. Explain that commas signal short pauses; periods, colons, and dashes represent longer pauses; and question marks and exclamation points show changes in tone of voice. Model reading aloud with the appropriate pacing and tone of voice, then have students practice with a partner.

Vocabulary (20 minutes)

Students practice using new vocabulary words.

> **STUDENT LEARNING OBJECTIVE**
>
> **READING COMPREHENSION: To understand and use new words in a variety of contexts**

SUGGESTED TARGET WORDS: **capable, occupation, reprimanding**

Choose the target words you want your class to learn, or use the suggested target words above. As you present a word, have students say it with you. Work on one word at a time, using these steps as a guide:

1. Place the word in context. Review how the word is used in the story.

2. Define the word. Use active language in your definition. Include a few examples of how to use the word in situations students will understand. For example:

    ◆ If you are **capable**, you are able to do many things well. We were not sure he could handle so many difficult tasks, but it turned out that he was a **capable** person. If you are a **capable** student, you might want to sign up for the spelling bee and the science fair.

    ◆ Your **occupation** is the job you do to earn a living. Being a doctor is a fine **occupation** because you can help people get well. His grandmother's **occupation** was teaching school, but her hobby was doing crossword puzzles.

    ◆ If someone is **reprimanding** you, that person is speaking to you in an angry way for doing something wrong. The teacher was **reprimanding** the boy for passing notes in class. The girl's father is always **reprimanding** her for slamming the door, but she keeps doing it.

3. Use the word. Encourage students to make the word their own by asking a few of them to use it in a sentence or to apply it to real-life situations.

REVIEW

REINFORCING TARGET WORDS

Use the target words in other subjects throughout the week and encourage students to use the words in conversation. If students have repeated opportunities to hear and use their new vocabulary words, they will be more likely to remember them.

4. Ask a question about the story, using the word. Have several students apply their knowledge of the word to answer the question.

5. Optional: Have students turn to Curious Words on page 153 of the Reader's Journal to write down some of their favorite words from the story.

REVIEW

NOTING CURIOUS WORDS

The Curious Words section of the Reader's Journal begins on page 152. There students can record and use a few interesting, funny, or intriguing words from the story.

OVERHEARD IN THE CLASSROOM

TARGET WORD: capable

PLACE THE WORD IN CONTEXT

" 'This girl is very clumsy,' said her sister Camila, who was very **capable** and quite conceited." (Refer students to page 10 in the student anthology.)

"Rogelia returned home, greeted everyone, and said that she had been learning to be **capable**" (page 20).

DEFINE THE WORD

If you are **capable**, you are able to do many things well. We were not sure he could handle so many difficult tasks, but it turned out that he was a **capable** person. If you are a **capable** student, you might want to sign up for the spelling bee and the science fair. Say the word with me.

USE THE WORD

Which of the following shows you are a **capable** person? Say "**capable**" or "not **capable**" for each task.

- Watching a movie
- Cooking a three-course meal
- Getting ready for bed
- Drawing a picture
- Studying hard

ASK A QUESTION ABOUT THE STORY

Why are Rogelia's sisters so concerned about Rogelia being **capable**?

Shared Inquiry Discussion (45 minutes)

Students discover meaning in the story by discussing an interpretive question.

> **STUDENT LEARNING OBJECTIVE**
>
> **CRITICAL THINKING: To clarify ideas in response to an interpretive question**
>
> **LOOK FOR STUDENTS TO**
>
> Give answers that show understanding of the question
>
> Offer answers that infer motives and causes in the story
>
> Explain how an idea answers the question

REVIEW

THE FIVE GUIDELINES FOR SHARED INQUIRY DISCUSSION

1. Read the story carefully before participating in the discussion.

2. Discuss only the story everyone has read.

3. Support your ideas with evidence from the story.

4. Listen to other participants and repond to them directly.

5. Expect the leader to only ask questions.

Use the Leader Discussion Planner on the facing page to prepare yourself for Shared Inquiry discussion. To prepare your group, have everyone sit in a circle or a square; remind them of the five discussion guidelines and any behavioral guidelines you want to share. Then follow these steps to conduct the discussion:

1. **Write the focus question** on the board and have students copy it on the Building Your Answer page of the Reader's Journal (page 5).

2. **Give students a few minutes** to review the story and to write down an answer.

3. **Begin the discussion** by asking the focus question. On your seating chart, keep track of students' participation and ideas (see Using the Seating Chart, page 19).

4. **Lead the discussion** by asking follow-up questions to help students clarify their ideas (see sample questions in your Leader Discussion Planner, page 17), provide evidence, and respond to one another. Aim to have the discussion last 20 to 30 minutes.

5. **As the discussion winds down**, have students finish the Building Your Answer page. Then ask volunteers to share what they wrote.

6. **Spend a few minutes** talking about the discussion. Ask students what they liked about it, what was hard about it, what they think makes a good discussion, and what might go better next time.

LEADER DISCUSSION PLANNER

After the first and second readings, use this section to keep track of:

◆ Questions that you and your students have about the story

◆ Characters, incidents, and ideas that interest you

◆ Passages that interest you

_____

_____

_____

_____

_____

Write down a focus question, cluster questions, and passages that you think you or your students will refer to in discussion. If you choose not to develop your own questions, see Suggested Interpretive Questions for Shared Inquiry Discussion on page 18.

CLUSTER QUESTION

_____

_____

_____

CLUSTER QUESTION

_____

_____

_____

FOCUS QUESTION FOR DISCUSSION

_____

_____

_____

RELATED PASSAGE   page _____

_____

_____

_____

_____

RELATED PASSAGE   page _____

_____

_____

_____

_____

In this Shared Inquiry discussion, look for opportunities to help your students clarify their ideas in response to an interpretive question.

FOLLOW-UP QUESTIONS: CLARIFYING IDEAS

◆ What do you mean by that phrase?

◆ Can you tell us more about what you mean?

◆ How does that idea help us answer the focus question?

SUGGESTED INTERPRETIVE QUESTIONS FOR SHARED INQUIRY DISCUSSION

OPTION 1 **Why are there so few dream weavers?**

◆ Why is Rogelia's family so unpleasant to her?

◆ Why does Gosvinda live so far from the village?

◆ Why does Gosvinda tell Rogelia that "if you say you weave dreams, people will laugh at you" when everyone who knows her orders dreams from her?

◆ Why is weaving dreams not on any list of occupations?

PASSAGE FOR DISCUSSION In the student anthology, from "Once upon a time there used to be seven of us weavers," on page 17, to "If you say you weave dreams, people will laugh at you," on page 18

OPTION 2 **Why is Rogelia so good at weaving dreams?**

◆ Why does Rogelia become "more and more inattentive" after she first meets Gosvinda?

◆ Why does Rogelia live without dreams when she is back at her family's house?

◆ Why does Rogelia never keep her dreams for herself?

◆ Why can Rogelia make beautiful lace after she learns to weave dreams?

PASSAGE FOR DISCUSSION In the student anthology, from "Little by little, Rogelia learned to make lovely woven fabrics of the color and shape of clouds," on page 17, to "'I shall weave the most beautiful one that has ever existed," on page 19

OVERHEARD IN THE CLASSROOM

LEADER   Why is Rogelia so good at weaving dreams?

TAMALA   Because it fits.

LEADER   How does it fit?

TAMALA   She's always daydreaming and can't even stop herself from daydreaming.

LEADER   Why does daydreaming all the time make her good at weaving dreams?

TAMALA   Some people are good at cooking or baseball and some are good at math. She's just good at dreams. When you're good at it you do it a lot.

LEADER   So does she do it because she's good at it, or does she become good at it because she's doing it all the time?

USING THE SEATING CHART

As you lead the discussion, use a seating chart to keep track of students' participation and ideas. Note students' participation by making a check mark next to their names, jot down a word or brief phrase from any comments that strike you, and use connecting lines to track agreement and disagreement. For more information about using the seating chart, please refer to your Shared Inquiry professional development materials.

SEATING CHART

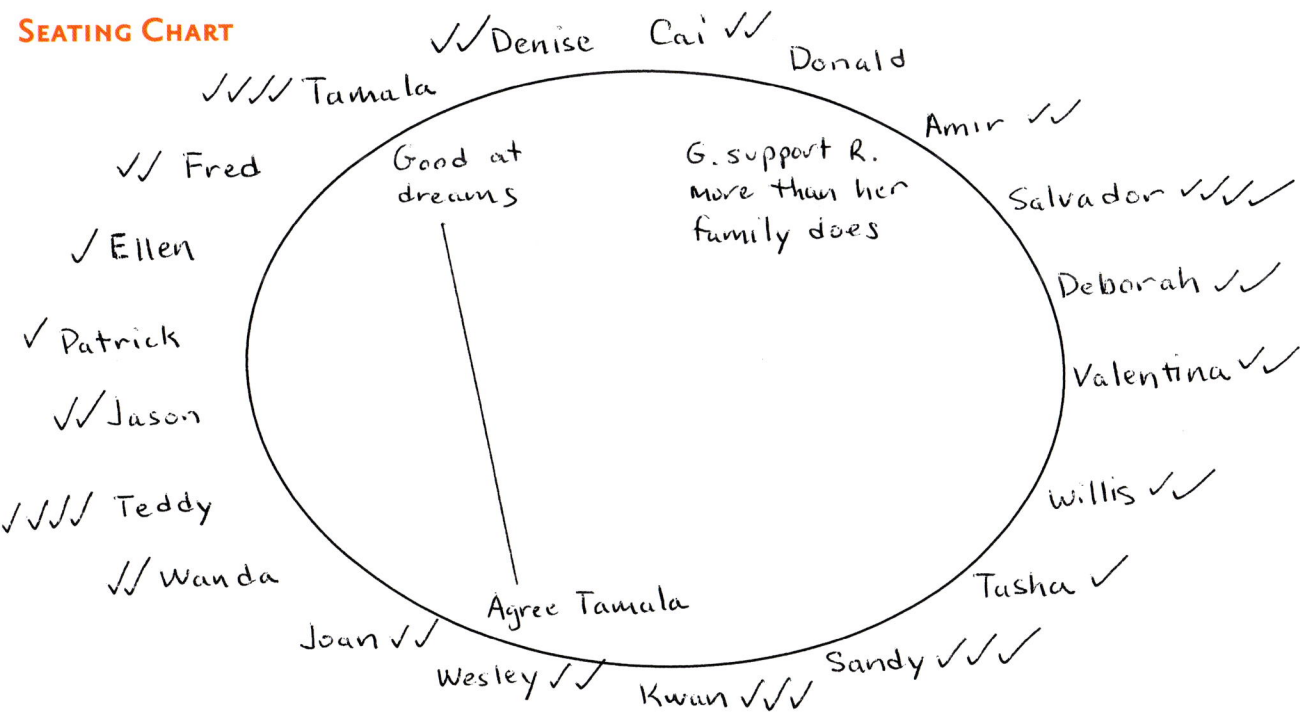

Expository Writing: Writing About Character (45 minutes)

Students choose words to describe the main character, then explain their word choices.

> **STUDENT LEARNING OBJECTIVE**
>
> **WRITING: To use a graphic organizer to record ideas about character traits**

GENERATING IDEAS IN STAGE 4

In Stage 4 writing activities, students practice generating ideas before writing, as they did in Book One, Stage 1. But now students are expected to use prewriting techniques with greater sophistication. Students still draw upon insights gained from Shared Inquiry discussion, but instead of writing about the focus question, students are asked to integrate their understanding of the story with something new—an important literary term or concept that lends itself well to the story. In all writing activities, students should continue to follow the writing process they learned in Book One of this series.

TEACHING LITERARY CONCEPTS: CHARACTER TRAITS

1. Ask volunteers to define the term *character traits,* then write this definition on the board:

   A character is someone in a story, play, or poem. **Character traits** tell what a character looks like, says, and does. They also tell how a character feels about people or things and how a character seems to other characters.

PREWRITING

2. Tell students that they will be writing to describe the character traits of Rogelia, the main character in "The Dream Weaver."

3. Draw a character web on the board similar to the one on page 7 of the Reader's Journal. Ask volunteers to name some of Rogelia's character traits, and begin a web about her as a class.

4. Ask students to turn to pages 6 and 7 in the Reader's Journal to find their own character web for Rogelia.

5. Have students work with a partner to complete their character webs. Ask students to think of as many descriptive words as they can, considering all of the parts of the character trait definition.

6. Encourage students to review the story as they describe Rogelia's character.

7. Have partners write one to two sentences near each descriptive word explaining why they chose that word.

Creative Writing:
Dream Weaving (45 minutes)

Students write a vivid paragraph about a dream.

STUDENT LEARNING OBJECTIVE

WRITING: To use vivid language to capture personal experiences

PREWRITING

1. Remind students that the author of the story used descriptive language to help form pictures in readers' minds as they read. As an example, read the paragraph the author uses to describe dream weaving, starting on page 17 with "Little by little, Rogelia learned how to make lovely woven fabrics . . . ."

2. Tell students that they will be weaving their own dreams with descriptive words rather than colorful thread.

3. Ask students to remember a dream or a daydream and to choose an especially interesting or exciting part of that dream.

4. Write a volunteer's example on the board, and have the class suggest details that would make a description of the dream more vivid and exciting. Help them by asking questions such as: What do you see, hear, smell, taste, and touch? How do you feel?

5. Have students complete page 8 of the Reader's Journal. Remind them to use as much detail as possible. For instance, the detail "There is a bird" can be elaborated upon to become "A beautiful white bird with giant wings stands on one leg."

WRITING A DRAFT

6. Have students use their prewriting notes to draft a vivid paragraph on page 9 of the Reader's Journal.

7. Optional: Have students copy a favorite sentence from their drafts onto strips of colored paper. Arrange them on a bulletin board in a criss-cross pattern as a literal example of woven dreams.

Curriculum Connections

Below are resources related to "The Dream Weaver" for further reading and investigation in a number of subject areas.

 Appropriate for classroom read-alouds; above-grade reading and interest levels

 Appropriate for independent reading; at- or near-grade reading and interest levels

OTHER WORKS BY THE AUTHOR

 Castroviejo, Concha. *The Garden with Seven Gates.* Lewisburg, PA: Bucknell University Press, 2003.

This collection of stories includes a dramatic version of the "Garden with the Seven Gates."

ARTS

 Ahiagble, Gilbert Bobbo, and Louise Meyer. *Master Weaver from Ghana.* Seattle: Open Hand Publishing, 1998.

A contemporary weaver from Ghana explains how his people maintain the tradition of weaving, including an explanation of the strip weaving of Kente cloth and its importance in the Ewe culture.

 Stalcup, Ann. *Mayan Weaving: A Living Tradition.* New York: PowerKids Press, 2000.

Briefly describes how the Maya wove their cloth, how they dyed the fabric, and how they created the clothing they wore.

FICTION AND FOLKLORE

 Heyer, Marilee. *The Weaving of a Dream: A Chinese Folktale.* New York: Puffin Books, 1989.

When the beautiful tapestry woven by a poor woman is stolen by fairies, her three sons set out on a magical journey to retrieve it. A retelling of a traditional Chinese tale.

Ⓘ Lyon, George Ella. *Weaving the Rainbow.* New York: Atheneum Books for Young Readers, 2004.

> An artist raises sheep, shears them, cards and spins the wool, dyes it, and then weaves a colorful picture of the Kentucky pasture where her lambs were born.

Ⓘ Musgrove, Margaret. *The Spider Weaver: A Legend of Kente Cloth.* New York: Blue Sky Press, 2001.

> In this retelling of a tale from Ghana, a wondrous spider shows two Ashanti weavers how to make intricate, colorful patterns in the cloth that they weave.

Ⓡ Ortega, Cristina. *Los ojos del tejedor/The Eyes of the Weaver.* Santa Fe: Clear Light Books, 1998.

> Ten-year-old Maria Cristina goes to visit her grandfather so that he can teach her to weave, as her family in northern New Mexico has done for seven generations.

SCIENCE

Ⓡ McGinty, Alice B. *The Orb Weaver.* New York: PowerKids Press, 2002.

> Describes the characteristics of the orb weaver spider, the web it spins, and its benefits to the ecosystem.

SOCIAL SCIENCE

Ⓡ Tull, Mary Herd. *Dreams: Mind Movies of the Night.* Brookfield, CT: Millbrook Press, 2000.

> Examines, in a question and answer format, the scientific and cultural aspects of dreams, including such topics as the physiological reasons for dreams, the connection between dreams and religion, and the dream life of animals.

"This girl is very clumsy," said her sister Camila, who was very <mark>capable</mark> and quite conceited.

"This girl is stupid," her sister Pepa would add.

"There's no telling whether this girl will learn or not," the schoolmistress sighed.

The worst of it was that Rogelia never learned how to make <u>bobbin</u> lace. Her granny, her sisters, and her aunts—all the women in her house—were very skillful with the bobbins and made beautiful lace with stars, birds, and flowers, fashioning all sorts of whimsical designs with the threads. This pleased Rogelia a great deal. She would sit down beside her granny, with her little sewing cushion full of pins, threads, and bobbins on her knees, and begin to dream of making wonderful designs. But she dreamed of her designs so intently, and planned them in her head so enthusiastically, that the bobbins collided, tangling the threads; the pins fell out of place, undoing the knots; and her handiwork ended up a sorry mess.

10

Think-Aloud

"Rogelia's sisters and teacher seem to be cruel toward Rogelia. I don't think they really understand her."

LEADER'S NOTES AND QUESTIONS

T **capable:** able to do things well

bobbin: a spool that holds yarn or thread for weaving or sewing

...

Rogelia burst into tears and felt ashamed as her older sisters began **reprimanding** her.

"Go get the tissue paper ready to wrap up our lacework," Camila would say to her. "That's all you're good for."

And that was how things went for Rogelia every day.

One afternoon she was peering out the window and saw a very old woman pass by the house, gazing at the sky. Rogelia, who was a very well-mannered girl, ran to the door and

reprimanding: speaking to someone in an angry way for doing something wrong

···

went out into the street, because it seemed that the old woman was about to trip and fall. But the old woman laughed and said to her, "Don't worry. I'm looking at the clouds. By doing so, the work I do later on turns out so nicely."

"What sort of work do you do?" Rogelia asked her.

The woman answered, "I'm a weaver of dreams."

Those words excited Rogelia.

"What a fine occupation!" she exclaimed, and then she asked, "What is your name, señora?"

"My name is Gosvinda."

Rogelia would have liked to follow along after old Gosvinda, but she did not dare. She remained at the door watching her, and saw her walk all the way down the long street, leave the town, and go into the woods. From that day on, Rogelia thought only of the dream weaver. At school she was more and more inattentive; she burned more and more clothes as she did the ironing, spilled more and more water as she watered the flower pots, and made an even worse tangle of the pins, threads, and bobbins when she sat down alongside her granny to make lace.

12

Think-Aloud

"Since Rogelia dreams so much of her own designs, I can see why the woman's work is so exciting to her. The lady might understand her better than her family does."

LEADER'S NOTES AND QUESTIONS

occupation: the job you do to earn a living

...

"This girl is going to have to be sent to a boarding school to see if they can manage to teach her something," her sister Pepa said one day.

"A place where they keep her locked up and punish her," her sister Camila added.

"Where they won't allow her to while away her time gazing at clouds," Pepa piped up again.

"She isn't good for anything," her aunt said.

Then Rogelia said to her sisters, "Since I must learn something, I'm going to learn how to weave dreams."

And her sisters laughed at her.

But Rogelia packed two changes of clothes, a jacket, and her rain boots into a cardboard box, put on a bonnet that she kept to wear on feast days, gave her granny a goodbye kiss, and took off on her own.

LEADER'S NOTES AND QUESTIONS

_____

_____

_____

_____

_____

_____

_____

_____

_____

_____

_____

_____

LEADER'S NOTES
AND QUESTIONS

...

Rogelia left the town and reached the woods. It was dark there because the tops of the trees were so dense. Rogelia walked on for a long time until at last she came upon an open meadow, and in the meadow was a house with its walls painted pink and its windows green, surrounded on every side with yellow flowers. The house had seven chimneys through which poured out lovely smoke that looked like no other, a different color puffing out from each chimney.

Rogelia pushed on the door, which was unlocked, and went into the house. From the kitchen, she climbed up to a bedroom, and from the bedroom, she climbed up to the loft, and from the loft, she saw the clouds and mountains in the distance. Old Gosvinda worked there in the loft all day, weaving one dream after another. The smoke of the dreams was what was escaping by way of the chimneys.

On reaching the loft, Rogelia said, "Good day, Señora Gosvinda."

The weaver was not surprised to see the little girl.

"I knew you'd come," she said, answering her greeting.

15

Rogelia looked all around. She saw the distaffs and the looms with threads of crystal, gold, and silver, with threads the color of emeralds and sapphires. In one corner there were twelve mice grooming their whiskers.

"I've come to stay, if you'll allow me to," she said to Gosvinda. "I wish to learn to weave dreams. At home they tell me I'm useless, but it may be that I'm suited for such a wonderful occupation."

Gosvinda replied that she could stay and explained to her that she needed a girl to help her because she had a great many orders to fill. People kept needing more and more dreams.

Rogelia remained in the house in the woods. Very early each morning, she went up to the loft

16

distaffs: sticks that hold wool ready to be spun into yarn or thread

and learned to thread the looms and ready the tufts to be spun into threads on the distaff. The threads glided in and out until they formed the <u>weft</u> under the old weaver's hand, and the distaff spun faster and faster, raising a breeze that made the mice sneeze. During the day the cuckoos, and at nightfall the <u>swifts</u>, came and went through the window, bringing in their beaks the orders sent by princes from their royal palaces and by miners from the depths of their caves. All the men and women who knew the weaver ordered dreams from her.

"Once upon a time there used to be seven of us weavers," Gosvinda said to Rogelia, "but my companions retired to take their rest and left me by myself. They were older than I. When I grow weary and retire, there will be no one left at all."

"And what will people do then?" Rogelia asked.

"They'll manufacture pills so they can have synthetic dreams. And children will weave their own dreams for themselves."

Little by little, Rogelia learned to make lovely woven fabrics of the color and shape of clouds. She learned how to make the rainbow <u>tarry</u> by

17

LEADER'S NOTES AND QUESTIONS

weft: woven fabric

swifts: small dark-colored birds

tarry: stay in a certain place for awhile

Think-Aloud

"It seems from the description that Rogelia enjoys her work with Gosvinda. The mood in this part seems happy."

LEADER'S NOTES
AND QUESTIONS

_____

_____

_____

_____

_____

_____

_____

_____

_____

_____

····

singing to it, and how to wrap it up in orange-colored dreams. She learned to weave pink and blue dreams for the young, and green ones to console those who were sick and those who were sad. And white dreams so that children could embroider them in color.

"You're a very clever little girl," old Gosvinda told her.

And that made Rogelia feel very happy.

"Oh, my!" she replied. "If only those back home could see me!"

"They would still find you useless. If you say you weave dreams, people will laugh at you."

···

Dreams, once they were woven, came out of the chimneys in a lacework of smoke, and the wind blew them to distant houses. Rogelia soon learned to sweep the floor and to put pots on the fire. Every week a bear brought old Gosvinda wood, rabbits took care of supplying her with vegetables, and blackbirds arrived with fruit.

"What a beautiful house!" Rogelia sighed.

Rogelia learned the weaver's craft so well that dreams now held no secrets for her. Because she worked with them so much with her hands, they no longer lodged in her head. She paid careful attention to the thin, fragile threads, to the delicate interweaving formed by the branches of the trees and the patterns made by the clouds, and to the colors of the rainbow that appeared above the sharp-pointed roof of the little house. Rogelia's mind was never in a daze now, for the dreams were no longer in her head, but in her hands. "When I want a dream for myself," she thought, "I shall weave the most beautiful one that has ever existed."

One day old Gosvinda said to her, "In order to find out if this is your true calling, you must put it to the test: return home and work there."

19

Rogelia realized that she was obliged to obey. She went to her cardboard box and put on a dress that she had woven with the leftovers from the distaff tufts and that gleamed with the colors of flowers.

Rogelia returned home, greeted everyone, and said that she had been learning to be capable. In the beginning her sisters laughed at her, but Rogelia's hands were blessed. If she sat down to make bobbin lace, the bobbins crossed back and forth like castanets and the threads turned into lace, with birds, flowers, and clouds in the white background that looked like a snow-covered

20

castanets: small musical instruments that you wear on your fingers and click together to the beat of a song

field. If she watered the plants, she did not spill a single drop. If she ironed, the glistening garment looked as good as new.

Everyone sang Rogelia's praises. The meters of lace she made were sought after by all the townspeople. For the grand fiesta of the year they ordered decorations for the balconies from her.

But Rogelia could no longer live without dreams. Each day she climbed to the very top of the house to see if she could make out the smoke coming from the chimneys of Gosvinda the weaver's house.

Rogelia readied her cardboard box once again, bade everyone goodbye, and headed for the woods one morning as day broke.

_____

_____

_____

_____

_____

_____

_____

_____

_____

_____

Think-Aloud

"I'd like to hear some of your inferences now. What does Rogelia think of visiting her family? What clues in the story tell you that?"

•••

"Good day!" she said as she entered the loft.

The weaver was seated in her corner, and the mice were holding in place the tufts that she was putting on the distaffs.

"I knew you would come," she said, answering Rogelia's greeting. "Now you will stay here forevermore."

Rogelia remained with old Gosvinda. She welcomed the cuckoos and the swifts, fed the mice, helped the bear unload the wood, and placed the vegetables and fruit that the rabbits and the blackbirds brought into their proper baskets. But above all, she kept weaving and weaving. She wove the most complicated and difficult dreams, the ones that tired old Gosvinda. She attended to everything, for she had so many dreams in her hands that none were left in her head. She was so fond of her dreams and so proud of her work that she never dared to keep them.

Each year she went to the town to visit her grandmother, her sisters, and her aunt. She greeted them and then went off once again.

One day a very serious looking gentleman, carrying a large briefcase full of registers with black oilcloth covers, came knocking at the door

22

registers: books in which official lists are kept

of Gosvinda's house. Rogelia came down from the loft to see what he wanted, and the gentleman told her that he had come to find out who lived there and what their occupation was, so he could write their names down in the tax registers.

"Old Gosvinda and I live here," Rogelia explained to him, "and we are weavers of dreams."

The gentleman looked through his registers and said that such an occupation was not on any list. Then he cleared his throat and left.

LEADER'S NOTES AND QUESTIONS

Unit Overview

SESSION 1: PAGE 43

PREREADING Students share their solutions to a problem they might have with a friend.

★ **FIRST READING** Students make inferences about the story as the leader reads it aloud.

★ **SHARING QUESTIONS** Students share different types of questions about the story.

SESSION 2: PAGE 48

★ **SECOND READING WITH DIRECTED NOTES** Students mark passages to note contrasting ideas in the story.

SPOTLIGHT ON FOLLOW-UP QUESTIONS The leader asks follow-up questions to help students become aware that evidence can support more than one conclusion.

SESSION 3: PAGE 50

VOCABULARY Students practice using new vocabulary words. Suggested target words: *broach*, *foreboding*, and *suspicious*

SESSION 4: PAGE 52

★ **SHARED INQUIRY DISCUSSION** Students discover meaning in the story by discussing an interpretive question.

SESSION 5 OPTIONS: PAGE 56

EXPOSITORY WRITING Students comment on a main character's problems and solutions.

CREATIVE WRITING Students write a vivid description of an imaginary character and read their descriptions aloud.

CURRICULUM CONNECTIONS The leader can use these resources to link the story to other subject areas.

★ Core activity

Prereading (5–10 minutes)

Students share their solutions to a problem they might have with a friend.

STUDENT LEARNING OBJECTIVE

READING COMPREHENSION: To recall experience with and knowledge about a concept in the story

1. Tell students that you are going to read a story about someone who thinks a neighbor is cheating him. Ask them to think about how a person might deal with a problem like that.

2. Have students imagine this situation:

   You are playing a game with a friend and you realize that the friend might be cheating. You want to stop the cheating, but you don't want to lose a friend. What might you do?

3. Ask students to share some of their ideas with the class. Help them consider the consequences of their actions by asking questions such as:
   ◆ What might your friend do or say in response?
   ◆ How might your friend act next time you get together?
   ◆ Why would doing that make your friend stop cheating?

First Reading (20–25 minutes)

Students make inferences about the story as the leader reads it aloud.

> **STUDENT LEARNING OBJECTIVE**
>
> **READING COMPREHENSION: To recognize and make inferences while reading**

BEFORE READING

1. Have students follow along in their books as they listen to you read "Jean Labadie's Big Black Dog," a story about a man who thinks a friend is stealing from him.

2. Explain to students that strong readers make inferences while reading to help them figure out things not directly stated in the story. Readers make inferences by combining their own ideas with clues from the story.

3. Tell students that as you read the story aloud, you will stop now and then to make an **inference** aloud or to ask them to make one. They should mark these places with an **I** in their books. They should also mark with a **?** places where they have a **question** about the story.

DURING READING

4. Read the story aloud with expression.

5. Pause several times while reading to model how you make inferences. Look up from the book and share your thinking aloud when you draw a conclusion about something that is not directly stated in the story or was not clear at first. After modeling a few of your own inferences, stop at an appropriate spot and ask a question to prompt students to make an inference. If you wish, use the Think-Alouds provided in the margins of the story in this Leader's Edition.

PROMPTING STUDENTS TO MAKE INFERENCES

Help students make inferences by stopping at appropriate places to ask questions such as:

- Why do you think he did that?
- What might she be feeling right now?
- What probably had to happen before this event?

AFTER READING

6. Ask students to review the story to find the places where they marked an **I** and to recall some of those inferences. Help students see that inferences are not facts written in the story, but are guesses or conclusions formed by combining story details with the reader's own ideas.

7. Tell students to review the story to find the passages they marked with a **?** and to think about questions they would like to share with the class.

MORE ON MAKING INFERENCES

When readers make inferences, they read between the lines to find meaning that is not directly stated in the words. Readers make inferences about all aspects of a story, such as characters, motives, events, themes, tone, and mood. There are various types of inferences, including predictions, generalizations, and deductions about story details. At first you may find that students make very simple inferences, or just restate or add a detail to something in the story. Over time, they will become more adept at recognizing, making, and articulating inferences.

Sharing Questions (20–30 minutes)

Students share different types of questions about the story.

STUDENT LEARNING OBJECTIVE

READING COMPREHENSION: To ask questions about the story, identifying those that are interpretive

LOOK FOR STUDENTS TO

Mention puzzling, confusing, or interesting aspects of the story

Ask questions about the story

Recognize interpretive questions about the story

---

1. Record questions on the board with students' names, or have students write their questions on strips of paper to post around the room.

2. Encourage students to identify and answer factual and vocabulary questions by using the text, the Reader's Journal glossary, a dictionary, or classmates for help.

3. Identify any evaluative, speculative, or background questions. Help the class revise, answer, or skip them, as appropriate.

4. Point to a remaining question that you think might be interpretive.

5. Test the question by asking students to offer possible answers that can be supported with evidence from the story.

6. If students are able to find support for two different answers, do not explore the question in detail. Tell students that they have identified an interpretive question—the kind of question you want them to keep in mind as they reread the story.

7. Repeat the process for as many questions as time allows.

REVIEW

IDENTIFYING INTERPRETIVE QUESTIONS

Your focus in this activity is to identify interpretive questions—questions that explore a story's meaning and inspire several different answers that can be supported with evidence from the story. Additional information about interpretive questions can be found in your Shared Inquiry professional development materials.

8. Tell students they are ready to choose their keeper question and that any of the interpretive questions they have identified would be a good choice. Have them write their keeper question on page 12 of the Reader's Journal, and encourage them to think about it as they read the story again.

9. Use your Leader Discussion Planner (page 53) to jot down posted questions that you will want to remember later for Shared Inquiry discussion.

10. Have students turn to page 13 in the Reader's Journal to practice making inferences as a reading strategy. This can also serve as homework.

Second Reading with Directed Notes (45 minutes)

Students mark passages to note contrasting ideas in the story.

STUDENT LEARNING OBJECTIVE

READING COMPREHENSION: To reread with a purpose and articulate ideas about the story

LOOK FOR STUDENTS TO

Explain marked passages by referring to specific events and characters in those passages

Explain why a passage means one thing and not another

Explain marked passages by pointing to words and phrases in those passages

SPOTLIGHT
on Follow-Up Questions

For this unit, the spotlight is on **asking follow-up questions to help students become aware that evidence can support more than one conclusion**. As students review their notes, read passages aloud, and explain their evidence, look for opportunities to help them consider how and why the same passage can be understood in different ways. With your questions, help students see that even written words can have multiple meanings, and that explaining the words and phrases they see as evidence can help them, as well as their classmates, understand the story.

FOLLOW-UP QUESTIONS: SEEING EVIDENCE IN DIFFERENT WAYS

- Is there a particular word or phrase that supports your opinion?
- How does that word or phrase support your opinion?
- Does anyone see this passage differently?

BEFORE READING

1. Explain to students that during the second reading they will be taking notes. Write the following on the board:

    B = A character **believes** something happened.   **NB** = A character does **not believe** something happened.

2. Tell students that as they reread the story, they should mark with a **B** places where they think a character **believes** something happened, and mark with an **NB** places where they think a character does **not believe** something happened.

3. Ask students to think about why they are choosing those places, as they make their notes.

DURING READING

4. Tell students to read the story on their own or with a partner, or have them listen to the story read aloud (by you or on the CD), making notes as they go.

AFTER READING

5. Have students read aloud passages they marked with a **B** or an **NB**, and ask them to explain why they chose those passages.

6. Ask follow-up questions to help students explain how their evidence supports their note. Remember to ask if anyone sees a passage another way. When two students have marked the same passage differently, ask follow-up questions to help students see how the same evidence can be understood in different ways.

7. Use your Leader Discussion Planner (page 53) to jot down questions or ideas to explore later.

8. Have students turn to Head in the Clouds on page 15 of the Reader's Journal and choose a topic for writing or drawing.

9. Optional: Have students perform a passage using reader's theater techniques (see sidebar).

READER'S THEATER

Performing a story passage for an audience brings the text to life. In reader's theater, students create a script based on the story, choose parts, and read the script in character and with expression. This is an enjoyable and effective way for students to understand the story and to practice reading aloud fluently. With no need for costumes, sets, or props, reader's theater is simple to implement in the classroom:

- In small groups, have students choose a page or two with plenty of dialogue.

- Have students write the selection in the form of a play, with separate speaking parts for each character, as well as a narrator.

- Encourage students to take turns reading each part before choosing roles.

- Have students practice reading their scripts until they are comfortable with their roles. Then have them perform their scripts for the class. Remind them to read in character and with expression.

Vocabulary (20 minutes)

Students practice using new vocabulary words.

> **STUDENT LEARNING OBJECTIVE**
>
> **READING COMPREHENSION: To understand and use new words in a variety of contexts**

SUGGESTED TARGET WORDS: broach, foreboding, suspicious

Choose the target words you want your class to learn, or use the suggested target words above. As you present a word, have students say it with you. Work on one word at a time, using these steps as a guide:

REVIEW

USING THE CONTEXT

To help students determine meaning from context, ask:

◆ Can you tell in your own words what is happening in this passage?

◆ What do you think this word means?

◆ Why do you think it means that?

◆ What else could it mean in this passage? Why can it mean that?

1. **Place the word in context.** Review how the word is used in the story.

2. **Define the word.** Use active language in your definition. Include a few examples of how to use the word in situations students will understand. For example:

   ◆ When you **broach** an idea or a subject as you speak to someone, you bring it up because you want to talk about it. You might not want to **broach** the subject of going to the playground with your parents if they are tired. If your friend said something mean behind your back, you might **broach** the problem by asking him if he is angry with you for something.

   ◆ **Foreboding** is a feeling that something bad is about to happen. If you are at a very scary movie, you might watch the screen with **foreboding**. She had a sense of **foreboding** when she heard her friend start to cry in the other room.

   ◆ When you feel **suspicious**, you don't trust someone because you think that person might be bad or wrong, but you don't have proof. If you think a friend is lying to you but you aren't sure, you might say that you are **suspicious** of him. My sister's guilty look when I asked her where my favorite book was made me **suspicious** that she took it.

3. **Use the word.** Encourage students to make the word their own by asking a few of them to use it in a sentence or to apply it to real-life situations.

4. Ask a question about the story, using the word. Have several students apply their knowledge of the word to answer the question.

5. Optional: Have students turn to Curious Words on page 154 of the Reader's Journal to write down some of their favorite words from the story.

OVERHEARD IN THE CLASSROOM

TARGET WORD: **suspicious**

PLACE THE WORD IN CONTEXT

" 'Now that you have seen him,' he said, 'you will know him if you should meet. Give him a wide path and don't do anything that will make him **suspicious**. He is a very fierce watchdog.' " (Refer students to page 29 in the student anthology.)

DEFINE THE WORD

When you feel **suspicious**, you don't trust someone because you think that person might be bad or wrong, but you don't have proof. If you think a friend is lying to you but you aren't sure, you might say that you are **suspicious** of him. My sister's guilty look when I asked her where my favorite book was made me **suspicious** that she took it. Let's say the word together.

USE THE WORD

Have students discuss a time when they felt **suspicious** and explain what made them feel that way. Begin by providing an example of your own, such as "When I heard my daughter and her friend laughing, I became **suspicious** that they were not doing their homework."

ASK A QUESTION ABOUT THE STORY

When does Jean become **suspicious** that André has been stealing his chickens?

Shared Inquiry Discussion (45 minutes)

Students discover meaning in the story by discussing an interpretive question.

STUDENT LEARNING OBJECTIVE

CRITICAL THINKING: To provide evidence that supports an answer to an interpretive question

LOOK FOR STUDENTS TO

Point to passages that they think show one answer is better than another

Point to relevant passages to support an independent conclusion

Explain how a passage supports a conclusion or answer

REVIEW

TIPS FOR DISCUSSION

Here are some tips for conducting an effective Shared Inquiry discussion:

- Tell students to keep their anthologies open and ready for reference.
- Ask students to read aloud from the story frequently, to supply evidence, and to examine specific passages.
- Return to your focus question regularly to ensure that students continue working on the same problem of meaning.
- Ask follow-up questions in such a way that students know you are genuinely curious and do not already have an answer in mind.
- Establish a measured pace to give students time to think, listen, and respond.
- Remind students that Shared Inquiry discussion is not a test, but rather a time to share ideas and learn from one another.

Use the Leader Discussion Planner on the facing page to prepare yourself for Shared Inquiry discussion. To prepare your group, have everyone sit in a circle or a square; remind them of the five discussion guidelines and any behavioral guidelines you want to share. Then follow these steps to conduct the discussion:

1. Write the focus question on the board and have students copy it on the Building Your Answer page of the Reader's Journal (page 17).

2. Give students a few minutes to review the story and to write down an answer.

3. Begin the discussion by asking the focus question. On your seating chart, keep track of students' participation and ideas (see Using the Seating Chart, page 55).

4. Lead the discussion by asking follow-up questions to help students clarify their ideas, provide evidence (see sample questions in your Leader Discussion Planner, page 53), and respond to one another. Aim to have the discussion last 20 to 30 minutes.

5. As the discussion winds down, have students finish the Building Your Answer page. Then ask volunteers to share what they wrote.

6. Spend a few minutes talking about the discussion. Ask students what they liked about it, what was hard about it, what they think makes a good discussion, and what might go better next time.

LEADER DISCUSSION PLANNER

After the first and second readings, use this section to keep track of:

◆ Questions that you and your students have about the story

◆ Characters, incidents, and ideas that interest you

◆ Passages that interest you

NOTES AND QUESTIONS

_____

_____

_____

_____

_____

Write down a focus question, cluster questions, and passages that you think you or your students will refer to in discussion. If you choose not to develop your own questions, see Suggested Interpretive Questions for Shared Inquiry Discussion on page 54.

CLUSTER QUESTION

_____
_____
_____

CLUSTER QUESTION

_____
_____
_____

FOCUS QUESTION FOR DISCUSSION

_____
_____
_____

RELATED PASSAGE   page _____

_____
_____
_____

RELATED PASSAGE   page _____

_____
_____
_____

In this Shared Inquiry discussion, look for opportunities to help students become aware that evidence can support more than one conclusion.

FOLLOW-UP QUESTIONS: SEEING EVIDENCE IN DIFFERENT WAYS

◆ Did anyone read that passage differently?

◆ Can you find a passage in the story that supports Fred's idea?

◆ Could that part of the story mean anything else?

SUGGESTED INTERPRETIVE QUESTIONS FOR SHARED INQUIRY DISCUSSION

R E V I E W

SUGGESTING A PASSAGE

If students need help exploring different interpretations of a story, suggest a specific passage for them to consider and ask related questions such as:

♦ How does this passage tie in with the part that you read?

♦ Does this passage help you understand the part that Wesley mentioned? Why or why not?

♦ Does this passage support your answer to the focus question? Why or why not?

OPTION 1 **Does André believe the big black dog is real?**

♦ When Jean first tells André about the big black dog, does he expect André to believe the story?

♦ Why does André compare the big black dog to the *loup-garou*?

♦ Why do the townspeople say they keep seeing the dog?

♦ At the end of the story, why does everyone agree that the dog is gone for good?

PASSAGE FOR DISCUSSION In the student anthology, from "André promised to stay a safe distance," on page 29, to " 'I would thank you to leave my dog alone, André Drouillard,' he said stiffly," on page 31

OPTION 2 **Why does the story have André end up with two hens while Jean gets into trouble with his neighbors?**

♦ According to the story, is Jean wrong to try to fool André?

♦ Why do the townspeople begin to complain to Jean about the big black dog?

♦ Why does André repeatedly tell Jean that he has seen the big black dog?

♦ Why does the author begin the incident of André's bleeding hand by telling us that Jean Labadie "left his neighbor chopping wood all by himself"?

PASSAGE FOR DISCUSSION In the student anthology, from "Then everyone grew angry at Jean Labadie," on page 37, to "the dog was gone for good," on page 39

OVERHEARD IN THE CLASSROOM

LEADER Why does the story have André end up with two hens while Jean gets into trouble with his neighbors?

DENISE Because he deserved to get in trouble.

LEADER Why did he deserve it?

DENISE Because it was mean to try to scare André.

LEADER Where in the story does it seem mean to try to scare André?

DENISE At the beginning, here, when he says how Jean had to stop telling stories about the *loup* . . . demon thing because everyone runs away all scared. It's on page 26.

LEADER (*To the group.*) Why does he have to stop just because they get scared?

DEBORAH Because they're just not very smart. They are scared so easily. It's not Jean's fault.

SEATING CHART

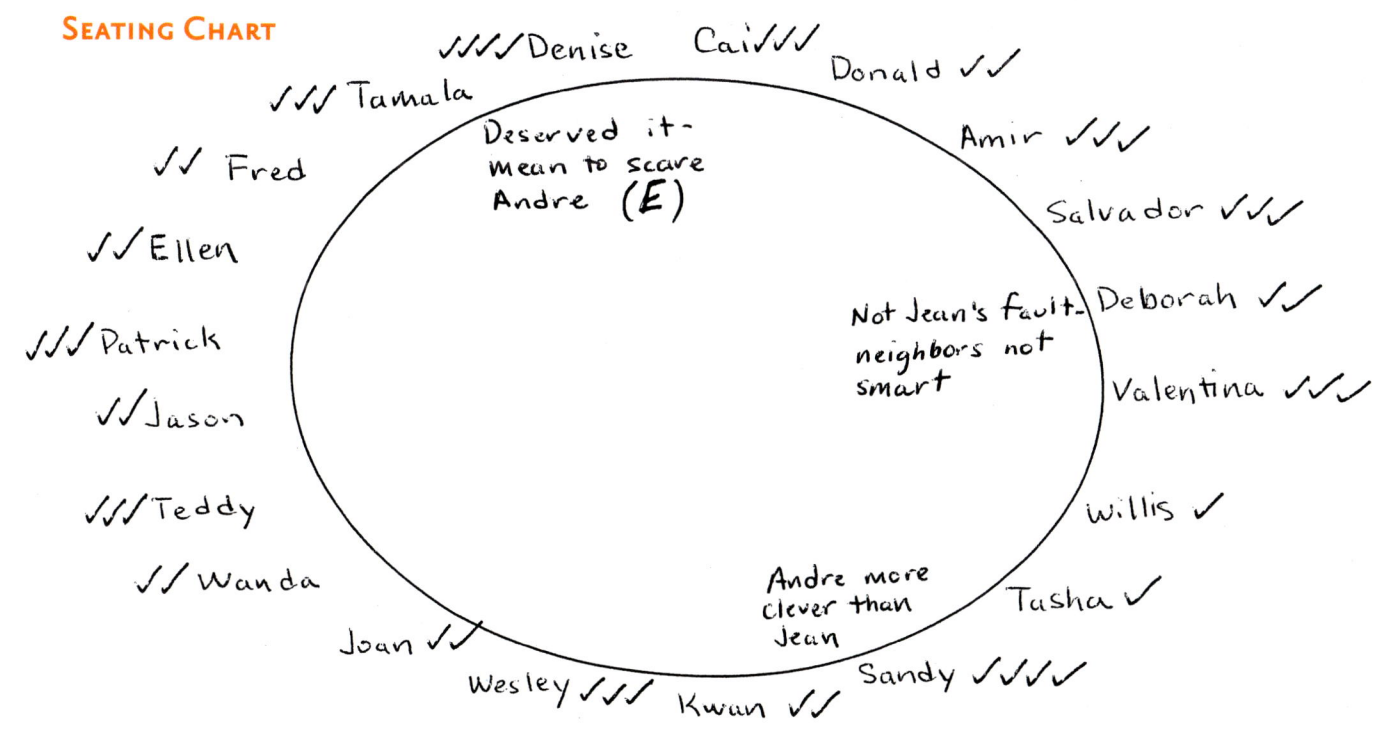

Expository Writing: Problems and Solutions (45 minutes)

Students comment on a main character's problems and solutions.

> **STUDENT LEARNING OBJECTIVE**
>
> **WRITING:** To use a graphic organizer to record problems and solutions in the story

TEACHING LITERARY CONCEPTS: PROBLEMS AND SOLUTIONS

PROBLEMS AND SOLUTIONS IN A STORY

Literature takes shape using a combination of story structures such as descriptive narrative, cause and effect, and problem and solution. It is hard to imagine a story that does not have a character trying to solve some sort of problem. A character may have to solve several problems within a story, and what this character does affects what other characters do. Isolating the problems and solutions a character encounters in a story will help students understand part of the story's structure and ultimately explain their own interpretation of the story.

1. Point out to students that stories have problems and solutions in them. Then post the following definitions on the board:

   A story **problem** happens when someone or something is working against a story character.

   A story **solution** happens when someone or something fixes the problem.

2. Discuss with students examples of problems and solutions from stories you have read together as a class.

PREWRITING

3. Make a chart on the board similar to the one on pages 18-19 of the Reader's Journal. Tell students to look in their books to find Jean Labadie's first problem in the story. Give students a few minutes before calling on volunteers. When the class has agreed on the first problem, write it in the corresponding box.

4. Help the class determine the solution to Jean Labadie's first problem and write it in the corresponding box.

5. Have students turn to pages 18-19 in the Reader's Journal to complete their own organizer for Jean Labadie's problems and solutions.

6. Ask students to look at their problem and solution organizers and to think of another way Jean Labadie could have solved some of his problems while remaining friends with André Drouillard. Have students share their ideas with the class.

Creative Writing: Great Storytellers (45 minutes)

Students write a description of an imaginary character and read their descriptions aloud.

> ### STUDENT LEARNING OBJECTIVE
>
> **WRITING: To use expressive language in vivid description**

PREWRITING

1. Remind students that in the story, the *loup-garou* is a monster that takes the form of a fierce animal. Tell students that they will pretend they saw the *loup-garou* and write about it.

2. Ask students to suggest animals the *loup-garou* might appear as, listing a few examples on the board. Lead students in making a web or list of important features of the *loup-garou,* such as what it looks, sounds, or smells like; what it eats; and where it can be found. A sample is shown below:

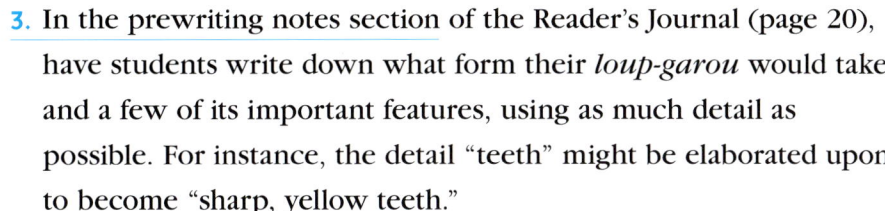

When I saw the loup-garou, it was . . .

A giant bird!   A big snake!

Some important features

Ten-foot wings	Eats children
Black and green feathers	Lives in the mud
Loud squawk	Smells like a swamp

3. In the prewriting notes section of the Reader's Journal (page 20), have students write down what form their *loup-garou* would take and a few of its important features, using as much detail as possible. For instance, the detail "teeth" might be elaborated upon to become "sharp, yellow teeth."

WRITING A DRAFT

4. Have students draft their descriptions on page 21 of the Reader's Journal and draw a picture of their *loup-garou* on the following page.

5. Optional: Have a storytelling festival (see sidebar).

A STORYTELLING FESTIVAL

An engaging storyteller uses vocal pitch, vocal speed, rhythm, expression, and gestures to communicate vividly with an audience. This story is not only about a good storyteller, but also describes dramatic storytelling techniques in a way that students can grasp.

A natural extension of this story is to have students read their own writing aloud, attempting to use some of the storytelling techniques outlined in the story. After students write their drafts, have a storytelling festival:

- Remind students that Jean Labadie was "the most popular storyteller in the parish" because he "acted out every story so that it would seem more real" (page 25). Have students find examples in the story.

- Ask students what makes a person a great storyteller, listing their ideas on the board. If students need help, ask them how the voice, hands, and body can be used to make a story more real.

- Have volunteers read their descriptions of the *loup-garou* aloud, using some of the techniques listed on the board.

Curriculum Connections

Below are resources related to "Jean Labadie's Big Black Dog" for further reading and investigation in a number of subject areas.

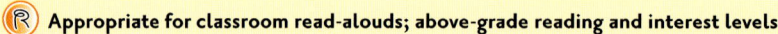 Appropriate for classroom read-alouds; above-grade reading and interest levels

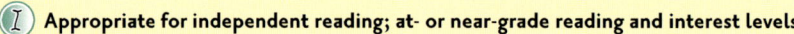 Appropriate for independent reading; at- or near-grade reading and interest levels

OTHER WORKS BY THE AUTHOR

Ⓡ Carlson, Natalie Savage. *The Family Under the Bridge.* New York: HarperCollins, 1989.

An old tramp, adopted by three fatherless children when their mother hides them under a bridge on the Seine, finds a home for the mother and children and a job for himself.

ART

Ⓘ Murawski, Laura. *How to Draw Dogs.* New York: PowerKids Press, 2001.

Describes how to draw various dogs, including the saluki, gray wolf, and golden retriever.

FOLKLORE

Ⓡ Amoss, Berthe. *The Loup Garou.* Gretna, LA: Pelican, 1980.

In eighteenth-century Nova Scotia as the English attempt to force out the French, one family draws upon its knowledge of the legendary werewolf, *loup-garou.*

Ⓘ Charles, Veronika Martenova. *The Maiden of the Mist: A Legend of Niagara Falls.* Toronto: Stoddart Kids, 2001.

Lelawala, a Seneca maiden, offers herself as a sacrifice to save her people from a great sickness.

SCIENCE

(I) Ganeri, Anita. *Dogs.* Chicago: Heinemann Library, 2003.

Provides information about the life cycles of dogs, looks at their physical characteristics, and offers advice on how to care for the animals, covering housing, food, and exercise.

(R) O'Hare, Jeffrey A. *Bogus Beasts: In Search of Imaginary Animals.* Honesdale, PA: Boyds Mills Press, 1999.

A nature book that asks children to choose which of several animals described on each page is actually imaginary.

(I) Stone, Lynn M. *Wildlife of Canada.* Vero Beach, FL: Rourke, 1995.

Photographs and simple text provide young readers with information about the animals that live in the different regions of Canada.

(I) Waters, Jo. *The Wild Side of Pet Dogs.* Chicago: Raintree, 2005.

Compares the bodies, senses, movements, diets, social behavior, and hunting instincts of the domesticated dog and its relative in the wild: the wolf.

SOCIAL STUDIES

(I) De Capua, Sarah. *Niagara Falls.* New York: Children's Press, 2002.

A brief introduction to Niagara Falls and some things to do there.

(I) Olson, Nathan. *Canada.* Mankato, MN: Capstone Press, 2005.

A brief introduction to Canada, following a simple question-and-answer format that discusses land features, government, housing, transportation, industries, education, sports, art forms, holidays, food, and family life.

(R) Tokunaga, Wendy. *Niagara Falls.* San Diego, CA: Kidhaven Press, 2004.

Describes the formation of the Niagara Falls, the efforts put forth to build a bridge across the falls, the daredevils who tempted fate, and how the falls are used today.

Highlighted words are the suggested target words in the vocabulary activity. Underlined words can be briefly explained as you read the story aloud, using the definitions provided.

LEADER'S NOTES AND QUESTIONS

• *Jean Labadie was the most popular storyteller.* •

JEAN LABADIE'S BIG BLACK DOG

French-Canadian folktale
as told by Natalie Savage Carlson

Once in another time, Jean Labadie was the most popular storyteller in the parish. He acted out every story so that it would seem more real.

When he told about the great falls in Niagara, he made a booming noise deep in his throat and whirled his fists around each other. Then each listener could plainly hear the falls and see the white water churning and splashing as if it were about to pour down on his own head. But Jean Labadie had to stop telling his stories about the *loup-garou*, the demon who takes the shape of a terrible animal and pounces upon those foolish people who go out alone at night.

25

LEADER'S NOTES
AND QUESTIONS

...

Every time the storyteller dropped down on all fours, rolled his eyes, snorted, and clawed at the floor, his listeners ran away from him in terror.

It was only on the long winter evenings that Jean had time to tell these tales. All the rest of the year, he worked hard with his cows and his pigs and his chickens.

One day Jean Labadie noticed that his flock of chickens was getting smaller and smaller. He began to suspect that his neighbor, André Drouillard, was stealing them. Yet he never could catch André in the act.

For three nights running, Jean took his gun down from the wall and slept in the henhouse with his chickens. But the only thing that happened was that his hens were disturbed by having their feeder roost with them, and they stopped laying well. So Jean sighed and put his gun back and climbed into his own bed again.

One afternoon when Jean went to help his neighbor mow the weeds around his barn, he found a bunch of gray chicken feathers near

26

the fence. Now he was sure that André was taking his chickens, for all of his neighbor's chickens were scrawny white things.

He did not know how to <mark>broach</mark> the matter to André without making an enemy of him. And when one lives in the country and needs help with many tasks, it is a great mistake to make an enemy of a close neighbor. Jean studied the matter as his <u>scythe</u> went swish, swish through the tall weeds. At last he thought of a way out.

"Have you seen my big black dog, André?" he asked his neighbor.

27

🎁 **broach:** bring an idea up because you want to talk about it

scythe: a tool with a curved blade, used to cut grass or crops

•••

"What big black dog?" asked André. "I didn't know you had a dog."

"I just got him from the Indians," said Jean. "Someone has been stealing my chickens so I got myself a dog to protect them. He is a very fierce dog, bigger than a wolf and twice as wild."

Jean took one hand off the scythe and pointed to the ridge behind the barn.

"There he goes now," he cried, "with his big red tongue hanging out of his mouth. See him!"

André looked but could see nothing.

"Surely you must see him. He runs along so fast. He lifts one paw this way and another paw that way."

As Jean said this, he dropped the scythe and lifted first one hand in its black glove and then the other.

28

...

André looked at the black gloves going up and down like the paws of a big black dog. Then he looked toward the ridge. He grew excited.

"Yes, yes," he cried, "I do see him now. He is running along the fence. He lifts one paw this way and another paw that way, just like you say."

Jean was pleased that he was such a good actor he could make André see a dog that didn't exist at all.

"Now that you have seen him," he said, "you will know him if you should meet. Give him a wide path and don't do anything that will make him <mark>suspicious.</mark> He is a very fierce watchdog."

André promised to stay a safe distance from the big black dog.

Jean Labadie was proud of himself over the success of his trick. No more chickens disappeared. It seemed that his problem was solved.

Then one day André greeted him with, "I saw your big black dog in the road today. He was running along lifting one paw this way and another paw that way. I got out of his way, you can bet my life!"

29

Think-Aloud

"Jean Labadie's plan appears to be working because no more chickens have disappeared and André seems to believe the story."

suspicious: not trusting someone because the person might be bad or wrong

• • •

Jean Labadie was pleased and annoyed at the same time. Pleased that André believed so completely in the big black dog that he could actually see him. He was also annoyed because the big black dog had been running down the road when he should have been on the farm.

Another day André leaned over the fence.

"Good day, Jean Labadie," he said. "I saw your big black dog on the other side of the village. He was jumping over fences and bushes. Isn't it a bad thing for him to wander so far away? Someone might take him for the *loup-garou*."

Jean Labadie was disgusted with his neighbor's good imagination.

"André," he asked, "how can my dog be on the other side of the village when he is right here at home? See him walking through the yard, lifting one paw this way and another paw that way?"

André looked in Jean's yard with surprise.

"And so he is," he agreed. "My faith, what a one he is! He must run like lightning to get home so fast. Perhaps you should chain him up. Someone will surely mistake such a fast dog for the *loup-garou*."

30

Think-Aloud

"Why does André talk like the dog is real? He can't be that easily fooled. Maybe he is being clever."

LEADER'S NOTES AND QUESTIONS

- mode: off—

Jean shrugged hopelessly.

"All right," he said, "perhaps you are right. I will chain him near the henhouse."

"They will be very happy to hear that in the village," said André. "Everyone is afraid of him. I have told them all about him, how big and fierce he is, how his long red tongue hangs out of his mouth, and how he lifts one paw this way and another paw that way."

Jean was angry.

"I would thank you to leave my dog alone, André Drouillard," he said stiffly.

"Oh, ho, and that I do," retorted André. "But today on the road he growled and snapped at me. I would not be here to tell the story if I hadn't taken to a tall maple tree."

LEADER'S NOTES AND QUESTIONS

...

Jean Labadie pressed his lips together.

"Then I will chain him up this very moment." He gave a long low whistle. "Come, fellow! Here, fellow!"

André took to his heels.

Of course, this should have ended the matter, and Jean Labadie thought that it had. But one day when he went to the village to buy some nails for his roof, he ran into Madame Villeneuve in a great how-does-it-make of excitement.

"Jean Labadie," she cried to him, "you should be ashamed of yourself, letting that fierce dog run loose in the village."

"But my dog is chained up in the yard at home," said Jean.

"So André Drouillard told me," said Madame, "but he has broken loose. He is running along lifting one paw this way and another paw that way, with the broken chain dragging in the dust. He growled at me and bared his fangs. It's a lucky thing his chain caught on a bush or I would not be talking to you now."

Jean sighed.

"Perhaps I should get rid of my big black dog," he said. "Tomorrow I will take him back to the Indians."

32

...

So next day Jean hitched his horse to the cart and waited until he saw André Drouillard at work in his garden. Then he whistled loudly toward the yard, made a great show of helping his dog climb up between the wheels and drove past André's house with one arm curved out in a bow, as if it were around the dog's neck.

"*Au revoir*, André!" he called. Then he looked at the empty half of the seat. "Bark goodbye to André Drouillard, fellow, for you are leaving here forever."

Jean drove out to the Indian village and spent the day with his friends, eating and talking. It seemed a bad waste of time when there was so much to be done on the farm, but on the other hand,

Think-Aloud

"I'd like to hear your inferences now. Why do you think Jean makes a great show of driving the dog away? What makes you think that?"

LEADER'S NOTES AND QUESTIONS

_____
_____
_____
_____
_____
_____
_____
_____
_____

au revoir: French for *goodbye*

•••

it was worth idling all day in order to end the big black dog matter.

Dusk was falling as he rounded the curve near his home. He saw the shadowy figure of André Drouillard waiting for him near his gate. A feeling of foreboding came over Jean.

"What is it?" he asked his neighbor. "Do you have some bad news for me?"

"It's about your big black dog," said André. "He has come back home. Indeed he beat you by an hour. It was that long ago I saw him running down the road to your house with his big red tongue hanging out of his mouth and lifting one paw this way and another paw that way."

Jean was filled with rage. For a twist of tobacco, he would have struck André with his horsewhip.

"André Drouillard," he shouted, "you are a liar! I just left the big black dog with the Indians. They have tied him up."

André sneered.

"A liar am I? We shall see who is the liar. Wait until the others see your big black dog running around again."

34

LEADER'S NOTES AND QUESTIONS

idling: being lazy and not doing any work

foreboding: a feeling that something bad is about to happen

...

So Jean might as well have accused André of being a chicken thief in the first place, for now they were enemies anyway. And he certainly might as well have stayed home and fixed his roof.

Things turned out as his neighbor had hinted. Madame Villeneuve saw the big black dog running behind her house. Henri Dupuis saw him running around the corner of the store. Delphine Langlois even saw him running through the graveyard among the tombstones. And always as he ran along, he lifted one paw this way and another paw that way.

•••

There came that day when Jean Labadie left his neighbor chopping wood all by himself, because they were no longer friends, and drove into the village to have his black mare shod. While he was sitting in front of the blacksmith shop, André Drouillard came galloping up at a great speed. He could scarcely hold the reins, for one hand was cut and bleeding.

A crowd quickly gathered. "What is wrong, André Drouillard?" they asked. "Have you cut yourself?"

"Where is Dr. Brisson? Someone fetch Dr. Brisson."

André Drouillard pointed his bleeding hand at Jean Labadie.

"His big black dog bit me," he accused. "Without warning, he jumped the fence as soon as Jean drove away and sank his teeth into my hand."

There was a gasp of horror from every throat. Jean Labadie reddened. He walked over to André and stared at the wound.

36

Think-Aloud

"I'd like to hear your inferences. What are some words to describe the townspeople? What in the story tells you that?"

LEADER'S NOTES AND QUESTIONS

shod: had horseshoes put on

"It looks like an ax cut to me," he said.

Then everyone grew angry at Jean Labadie and his big black dog. They threatened to drive them both out of the parish.

"My friends," said Jean wearily, "I think it is time for this matter to be ended. The truth of it is that I have no big black dog. I never had a big black dog. It was all a joke."

"Aha!" cried André. "Now he is trying to crawl out of the blame. He says he has no big black dog. Yet I have seen it with my own eyes, running around and lifting one paw this way and another paw that way."

"I have seen it, too," cried Madame Villeneuve. "It ran up and growled at me."

"And I."

"And I."

Jean Labadie bowed his head.

"All right, my friends," he said. "There is nothing more I can do about it. I guess that big black dog will eat me out of house and home for the rest of my life."

"You mean you won't make things right about this hand?" demanded André Drouillard.

"What do you want me to do?" asked Jean.

37

LEADER'S NOTES AND QUESTIONS

• • •

"I will be laid up for a week at least," said André Drouillard, "and right at harvest time. Then, too, there may be a scar. But for two of your plumpest pullets, I am willing to overlook the matter and be friends again."

"That is fair," cried Henri Dupuis.

"It is just," cried the blacksmith.

"A generous proposal," agreed everyone.

"And now we will return to my farm," said Jean Labadie, "and I will give André two of my pullets. But all of you must come. I want witnesses."

A crowd trooped down the road to watch the transaction.

After Jean had given his neighbor two of his best pullets, he commanded the crowd, "Wait!"

He went into the house. When he returned, he was carrying his gun.

"I want witnesses," explained Jean, "because I am going to shoot my big black dog. I want everyone to see this happen."

The crowd murmured and surged. Jean gave a long low whistle toward the henhouse.

"Here comes my big black dog," he pointed.

38

pullets: young hens

LEADER'S NOTES AND QUESTIONS

···

"You can see how he runs to me with his big red tongue hanging out and lifting one paw this way and another paw that way."

Everyone saw the big black dog.

Jean Labadie lifted his gun to his shoulder, pointed it at nothing and pulled the trigger. There was a deafening roar and the gun kicked Jean to the ground. He arose and brushed off his blouse. Madame Villeneuve screamed and Delphine Langlois fainted.

"There," said Jean, brushing away a tear, "it is done. That is the end of my big black dog. Isn't that true?"

And everyone agreed that the dog was gone for good.

LEADER'S NOTES AND QUESTIONS

Caporushes

English folktale as told by Flora Annie Steel

STORY LENGTH: 16 pages   READ-ALOUD TIME: About 19 minutes

◆ ABOUT THE STORY

Caporushes works as a scullery maid, hiding her beautiful dress and hair. She tells no one that she is the daughter of a rich gentleman or that her father, doubting her love for him, banished her from their home. When the master for whom she works throws a ball, she attends it without her disguise and captures the heart of the master's son. But Caporushes waits to reveal her true identity until she has tested the young man's love, and given her father another chance.

◆ ABOUT THE AUTHOR

Flora Annie Steel was born in 1847 in Harrow, England, and lived in India for many years. She authored a variety of books for adults as well as children, including retellings of traditional Indian and English stories. She was the first female school inspector in India and an advocate for Indian women's education. After returning to England, Steel published *English Fairy Tales*, from which "Caporushes" is taken. She died in 1929.

The story starts on page 96 of the Leader's Edition, and on page 40 of the student anthology.

STAGE 4 ASSESSMENT

The Stage 4 story comprehension test
(appendix A) is based on this unit.

Unit Overview

❖ **SESSION 1:** PAGE 79

> **PREREADING** Students use similes to express love.
>
> ☆ **FIRST READING** Students make inferences about the story as the leader reads it aloud.
>
> ☆ **SHARING QUESTIONS** Students share different types of questions about the story.

SESSION 2: PAGE 84

> ☆ **SECOND READING WITH DIRECTED NOTES** Students mark passages to note contrasting ideas in the story.
>
> **SPOTLIGHT ON FOLLOW-UP QUESTIONS** The leader asks follow-up questions to help students reflect and comment on their classmates' ideas.

SESSION 3: PAGE 86

> **VOCABULARY** Students practice using new vocabulary words. Suggested target words: *exceedingly*, *implored*, and *mindful*

SESSION 4: PAGE 88

> ☆ **SHARED INQUIRY DISCUSSION** Students discover meaning in the story by discussing an interpretive question.

SESSION 5 OPTIONS: PAGE 92

> **EXPOSITORY WRITING** Students use similes to tell the story.
>
> **CREATIVE WRITING** Students write a description of a character, using similes.
>
> **CURRICULUM CONNECTIONS** The leader can use these resources to link the story to other subject areas.

❖ May require two class periods

☆ Core activity

Prereading (5–10 minutes)

Students use similes to express love.

> **STUDENT LEARNING OBJECTIVE**
>
> **READING COMPREHENSION: To become familiar with a concept in the story**

1. Tell students that you are going to read a story about a girl who finds an unusual way to tell her father she loves him. Explain to students that you would like them to try to express their love for a family member in a similar way.

2. Write the following on the board:

   I love you as _____ loves _____.

   Ask students to supply words to complete the sentence. Offer examples such as:

   - I love you as <u>grass</u> loves <u>rain</u>.
   - I love you as <u>paper</u> loves <u>paint</u>.
   - I love you as <u>toast</u> loves <u>jelly</u>.

3. Collect additional examples from students, writing them on the board.

4. Ask students whether they think their family members would have trouble understanding their sentences. Help students share their ideas by asking questions such as:

   - How long do you think it would take your family member to understand what you are trying to say?
   - Would your family member like your sentence? Or would the person rather just hear you say, "I love you"?

First Reading (25–30 minutes)

Students make inferences about the story as the leader reads it aloud.

> **STUDENT LEARNING OBJECTIVE**
>
> **READING COMPREHENSION: To recognize and make inferences while reading**

BEFORE READING

1. Have students follow along in their books as they listen to you read "Caporushes," a story about a girl who finds an unusual way to tell her father that she loves him.

2. Remind students that strong readers make inferences while reading to help them figure out things not directly stated in the story. Readers make inferences by combining their own ideas with clues from the story.

3. Ask students to mark with an **I** at least one place where they make an **inference** about something not directly stated in the story. They should also mark with a **?** places where they have a **question** about the story. After listening to the story they will have a chance to share their inferences and questions.

DURING READING

4. Read the story aloud with expression.

5. Pause several times while reading to model how you make inferences. Look up from the book and share your thinking aloud when you draw a conclusion about something that is not directly stated in the story or was not clear at first. After modeling a few of your own inferences, stop at an appropriate spot and ask a question to prompt students to make inferences. If you wish, use the Think-Alouds provided in the margins of the story in this Leader's Edition.

PRACTICE WITH INFERENCES

Students need repeated and varied instruction—explicit teaching, modeling, guided practice, mini-lessons, and independent practice—to become proficient at using reading strategies. Encourage students to practice making inferences and to mark passages with an I while reading other stories. Have them share their inferences in small group discussions, or individually in conferences with you. Ask students to identify words or passages in the story and background knowledge they used to make their inferences.

AFTER READING

6. Ask students to review the story to find the places where they marked an **I** and to recall some of those inferences. Remind students that inferences are not facts written in the story but are guesses or conclusions formed by combining story details with the reader's own ideas.

7. Have a few students share a passage and their inference with the class and ask them to explain which story clues they used to make their inference.

8. Ask students to review the story to find the passages they marked with a **?** and to think about questions they would like to share with the class.

SHARING QUESTIONS AT A DIFFERENT TIME

Due to the length of this story and of the sharing questions activity, you may wish to wait until the next class meeting to move on to sharing questions. In that case, be sure to collect your students' questions (step 1 of the sharing questions activity on page 82) at the end of this class period, when their questions and curiosity are fresh. The next time you meet, you can briefly review the story before addressing students' questions. Note: You can skip or shorten the prereading, vocabulary, or writing activities in order to devote more time to the first reading and sharing questions activities.

Sharing Questions (20–30 minutes)

Students share different types of questions about the story.

> **STUDENT LEARNING OBJECTIVE**
>
> **READING COMPREHENSION: To ask questions about the story, identifying those that are interpretive**
>
> **LOOK FOR STUDENTS TO**
>
> Mention puzzling, confusing, or interesting aspects of the story
>
> Ask questions about the story
>
> Recognize interpretive questions about the story

MAKING QUESTIONS INTERPRETIVE

You may occasionally find that students express enthusiasm for a factual, evaluative, or speculative question. Help students revise the question to make it interpretive. Often, simply asking students to explain why they find the question interesting or where the question comes from in the story, will help you identify the interpretive issue underlying their curiosity. Additional information about different types of questions can be found in the sharing questions activity in Unit I of this Leader's Edition (page IO).

I. Record questions on the board with students' names, or have students write out their questions on strips of paper to post around the room.

2. Encourage students to identify and answer factual and vocabulary questions by using the text, the Reader's Journal glossary, a dictionary, or classmates for help.

3. Identify any evaluative, speculative, or background questions. Help the class revise, answer, or skip them as appropriate.

4. Point to a remaining question that you think might be interpretive.

5. Test the question by asking students to offer possible answers that can be supported with evidence from the story.

6. If students are able to find support for two different answers, do not explore the question in detail. Tell students that they have identified an interpretive question—the kind of question you want them to keep in mind as they reread the story.

7. Repeat the process for as many questions as time allows.

8. Tell students that they are ready to choose their keeper question and that any of the interpretive questions they have identified would be a good choice. Have them write their keeper question on page 24 of the Reader's Journal, and encourage them to think about it as they read the story again.

9. Use your Leader Discussion Planner (page 89) to jot down posted questions that you will want to remember later for Shared Inquiry discussion.

10. Have students turn to page 25 in the Reader's Journal to practice making inferences as a reading strategy. This can also serve as homework.

TURNING QUESTIONS INTO POSTDISCUSSION ACTIVITIES

Questions that emerge during this activity can sometimes inspire additional activities for later use. For example, if a student asks a particularly intriguing speculative question, you can set it aside to use for creative writing or other imaginative activities after the Shared Inquiry discussion.

Second Reading with Directed Notes (45 minutes)

Students mark passages to note contrasting ideas in the story.

STUDENT LEARNING OBJECTIVE

READING COMPREHENSION: To reread with a purpose and articulate ideas about the story

LOOK FOR STUDENTS TO

Recognize differing opinions within the group

Agree or disagree with other students' ideas

Give reasons for agreement or disagreement

SPOTLIGHT
on Follow-Up Questions

For this unit, the spotlight is on **asking follow-up questions to help students reflect and comment on their classmates' ideas.** Encourage students to speak and respond directly to each other instead of to you, and to consider how other students viewed the same passage, by asking follow-up questions related to other students' ideas.

FOLLOW-UP QUESTIONS: COMMENTING ON CLASSMATES' IDEAS

- Why did you mark this place with a different note than Amir did?
- Do you have a question for Kwan about the way he marked that passage?
- Did you mark this place for the same reason Joan did?

BEFORE READING

1. Explain to students that during the second reading, they will be taking notes. Write the following on the board:

    R = Caporushes is taking a **risk**.   **C** = Caporushes is being **careful**.

2. Tell students that as they reread the story, they should mark with an **R** places where Caporushes is taking a **risk**, and mark with a **C** places where she is being **careful**.

3. Ask students to think about why they are choosing those places, as they make their notes.

DURING READING

4. Tell students to read the story on their own or with a partner, or have them listen to the story read aloud (by you or on the CD), making notes as they go.

AFTER READING

5. Have students read aloud passages they marked with an **R** or a **C**, and ask them to explain why they chose to mark those passages.

6. Ask follow-up questions to help students consider their own ideas in light of their classmates' conclusions about the passages in question. Remember to ask if anyone sees a passage differently. Examine as many passages and notations as time allows.

7. Use your Leader Discussion Planner (page 89) to jot down questions or ideas to explore later.

8. Have students turn to Head in the Clouds on page 27 of the Reader's Journal and choose a topic for writing or drawing.

FLUENCY TIP

Sometimes reading a passage aloud gives students new ideas about the story. After students share a passage and explain it, have them read it aloud a second time. Did they read it differently? Ask volunteers to share any differences they heard in the reader's tone of voice.

Vocabulary (20 minutes)

Students practice using new vocabulary words.

> **STUDENT LEARNING OBJECTIVE**
>
> **READING COMPREHENSION: To understand and use new words in a variety of contexts**

REVIEW

USING TARGET WORDS IN WRITING

Follow up vocabulary lessons with practice using target words in writing. A simple way to do this is to write questions on the board incorporating a target word. Base questions on the sentences in the vocabulary activity, or use questions of your own. Have students incorporate the target word into their written answers. You can also encourage students to use target words as they complete other written activities related to the story, such as the Building Your Answer page in the Reader's Journal and the expository and creative writing activities.

SUGGESTED TARGET WORDS: exceedingly, implored, mindful

Choose the target words you want your class to learn, or use the suggested target words above. As you present a word, have students say it with you. Work on one word at a time, using these steps as a guide:

1. Place the word in context. Review how the word is used in the story.

2. Define the word. Use active language in your definition. Include a few examples of how to use the word in situations students will understand. For example:

   - **Exceedingly** means very, very much or more than is usual. The man who owns that big house is **exceedingly** rich. Even though it was the first day of winter, it was **exceedingly** warm.
   - If I **implored** you to do something, I begged you or asked you very seriously. You might **implore** your parents for a later bedtime. The prisoner **implored** the judge to let him go free.
   - To be **mindful** is to be aware of or to pay careful attention to something. If you have to be home at six o'clock, you should be **mindful** of the time when you are playing outside. When I put away the dishes after dinner, I try to be **mindful** of how easily they can break.

3. Use the word. Encourage students to make the word their own by asking a few of them to use it in a sentence or to apply it to real-life situations.

4. Ask a question about the story, using the word. Have several students apply their knowledge of the word to answer the question.

5. Optional: Have students turn to Curious Words on page 155 of the Reader's Journal to write down some of their favorite words from the story.

OVERHEARD IN THE CLASSROOM

TARGET WORD: mindful

PLACE THE WORD IN CONTEXT

"But ne'er a cottage or a hamlet did she see, till just at sunsetting she came on a great house on the edge of the fen. It had a fine front door to it, but **mindful** of her dress of rushes she went round to the back." (Refer students to page 43 in the student anthology.)

DEFINE THE WORD

To be **mindful** is to be aware of or to pay careful attention to something. If you have to be home at six o'clock, you should be **mindful** of the time when you are playing outside. When I put away the dishes after dinner, I try to be **mindful** of how easily they can break. Say the word with me.

USE THE WORD

Which of the following makes you think of our target word **mindful**? Say "**mindful**" or "not **mindful**."

- ◆ Looking both ways before crossing the street
- ◆ Reading a test question twice before writing an answer
- ◆ Looking out the window during silent reading time
- ◆ Trying to wash the dishes in record-breaking time

ASK A QUESTION ABOUT THE STORY

Why is Caporushes **mindful** of scouring the pots and pans so well?

Shared Inquiry Discussion (45 minutes)

Students discover meaning in the story by discussing an interpretive question.

> ### STUDENT LEARNING OBJECTIVE
>
> CRITICAL THINKING: To refer to other students' ideas when responding to an interpretive question
>
> ### LOOK FOR STUDENTS TO
>
> Comment in ways that show they remember what others said
>
> Agree or disagree with other students' ideas
>
> Give reasons for agreement or disagreement

REVIEW

MEETING CHALLENGES

Anticipating and addressing potential challenges in group dynamics will make your discussion smoother and more productive. Here are some ideas:

- If you have shy students, create opportunities for them to participate by asking them to repeat an idea they agree with in discussion.

- If a few talkative students dominate, encourage them to listen by asking them why they agree or disagree with someone else's idea.

- If group size is an issue (25 students or more), try forming an inside and an outside circle. Lead the inside group in a discussion while the outside group listens for ideas they agree and disagree with. After the discussion, ask a few students from the outside circle to share what they heard. Then switch the groups and lead a discussion with a different focus question.

Use the Leader Discussion Planner on the facing page to prepare yourself for Shared Inquiry discussion. To prepare your group, have everyone sit in a circle or a square; remind them of the five discussion guidelines and any behavioral guidelines you want to share. Then follow these steps to conduct the discussion:

1. Write the focus question on the board and have students copy it on the Building Your Answer page of the Reader's Journal (page 28).

2. Give students a few minutes to review the story and to write down an answer.

3. Begin the discussion by asking the focus question. On your seating chart, keep track of students' participation and ideas (see Using the Seating Chart, page 91).

4. Lead the discussion by asking follow-up questions to help students clarify their ideas, provide evidence, and respond to one another (see sample questions in your Leader Discussion Planner, page 89). Aim to have the discussion last 20 to 30 minutes.

5. As the discussion winds down, have students finish the Building Your Answer page. Then ask volunteers to share what they wrote.

6. Spend a few minutes talking about the discussion. Ask students what they liked about it, what was hard about it, what they think makes a good discussion, and what might go better next time.

LEADER DISCUSSION PLANNER

After the first and second readings, use this section to keep track of:

◆ Questions that you and your students have about the story

◆ Characters, incidents, and ideas that interest you

◆ Passages that interest you

NOTES AND QUESTIONS

_____

_____

_____

_____

_____

Write down a focus question, cluster questions, and passages that you think you or your students will refer to in discussion. If you choose not to develop your own questions, see Suggested Interpretive Questions for Shared Inquiry Discussion on page 90.

CLUSTER QUESTION

_____

_____

_____

_____

CLUSTER QUESTION

_____

_____

_____

_____

FOCUS QUESTION FOR DISCUSSION

_____

_____

_____

RELATED PASSAGE   page _____

_____

_____

_____

_____

RELATED PASSAGE   page _____

_____

_____

_____

_____

In this Shared Inquiry discussion, look for opportunities to help your students listen and respond to their classmates' ideas.

FOLLOW-UP QUESTIONS: COMMENTING ON CLASSMATES' IDEAS

◆ Do you agree with what Deborah just said?

◆ What is it about Sandy's idea that you agree with?

◆ Is your answer the same as or different from Salvador's?

SUGGESTED INTERPRETIVE QUESTIONS FOR SHARED INQUIRY DISCUSSION

JUMPING RIGHT INTO DISCUSSION

Effective discussion questions are very specific. Questions such as *What is the theme of this story?* leave participants unsure what they are being asked to figure out. When a question is specific, students are able to jump right into discussion and refer back to the story for explicit supporting evidence.

OPTION I **When her father asks how much she loves him, why does Caporushes tell him she loves him "as fresh meat loves salt," instead of something easier to understand?**

◆ Why does the father get so angry at Caporushes when he loves her more than the other daughters?

◆ Why does Caporushes think before she speaks and answer slowly, while the other daughters answer "as pat as may be" and "as swift as thought"?

◆ Why doesn't Caporushes tell the young master who she is even after she has agreed to marry him?

◆ Why does Caporushes arrange the wedding food to show her father what she meant, even though it spoils the wedding breakfast?

PASSAGE FOR DISCUSSION In the student anthology, from "Once upon a time," on page 40, to "shut the door in her face," on page 41

OPTION 2 **Why does Caporushes wait until the young master is dying to reveal that she is the beautiful dancer?**

◆ Why does Caporushes go around to the back of the young master's house in her dress of rushes, rather than taking off her disguise and knocking on the front door?

◆ Why can't Caporushes keep from dancing with the young master, even though she thinks she shouldn't?

◆ Why is Caporushes so sure that young men don't die of love?

◆ Why does Caporushes hide the young master's ring in the gruel, instead of just giving it back to him?

PASSAGE FOR DISCUSSION In the student anthology, from "Then Caporushes told herself she would not dance again," on page 49, to "From him that gave it me," on page 53

OVERHEARD IN THE CLASSROOM

LEADER Why does Caporushes wait until the young master is dying to reveal that she is the beautiful dancer?

SANDY She's sort of afraid.

LEADER What is she afraid of?

SANDY How he might react. When she told her father that she loved him, he got really mad and kicked her out of the house. It says so on page 41.

LEADER Fred, do you agree that Caporushes is somewhat afraid?

FRED Partly.

LEADER Why partly?

FRED I don't think she's afraid of the young master kicking her out of the house. I think she doesn't want her own feelings to get hurt.

USING THE SEATING CHART

You will probably find that the more comfortable you become using the seating chart, the more your chart may differ from those in this book. The chart is your discussion tool—let it evolve to fit your note-taking style and discussion goals.

SEATING CHART

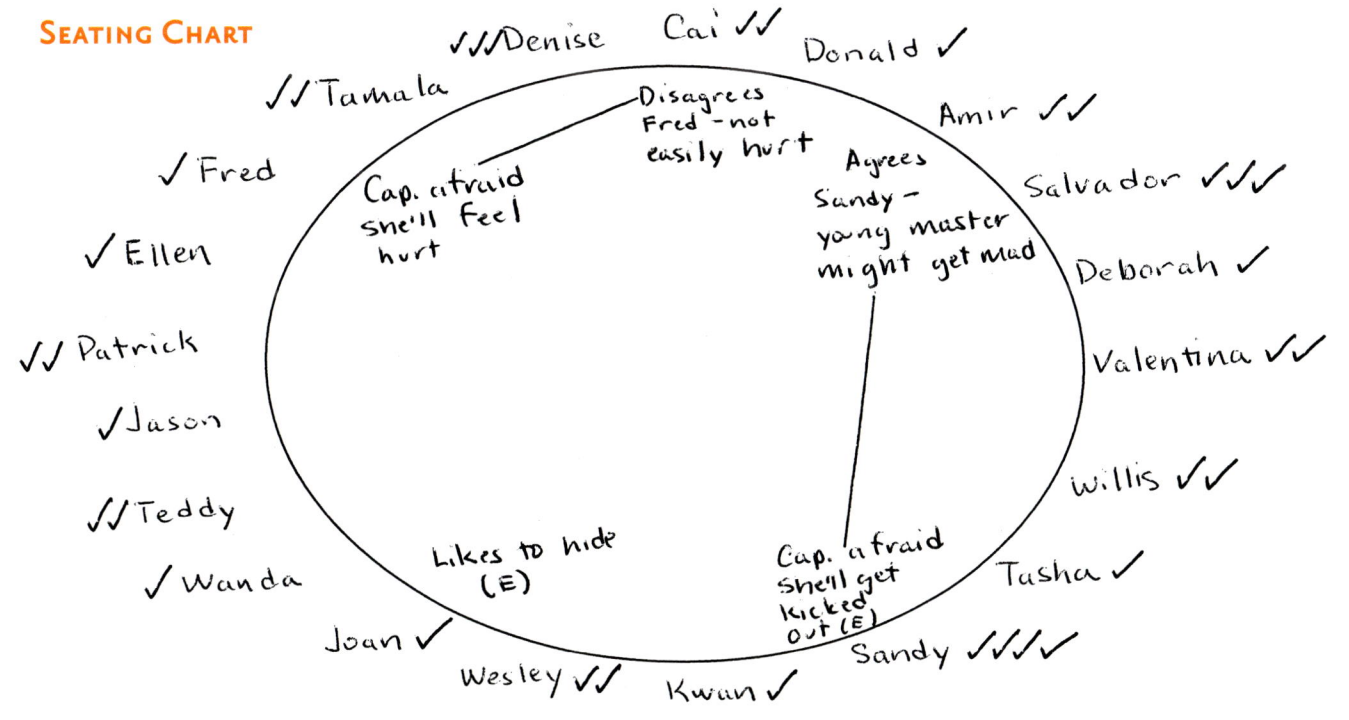

Expository Writing: Retelling with Similes (45 minutes)

Students use similes to tell the story.

> **STUDENT LEARNING OBJECTIVE**
>
> **WRITING:** To use similes in a narrative retelling

STAGE 4 ASSESSMENT

In the Reflect and Connect activity following this unit, students will have the opportunity to revise a piece of writing from Stage 4, which you may then choose to assess.

FIGURATIVE LANGUAGE IN EXPOSITORY WRITING

Creating their own similes will help students become more aware of how language is used in stories. This lesson allows students to incorporate creative language into story sequencing, an expository task.

TEACHING LITERARY CONCEPTS: SIMILES

1. Write this definition of the term *simile* on the board:

   A **simile** is a poetic comparison using the word **like** or **as**.

   Then write these examples on the board:
   - Her smile is like the sun.
   - The wind was as quiet as a whisper.

2. Remind students that Caporushes makes up a simile to tell her father how much she loves him. Tell students that they will learn how similes express ideas and then write some of their own.

3. Ask students to look at the example similes and to suggest words that come to mind. Summarize the meaning of the simile by saying, for example, "Her smile is like the sun. This is a poetic way of saying that her smile is bright, pleasant, full of light, and warm."

PREWRITING

4. Write Caporushes' simile on the board in a simile organizer:

   Caporushes loves her father ╱ as ╲ fresh meat loves salt.

5. Next, ask students to explain what the simile means, using evidence from the story. Write an explanation on the board.

6. Have students complete pages 29 and 30 in the Reader's Journal, working independently or in pairs.

WRITING A DRAFT

7. Have students retell "Caporushes" on page 31 of the Reader's Journal, incorporating their own similes.

Creative Writing:
Have You Seen Caporushes? (45 minutes)

Students write a description of a character, using similes.

> **STUDENT LEARNING OBJECTIVE**
>
> **WRITING: To use similes to describe a character**

PREWRITING

1. Tell students that Caporushes and her sisters use similes to describe their love for their father (pages 40 and 41).

2. Remind students that after Caporushes disappears for the last time, the master's son spends all his time trying to find her again. Tell students that they will create a poster seeking information about Caporushes, from the point of view of the master's son, writing their own similes to use in their description.

3. Ask students to review the story to find phrases or words used to describe Caporushes. List them on the board in the left-hand column of a two-column chart. In the right-hand column, help the class create similes to describe Caporushes from the point of view of the master's son, using organizers like the ones below.

SIMILES DEFINED

Similes are statements or sentences that compare two things using the words *like* or *as*. (For a thorough description and teaching notes, see the Teaching a Literary Concept section in the Expository Writing activity for this unit.)

Description of Caporushes	Simile
"... [She was] not only pretty, she was clever" (page 41) →	She is as clever **as** a magician's trick.
"Beautiful golden hair" (page 42) →	Her hair is **like** a sunflower.

4. Tell students to complete the descriptions in the Reader's Journal (page 33). Have them work in pairs to create similes out of these descriptions.

WRITING A DRAFT

5. Have students draft a description and draw a picture of Caporushes on page 34 of the Reader's Journal.

Curriculum Connections

Below are resources related to "Caporushes" for further reading and investigation in a number of subject areas.

 Appropriate for classroom read-alouds; above-grade reading and interest levels

 Appropriate for independent reading; at- or near-grade reading and interest levels

OTHER WORKS BY THE AUTHOR

 Steel, Flora Annie. *Goldilocks and the Three Bears and Other Classic English Fairy Tales.* New York: Children's Classics, 1994.

Presents a collection of both familiar and lesser known English fairy tales, including "Tattercoats," "Jack and the Beanstalk," and "Mollie Whuppie and the Double-Faced Giant."

APPLIED ARTS

 Dawson, Imogen. *Clothes and Crafts in the Middle Ages.* Milwaukee: Gareth Stevens, 2000.

Surveys the clothing and crafts of Europe during the Middle Ages and includes activities for making similar items with modern materials.

 Elliott, Lynne. *Food and Feasts in the Middle Ages.* New York: Crabtree, 2004.

Provides an overview of food, hunting, and cooking in the Middle Ages, including farming, markets, the spice trade, food shops, feasts and fasts, and the differences between the food available to peasants and nobles.

 Lilly, Melinda. *Salt.* Vero Beach, FL: Rourke, 2002.

Provides a variety of historical and scientific facts about salt.

FINE ARTS

 Craig-Quijada, Balinda. *Dance for Fun!* Minneapolis: Compass Point Books, 2004.

A survey of dance, including tap, modern, jazz, and ballet, and a timeline of the history of dance and the place it holds in cultures around the world.

 Gibson, Barry. *Dance.* Chicago: Heinemann Library, 2000.

An introduction to dance, describing styles and steps, with tips on safety, warm-ups, and cooldowns.

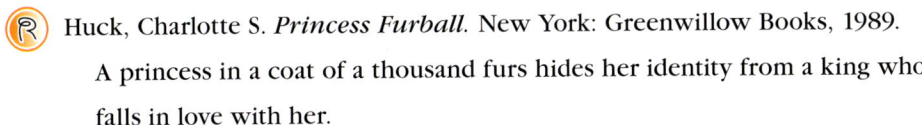

FOLLORE

(R) Huck, Charlotte S. *Princess Furball*. New York: Greenwillow Books, 1989.

A princess in a coat of a thousand furs hides her identity from a king who falls in love with her.

(R) Jaffe. Nina. *The Way Meat Loves Salt: A Cinderella Tale from the Jewish Tradition*. New York: Holt, 1998.

In this Eastern European variant of the Cinderella story, the youngest daughter of a rabbi is sent away from home in disgrace, but thanks to the help of the prophet Elijah, marries the son of a renowned scholar and is reunited with her family.

RECREATION

(I) Wilkes, Angela. *Dazzling Disguises and Clever Costumes*. New York: DK, 1996.

Projects for creating a variety of disguises using false features, fake hair, and masks, as well as such costume items and accessories as hats, cloaks, swords, and fairy wands.

SOCIAL STUDIES

(R) Eastwood, Kay. *Life in a Castle*. New York: Crabtree, 2004.

Describes different kinds of castles, their purposes, how they were built, and what it was like to live in a castle, especially for women and children.

Highlighted words are the suggested target words in the vocabulary activity. Underlined words can be briefly explained as you read the story aloud, using the definitions provided.

LEADER'S NOTES AND QUESTIONS

CAPORUSHES

*English folktale
as told by Flora Annie Steel*

Once upon a time, a long, long while ago, when all the world was young and all sorts of strange things happened, there lived a very rich gentleman whose wife had died, leaving him three lovely daughters. They were as the apple of his eye, and he loved them exceedingly.

Now one day he wanted to find out if they loved him in return, so he said to the eldest, "How much do you love me, my dear?"

And she answered as pat as may be, "As I love my life."

40

🎁 **exceedingly:** very, very much

"Very good, my dear," said he, and gave her a kiss. Then he said to the second girl, "How much do you love me, my dear?"

And she answered as swift as thought, "Better than all the world beside."

"Good!" he replied, and patted her on the cheek. Then he turned to the youngest, who was also the prettiest.

"And how much do *you* love me, my dearest?"

Now the youngest daughter was not only pretty, she was clever. So she thought a moment, then she said slowly, "I love you as fresh meat loves salt!"

Now when her father heard this he was very angry, because he really loved her more than the others.

"What!" he said. "If that is all you give me in return for all I've given you, out of my house you go." So there and then he turned her out of the home where she had been born and bred, and shut the door in her face.

Not knowing where to go, she wandered on, and she wandered on, till she came to a big <u>fen</u> where the reeds grew ever so tall and the rushes swayed in the wind like a field of corn. There she sat down and <u>plaited</u> herself an overall

41

Think-Aloud

"Caporushes' father seems out of control."

fen: a low, wet area of land

plaited: braided

•••

of rushes and a cap to match, so as to hide her fine clothes and her beautiful golden hair that was all set with milk-white pearls. For she was a wise girl and thought that in such lonely country, mayhap, some robber might fall in with her and kill her to get her fine clothes and jewels.

It took a long time to plait the dress and cap, and while she plaited she sang a little song:

Hide my hair, O cap o' rushes,
Hide my heart, O robe o' rushes.
Sure! my answer had no fault
I love him more than he loves salt.

And the fen birds sat and listened and sang back to her:

Cap o' rushes, shed no tear,
Robe o' rushes, have no fear.
With these words if fault he'd find,
Sure your father must be blind.

When her task was finished she put on her robe of rushes, and it hid all her fine clothes. And she put on the cap, and it hid all her beautiful hair, so that she looked quite a common country girl. But the fen birds flew away, singing as they flew:

42

_____
_____
_____
_____
_____
_____
_____
_____
_____
_____

...

Cap o' rushes! we can see,
Robe o' rushes! what you be,
Fair and clean, and fine and tidy,
So you'll be whate'er betide ye.

By this time she was very, very hungry, so she wandered on, and she wandered on. But ne'er a cottage or a hamlet did she see, till just at sunsetting she came on a great house on the

edge of the fen. It had a fine front door to it, but mindful of her dress of rushes she went round to the back. And there she saw a strapping fat scullion washing pots and pans with a very sulky face. So, being a clever girl, she guessed what

43

whate'er betide ye: whatever happens to you

hamlet: a small village

mindful: paying careful attention to something

scullion: a servant who does hard work in a kitchen

···

the maid was wanting and said, "If I may have a night's lodging, I will scrub the pots and pans for you."

"Why! Here's luck," replied the scullery maid, ever so pleased. "I was just wanting badly to go walking with my sweetheart. So if you will do my work you shall share my bed and have a bite of my supper. Only mind you scrub the pots clean, or Cook will be at me."

Now next morning the pots were scraped so clean that they looked like new, and the saucepans were polished like silver, and the cook said to the scullion, "Who cleaned these pots? Not you, I'll swear." So the maid had to up and out with the truth. Then the cook would have turned away the old maid and put on the new, but the latter would not hear of it.

"The maid was kind to me and gave me a night's lodging," she said. "So now I will stay without wages and do the dirty work for her."

So Caporushes—for so they called her since she would give no other name—stayed on and cleaned the pots and scraped the saucepans.

Now it so happened that her master's son came of age, and to celebrate the occasion a ball

Think-Aloud

"What kind of person does Caporushes seem like? Why do you say that?"

44

• • •

was given to the neighbourhood, for the young man was a grand dancer and loved nothing so well as a country <u>measure</u>. It was a very fine party, and after supper was served, the servants were allowed to go and watch the quality from the <u>gallery</u> of the ballroom.

But Caporushes refused to go, for she also was a grand dancer, and she was afraid that when she heard the fiddles starting a merry jig, she might start dancing. So she excused herself by saying she was too tired with scraping pots and washing saucepans, and when the others went off she crept up to her bed.

But alas! And alack-a-day! The door had been left open, and as she lay in her bed she could hear the fiddlers fiddling away and the tramp of dancing feet.

Then she upped and off with her cap and robe of rushes, and there she was, ever so fine and tidy.

45

measure: a kind of dance

gallery: an upstairs sitting or standing area that looks down on a large room

· · ·

She was in the ballroom in a <u>trice</u>, joining in the jig, and none was more beautiful or better dressed than she. While as for her dancing . . . !

Her master's son singled her out at once and with the finest of bows engaged her as his partner for the rest of the night. So she danced away to her heart's content, while the whole room was <u>agog</u>, trying to find out who the beautiful young stranger could be. But she kept her own <u>counsel</u> and, making some excuse, slipped away before the ball finished. So when her fellow servants came to bed, there she was in hers, in her cap and robe of rushes, pretending to be fast asleep.

Next morning, however, the maids could talk of nothing but the beautiful stranger.

46

LEADER'S NOTES AND QUESTIONS

trice: a very short amount of time

agog: very excited about something

counsel: advice or a plan about what to do; when you keep your own **counsel**, you follow your own plans or ideas

···

"You should have seen her," they said. "She was the loveliest young lady as ever you see, not a bit like the likes o' we. Her golden hair was all silvered with pearls, and her dress—law! You wouldn't believe how she was dressed. Young master never took his eyes off her."

And Caporushes only smiled and said, with a twinkle in her eye, "I should like to see her, but I don't think I ever shall."

"Oh, yes, you will," they replied, "for young master has ordered another ball tonight in hopes she will come to dance again."

But that evening Caporushes refused once more to go to the gallery, saying she was too tired with cleaning pots and scraping saucepans. And once more when she heard the fiddlers fiddling she said to herself, "I must have one dance—just one with the young master: he dances so beautifully." For she felt certain he would dance with her.

And sure enough, when she had upped and offed with her cap and robe of rushes, there he was at the door waiting for her to come. For he had determined to dance with no one else.

47

...

So he took her by the hand, and they danced down the ballroom. It was a sight of all sights! Never were such dancers! So young, so handsome, so fine, so gay!

But once again Caporushes kept her own counsel and just slipped away on some excuse in time, so that when her fellow servants came to their beds they found her in hers, pretending to be fast asleep; but her cheeks were all flushed and her breath came fast. So they said, "She is dreaming. We hope her dreams are happy."

But next morning they were full of what she had missed. Never was such a beautiful young gentleman as young master! Never was such a beautiful young lady! Never was such beautiful dancing! Everyone else had stopped theirs to look on.

And Caporushes, with a twinkle in her eyes, said, "I should like to see her, but I'm *sure* I never shall!"

"Oh yes!" they replied. "If you come tonight you're sure to see her, for young master has ordered another ball in hopes the beautiful stranger will come again. For it's easy to see he is madly in love with her."

48

...

Then Caporushes told herself she would not dance again, since it was not fit for a gay young master to be in love with his scullery maid. But, alas! The moment she heard the fiddlers fiddling, she just upped and offed with her rushes, and there she was, fine and tidy as ever! She didn't even have to brush her beautiful golden hair!

And once again she was in the ballroom in a trice, dancing away with young master, who never took his eyes off her and implored her to tell him who she was. But she kept her own counsel and only told him that she never, never, never would come to dance anymore, and that he must say goodbye. And he held her hand so

49

implored: begged or asked very seriously

Think-Aloud

"What does the young man's reaction tell us? How do you know?"

• • •

fast that she had a job to get away. And lo and behold! His ring came off his finger, and as she ran up to her bed there it was in her hand! She had just time to put on her cap and robe of rushes, when her fellow servants came trooping in and found her awake.

"It was the noise you made coming upstairs," she made excuse. But they said, "Not we! It is the whole place that is in an uproar searching for the beautiful stranger. Young master he tried to detain her, but she slipped from him like an eel. But he declares he will find her, for if he doesn't he will die of love for her."

Then Caporushes laughed. "Young men don't die of love," said she. "He will find someone else."

But he didn't. He spent his whole time looking for his beautiful dancer, but go where he might, and ask whom he would, he never heard anything about her. And day by day he grew thinner and thinner, and paler and paler, until at last he took to his bed.

And the housekeeper came to the cook and said, "Cook the nicest dinner you can cook, for young master eats nothing."

50

...

Then the cook prepared soups and jellies and creams and roast chicken and bread sauce, but the young man would none of them.

And Caporushes cleaned the pots and scraped the saucepans and said nothing.

Then the housekeeper came crying and said to the cook, "Prepare some gruel for young master. Mayhap he'd take that. If not he will die for love of the beautiful dancer. If she could see him now, she would have pity on him."

So the cook began to make the gruel, and Caporushes left scraping saucepans and watched her.

"Let me stir it," she said, "while you fetch a cup from the pantry room."

So Caporushes stirred the gruel, and what did she do but slip young master's ring into it before the cook came back!

Then the butler took the cup upstairs on a silver salver. But when the young master saw it he waved it away, till the butler, with tears, begged him just to taste it.

So the young master took a silver spoon and stirred the gruel, and he felt something hard at the bottom of the cup. And when he fished it

51

gruel: very thin porridge or soup

salver: a tray for serving food or drinks

up, lo, it was his own ring! Then he sat up in bed and said quite loud, "Send for the cook!"

And when she came he asked her who made the gruel.

"I did," she said, for she was half-pleased and half-frightened.

Then he looked at her all over and said, "No, you didn't! You're too stout! Tell me who made it and you shan't be harmed!"

Then the cook began to cry. "If you please, sir, I *did* make it. But Caporushes stirred it."

"And who is Caporushes?" asked the young man.

52

"If you please, sir, Caporushes is the scullion," whimpered the cook.

Then the young man sighed and fell back on his pillow. "Send Caporushes here," he said in a faint voice, for he really was very near dying.

And when Caporushes came he just looked at her cap and her robe of rushes and turned his face to the wall. But he asked her in a weak little voice, "From whom did you get that ring?"

Now when Caporushes saw the poor young man so weak and worn with love for her, her heart melted, and she replied softly, "From him that gave it me," and offed with her cap and robe of rushes. And there she was as fine and tidy as ever, with her beautiful golden hair all silvered over with pearls.

And the young man caught sight of her with the tail of his eye, and sat up in bed as strong as may be, and drew her to him and gave her a great big kiss. So, of course, they were to be married in spite of her being only a scullery maid, for she told no one who she was.

Now everyone far and near was asked to the wedding. Among the invited guests was Caporushes' father, who from grief at losing his

53

LEADER'S NOTES
AND QUESTIONS

...

favourite daughter had lost his sight and was very dull and miserable. However, as a friend of the family, he had to come to the young master's wedding.

Now the marriage feast was to be the finest ever seen. But Caporushes went to her friend the cook and said, "Dress every dish without one mite of salt."

"That'll be rare and nasty," replied the cook. But because she prided herself on having let Caporushes stir the gruel and so saved the young master's life, she did as she was asked and dressed every dish for the wedding breakfast without one mite of salt.

Now when the company sat down to table their faces were full of smiles and content, for all the dishes looked so nice and tasty. But no sooner had the guests begun to eat than their faces fell, for nothing can be tasty without salt.

Then Caporushes' blind father, whom his daughter had seated next to her, burst out crying.

"What is the matter?" she asked.

Then the old man sobbed, "I had a daughter whom I loved dearly, dearly. And I asked her how much she loved me, and she replied,

54

'As fresh meat loves salt.' And I was angry with
her and turned her out of house and home,
for I thought she didn't love me at all. But now
I see she loved me best of all."

    And as he said the words his eyes were
opened, and there beside him was his daughter,
lovelier than ever.

    And she gave him one hand, and her husband
the young master the other, and laughed, saying,
"I love you both as fresh meat loves salt." And
after that they were all happy forevermore.

55

STUDENT LEARNING OBJECTIVES IN STAGE 4

The following list is a collection of the student learning objectives from all activities in units 1 through 3 (Stage 4).

READING COMPREHENSION

- To preview text features before reading the story
- To recall experience with and knowledge about a concept in the story
- To become familiar with a concept in the story
- To recognize and make inferences while reading
- To ask questions about the story, identifying those that are interpretive
- To reread with a purpose and articulate ideas about the story
- To understand and use new words in a variety of contexts

CRITICAL THINKING

- To clarify ideas in response to an interpretive question
- To provide evidence that supports an answer to an interpretive question
- To refer to other students' ideas when responding to an interpretive question

WRITING

- To use a graphic organizer to record ideas about character traits
- To use vivid language to capture personal experiences
- To use a graphic organizer to record problems and solutions in the story
- To use expressive language in vivid description
- To use similes in a narrative retelling
- To use similes to describe a character

STAGE 4: REFLECT AND CONNECT

Each of the activities below will give your students an opportunity to reflect on their learning process in relation to the student learning objectives in Stage 4. Students will also review the concepts and strategies they learned in this stage and make connections between the stories. Choose any or all of the following topics: reading comprehension strategies, Shared Inquiry discussion, story-to-story comparison, and writing revision.

Reading Comprehension Strategies (45 minutes)

Before class, make a copy of the handout on pages 428–429 of appendix C for each student. Be sure to copy the front and back of the master. Choose a story from Stage 4. Briefly review with students the reading strategy of making inferences. Then ask students to review the story and the Reader's Journal to help them locate places where they made an inference during the first or second reading. Help students by asking questions such as:

- Can anyone share an inference about a passage that helped you figure out something about the story that is not directly stated?
- What words in the passage gave you the clues you needed to make the inference?
- Did anyone make a similar inference about this passage? What clues did you use?
- Did anyone make a different inference about this passage? What clues did you use?

Next, have partners choose two new stories or books they would like to read. You may wish to use works from your classroom or school library, or books listed on the Curriculum Connections pages in this Leader's Edition. If students choose a lengthy book, have them select one section for this exercise.

Distribute the handout you photocopied earlier. Tell students they will be reading silently for ten minutes, noting on the handout two inferences they make as they read (including page and paragraph numbers for reference). Then they will switch books with their partner and repeat the process.

Give partners time to share with each other the inferences they made, along with the place in the story where they made each inference. Then have students note on their handouts how their inferences are similar to or different from their partners' inferences.

Shared Inquiry Discussion (30 minutes)

To allow students to reflect on discussions so far, ask the class, "How does discussing a story help us understand it better?" Tell students to look through their Building Your Answer pages in Stage 4 to help them remember what happened during discussions. Ask questions such as:

- What was the focus question we used for our discussion of that story?
- How did our answers to the question change as we discussed it?
- While answering this question, what other questions did we think of?
- What questions do we still have about the story?

On the board, write the following questions for students to answer on a piece of paper:

- What did you do to prepare for the discussion?
- What do you plan to do in the next discussion?

Ask students to share what they wrote with a partner and to listen closely so they can report what their partner wrote. Call on students to recount their partner's ideas.

Story-to-Story Comparison (20 minutes)

Tell students they will be thinking about how each story in Stage 4 contains things that could only happen in a make-believe world and things that could happen in real life. Create the following chart on the board:

Story title	Something that could only happen in a make-believe world	Something that could happen in real life
The Dream Weaver		
Jean Labadie's Big Black Dog		
Caporushes		

Go over the concepts of make-believe and real-life events with students. Then ask them to look through "The Dream Weaver" and find examples of things that could only happen in a make-believe world and things that could only happen in real life. Write students' responses in the chart. Repeat this for the next two stories until you have completed the chart. Encourage students to come up with as many examples in each category as they can.

Writing Revision (45 minutes)

Have your students turn to page 140 in the Reader's Journal to revise one of their expository writing pieces from Stage 4. Review the revision steps on page 139 of the Reader's Journal with students.

ASSESSMENT KIT

When your class completes a stage, you may want to assess your students' progress and evaluate your own progress as a leader. In appendix A, you will find an assessment kit with the story comprehension tests (page 398), rubrics and instructions for grading students' participation in Shared Inquiry discussion (page 410) and their writing (page 412), and leader reflection forms (page 418). In appendix C, you will find a form called Our Collaboration (page 427). Distribute this form to your students to guide them in reflecting on the group's discussion habits and to create a record of their progress.

The Upside-Down Boy

Juan Felipe Herrera

Juanito feels upside down when he moves with his family and is introduced to a new life, a new school, and a new language.

The Green Man

Gail E. Haley

Selfish Claude gets lost in the forest and lives there for an entire year, returning home a changed man.

The Ugly Duckling

Hans Christian Andersen

Harassed for his ugliness, a duckling flees his family and barnyard only to find himself bouncing from one place to another. He does not fit in anywhere until he meets a group of swans.

STAGE 5: EXPLORING IDEAS

You and your students will be able to identify interpretive questions fairly easily by Stage 5. You will now focus on refining answers. Students will explain their interpretations of a story in more detail, provide more precise evidence to support their ideas, and consider their classmates' ideas when responding to interpretive questions. Due to longer stories and more advanced activities, some sessions require more time than a traditional class period. Suggested time allotments and tips on how to handle longer sessions appear in the relevant activities.

| | Student Learning Objectives | | | Leader Learning Objectives |
	READING COMPREHENSION	CRITICAL THINKING	EXPOSITORY AND CREATIVE WRITING	SPOTLIGHT ON FOLLOW-UP QUESTIONS
STAGE 4: CONSIDERING INTERPRETATIONS	• To recognize and make inferences while reading • To reread with a purpose and articulate ideas about the story • To identify different types of questions about the story	To recognize multiple interpretations of the story	• To practice prewriting strategies and drafting methods • To integrate literary terms and concepts into writing	To ask follow-up questions that help students recognize differing ideas
STAGE 5: EXPLORING IDEAS	• To determine important ideas in the story • To reread with a purpose and articulate ideas about the story • To identify interpretive questions about important issues in the story	To consider multiple interpretations of the story	• To develop prewriting strategies and drafting methods • To integrate literary terms and concepts into writing	To ask questions that help students explore ideas
STAGE 6: PUTTING THE PUZZLE TOGETHER	• To begin to synthesize information in the story • To reread with a purpose and articulate ideas about a story • To explore interpretive questions about the story	To discuss multiple interpretations of the story	• To hone drafting methods • To integrate literary terms and concepts into writing	• To ask questions that help students add depth to their reasoning • To choose a target area for follow-up questions

Reading Comprehension

In Stage 5, students practice determining important ideas in a story, a strategy you model during the first reading. The sharing questions activities in Stage 5 guide students toward supporting various answers to questions about important issues in a story. During the second reading, students continue to find evidence in the story and to practice clarifying and explaining their ideas about those parts of the story.

Critical Thinking

Students strengthen the critical-thinking skills practiced in Stage 4 while more thoroughly explaining their interpretations of a story, supporting their interpretations by referring to specific passages in the story, and drawing upon other students' ideas to help bolster their own.

Expository and Creative Writing

In Stage 5 expository writing, students continue to practice prewriting and drafting strategies, with an emphasis on developing solid essays. They also learn how to sequence story events and write about story setting. The creative writing activities allow students to experiment with figurative language as well as different writing forms, such as letters and sets of instructions.

Spotlight on Follow-Up Questions

The Spotlight on Follow-Up Questions in Stage 5 features questions that help students explore their ideas and supporting evidence. Your questions will help students with these elements of critical thinking:

◆ Idea—Explaining ideas in more detail
◆ Evidence—Providing more precise evidence to support ideas
◆ Response—Considering other students' ideas when responding to interpretive questions

Curriculum Connections

Use Curriculum Connections to find books by the authors of the Stage 5 stories, as well as resources linking the stories to biography, folklore, science, social studies, and other subjects. Icons designate whether books are appropriate for classroom read-alouds or independent reading, according to each book's reading and interest level.

Reflect and Connect

Reflect and Connect allows your students to compare concepts across stories and reinforces what they have learned in Stage 5. It also contains guidelines to help you evaluate your students' progress in meeting the learning objectives thus far.

The Upside-Down Boy

Juan Felipe Herrera

STORY LENGTH: 15 pages   **READ-ALOUD TIME:** About 13 minutes

◆ ABOUT THE STORY

Juanito and his family move from the country to the city, where he begins school for the first time. Everything about his new life seems strange and new—the city, his school, and especially learning English. Juanito feels upside down as he tries to learn English and adapt to school.

◆ ABOUT THE AUTHOR

Juan Felipe Herrera was born in 1948 in Fowler, California. His parents were farmworkers, immigrants from Mexico. Herrera is the author of numerous poetry collections for adults, as well as books for young adults and children. Many of his works are written in a mixture of Spanish and English, and draw upon his personal experiences. When Herrera was eight years old, his parents moved into a small house and he started school. "The Upside-Down Boy" is based on these events.

The story starts on page 141 of the Leader's Edition, and on page 57 of the student anthology.

Unit Overview

SESSION 1: PAGE 123

PREREADING Students share their experiences with being the outsider in a new situation.

☆ **FIRST READING** Students note important ideas in the story as the leader reads it aloud.

☆ **SHARING QUESTIONS** Students share their questions about the story, concentrating on interpretive questions.

SESSION 2: PAGE 128

☆ **SECOND READING WITH DIRECTED NOTES** Students mark words or phrases to note an element in the story.

SPOTLIGHT ON FOLLOW-UP QUESTIONS The leader asks follow-up questions to help students explain their ideas.

SESSION 3: PAGE 130

VOCABULARY Students practice using new vocabulary words. Suggested target words: *admires*, *symphony*, and *weave*

SESSION 4: PAGE 132

☆ **SHARED INQUIRY DISCUSSION** Students discover meaning in the story by discussing an interpretive question.

SESSION 5 OPTIONS: PAGE 136

EXPOSITORY WRITING Students explain how imagery helps them understand a character.

CREATIVE WRITING Students write a poem using metaphors.

CURRICULUM CONNECTIONS The leader can use these resources to link the story to other subject areas.

☆ Core activity

Prereading (5–10 minutes)

Students share their experiences with being the outsider in a new situation.

> **STUDENT LEARNING OBJECTIVE**
>
> **READING COMPREHENSION: To recall experience with and knowledge about a concept in the story**

1. Tell students that you are going to read a story about a boy who has moved to a new home and a new school, in a city where people speak a different language.

2. Have students recall times when they felt out of place in new surroundings. If students have difficulty, suggest situations such as:
   - Moving to a new neighborhood
   - The first day at camp
   - Joining a new team or activity

3. Ask students to share how they felt in their new situations, writing their words or phrases on the board. Help them by asking questions such as:
   - What were you new at?
   - How did it feel to be new?
   - What were some good things about being new?
   - What were some difficult things about being new?

First Reading (15–20 minutes)

Students note important ideas in the story as the leader reads it aloud.

> **STUDENT LEARNING OBJECTIVE**
>
> **READING COMPREHENSION: To determine important ideas in the story**

BEFORE READING

DETERMINING IMPORTANT IDEAS: A READING COMPREHENSION STRATEGY

Strong readers continuously make decisions and change their opinions about what is important as they read and reread. As you read aloud, model this strategy by stopping to explain why you think certain words, phrases, sentences, or events could be important. Demonstrate how you make these decisions based on your own personal experience, including knowledge of story structure.

1. Have students follow along in their books as they listen to you read "The Upside-Down Boy," a story about a boy who moves to a new school and city, where people speak a language different from his own. Tell students that the story is arranged in lines similar to poetry. The author uses language in a poetic way to show how the characters think and feel.

2. Explain to students that in a story some of the information is important to understanding the story's meaning, and other information, while enjoyable or interesting, is not as important. Figuring out what is important in a story helps readers discover the main ideas or themes.

3. Ask students to mark with an **!** places where they think something is **important** in the story, and to mark with a **?** places where they have a **question** about the story. After listening to the story, they will have a chance to share important passages and questions.

DURING READING

4. Read the story aloud with expression.

5. Pause several times while reading to model how you determine whether something is important. Look away from the book to share why something in the story seems important to you, explaining how you arrived at your decision. Use your own ideas or the Think-Alouds provided in the margins of the story.

AFTER READING

6. Ask students to review the story to find passages they marked as important.

7. Have students take a few minutes to share with a partner a passage that they think is important and why. If time allows, have a few students share their ideas with the class.

8. Tell students to review the story to find the passages they marked with a **?** and to think about questions they would like to share with the class.

Sharing Questions (25–35 minutes)

Students share their questions about the story, concentrating on interpretive questions.

STUDENT LEARNING OBJECTIVE

READING COMPREHENSION: To identify interpretive questions that address important issues in the story

LOOK FOR STUDENTS TO

Ask questions about the story

Recognize interpretive questions about the story

Identify interpretive questions about important ideas in the story

TAKING THE TIME YOU NEED

Sharing questions is essential preparation for Shared Inquiry discussion. However, since students are identifying and exploring many types of questions and time can run short, you can and should tailor this activity to suit your class. Here are some options:

◆ Assign steps 2 and 3 as homework.

◆ Finish the activity in your next class period.

◆ Complete steps 4 and 5 after the second reading (especially if your students would benefit from rereading before identifying interpretive or keeper questions).

◆ Forgo steps 4, 5, and 6 and concentrate on earlier steps (especially if your students are still learning to identify different types of questions).

1. Record questions on the board with students' names, or have students write out their questions on strips of paper to post around the room.

2. Encourage students to answer factual and vocabulary questions by using the text, the Reader's Journal glossary, a dictionary, or classmates for help.

3. Identify any evaluative, speculative, or background questions. Help the class revise, answer, or skip them as appropriate.

4. Have students identify a few questions that they think might be interpretive.

5. Test one of the questions by asking students to offer possible answers that can be supported with evidence from the story.

6. If students are able to find support for two different answers, do not explore the question in detail. Tell students that they have identified an interpretive question.

7. Repeat the process for as many questions as time allows.

8. Tell students that any of the interpretive questions they have identified would be a good choice for a keeper question. Ask students to think about what makes a good keeper question. Lead a brief discussion, asking questions such as:

   ◆ What makes a good keeper question?

   ◆ How do you decide which question to choose?

   ◆ How might thinking about your keeper question help you during your second reading?

9. Have students choose their keeper question and write it on page 36 of the Reader's Journal. Then ask students to write about how they decided to choose that question.

10. Use your Leader Discussion Planner (page 133) to jot down posted questions that you will want to remember later for Shared Inquiry discussion.

11. Have students turn to page 37 in the Reader's Journal to practice determining important ideas as a reading strategy. This can also serve as homework.

RECOGNIZING IMPORTANT ISSUES IN THE STORY

In Stage 5, the goal in the sharing questions activity is for students to begin to concentrate on an interpretive question to explore further. Talking about their keeper questions can help students recognize which questions are most compelling to them. In subsequent units, students begin to identify questions that are not only interpretive but are more central to the story's meaning, thus making good focus questions for discussion.

Second Reading with Directed Notes (45 minutes)

Students mark words or phrases to note an element in the story.

STUDENT LEARNING OBJECTIVE

READING COMPREHENSION: To reread with a purpose and articulate ideas about the story

LOOK FOR STUDENTS TO

Identify meaningful and interesting words or phrases in the story

Explain why the word or phrase is interesting

Explain the meaning or implication of the word or phrase

OPEN NOTES

By now you are familiar with using contrasting notes—notes about different sides of a story-specific issue. In Stage 5, the second reading note-taking activity features open notes—notes about a general concept common to narrative structure (such as the use of vivid language or surprise as a plot device) or narrative content (such as evidence of strength or change in a character). Whether students are taking contrasting or open notes during the second reading, the purpose of the activity should be to guide students toward selecting passages that can be understood in multiple ways and supporting their choices with evidence from the story.

SPOTLIGHT
on Follow-Up Questions

For this unit, the spotlight is on **asking follow-up questions to help students explain their ideas.** Not everything a student says must be explained, but if certain words, phrases, or assumptions are not explored, meaning might be misunderstood or an important point lost. As you ask students to explain their notes and comments, you are also helping them determine what does and does not need explanation.

FOLLOW-UP QUESTIONS: EXPLAINING IDEAS

- What part of that passage made you mark it with a note?

- What makes that phrase interesting to you?

- What is another way for you to say that?

BEFORE READING

1. Explain to students that during the second reading they will be taking notes. Write the following on the board:

    ✱ = This is a word or phrase that is **interesting**.

2. Tell students that as they reread the story, they should mark with a ✱ words or phrases that they think are **interesting**.

3. Ask students to think about why they are choosing those places, as they make their notes.

DURING READING

4. Tell students to read the story on their own or with a partner, or have them listen to the story read aloud (by you or on the CD), making notes as they go.

AFTER READING

5. Have students read aloud parts of the story they marked with a ✱, and ask them to explain why they chose those words or phrases and what they think those words or phrases mean.

6. Ask follow-up questions to help students explain their ideas. Remember to ask if anyone sees those parts of the story differently. Examine as many notations as possible.

7. Use your Leader Discussion Planner (page 133) to jot down questions or ideas to explore later.

8. Have students turn to Head in the Clouds on page 39 of the Reader's Journal and choose a topic for writing or drawing.

9. Optional: Have students perform a passage using reader's theater techniques (see sidebar).

EXPLORING LANGUAGE

"The Upside-Down Boy," which incorporates poetic devices as well as Spanish words, provides an excellent opportunity to explore language, and to notice the effects of language on other story elements. For this activity, students can note similes, metaphors, vivid imagery, and Spanish words.

READER'S THEATER

Students can interpret this story's expressive poetic text by acting out certain passages. As they create a script, ask students to add the sounds and actions mentioned in the story.

◆ In small groups, have students choose a page or two from the story.

◆ Ask students to write the selection in script form, with separate speaking parts for each character, as well as a narrator.

◆ Have students take turns reading each part before choosing roles.

◆ Encourage students to add stage directions such as "kids laugh" or "jumps up while everyone else sits," as well as sound effects. Tell students to write them into their scripts using a different color pencil or set them off with brackets.

◆ Have students practice reading their scripts until they are comfortable with their roles. Then have them perform their scripts for the class.

Vocabulary (20 minutes)

Students practice using new vocabulary words.

> **STUDENT LEARNING OBJECTIVE**
>
> **READING COMPREHENSION: To understand and use new words in a variety of contexts**

SUGGESTED TARGET WORDS: admires, symphony, weave

Choose the target words you want your class to learn, or use the suggested target words above. As you present a word, have students say it with you. Work on one word at a time, using these steps as a guide:

1. Place the word in context. Review how the word is used in the story.

2. Define the word. Use active language in your definition. Include a few examples of how to use the word in situations students will understand. For example:

   ♦ To **admire** something is to look at it with pleasure and to like it. My parents stopped to **admire** the beautiful sunset. My best friend always **admires** the cakes in the bakery window.

   ♦ A **symphony** is a long piece of music played by many different musical instruments. A **symphony** usually has three or four parts, called *movements*. My favorite part of the **symphony** is when the tuba plays.

   ♦ To **weave** is to make a path through something by moving from side to side or in and out. You might **weave** through a crowd of people to get to the door.

3. Use the word. Encourage students to make the word their own by asking a few of them to use it in a sentence or to apply it to real-life situations.

4. Ask a question about the story, using the word. Have several students apply their knowledge of the word to answer the question.

5. Optional: Have students turn to Curious Words on page 156 of the Reader's Journal to write down some of their favorite words from the story.

OVERHEARD IN THE CLASSROOM

TARGET WORD: admires

PLACE THE WORD IN CONTEXT

"On Open House Day, Mama and Papi sit in the front row. Mrs. Andasola **admires** our drawings on the walls, Gabino on her shoulder." (Refer students to page 71 in the student anthology.)

DEFINE THE WORD

To **admire** something is to look at it with pleasure and to like it. My parents stopped to **admire** the beautiful sunset. My best friend always **admires** the cakes in the bakery window. Let's say the word together.

USE THE WORD

Which of these is something you would **admire**?

- ◆ A view from a mountaintop
- ◆ A box of cereal
- ◆ A song by your favorite singer
- ◆ A dog catching a ball in the air
- ◆ A stoplight

ASK A QUESTION ABOUT THE STORY

Why does Juanito change after Mrs. Sampson **admires** his singing voice?

Shared Inquiry Discussion (45 minutes)

Students discover meaning in the story by discussing an interpretive question.

STUDENT LEARNING OBJECTIVE

CRITICAL THINKING: To answer an interpretive question with clear and specific ideas

LOOK FOR STUDENTS TO

Offer a thoughtful answer to an interpretive question

Explain their answer to an interpretive question

Elaborate on their ideas about an interpretive question

MODELING CURIOSITY

During the discussion, take advantage of the chance to be yourself. Allow your students' ideas to delight, overwhelm, confuse, or enlighten you. You are providing them with a model of an active, curious mind, eager to learn alongside them as everyone works together to figure out the story's meaning. Asking follow-up questions not only challenges your students to do their own thinking—it lets them know that you take their ideas seriously.

Use the Leader Discussion Planner on the facing page to prepare yourself for Shared Inquiry discussion. To prepare your group, have everyone sit in a circle or a square; remind them of the five discussion guidelines and any behavioral guidelines you want to share. Then follow these steps to conduct the discussion:

1. Write the focus question on the board and have students copy it on the Building Your Answer page of the Reader's Journal (page 40).

2. Give students a few minutes to review the story and to write down an answer.

3. Begin the discussion by asking the focus question. On your seating chart, keep track of students' participation and ideas.

4. Lead the discussion by asking follow-up questions to help students explain their ideas (see sample questions in your Leader Discussion Planner, page 133), provide evidence, and respond to one another. Aim to have the discussion last 20 to 30 minutes.

5. As the discussion winds down, have students finish the Building Your Answer page. Then ask volunteers to share what they wrote.

6. Spend a few minutes talking about the discussion. Ask students what they liked about it, what was hard about it, what they think makes a good discussion, and what might go better next time.

LEADER DISCUSSION PLANNER

After the first and second readings, use this section to keep track of:

◆ Questions that you and your students have about the story

◆ Characters, incidents, and ideas that interest you

◆ Passages that interest you

NOTES AND QUESTIONS

_____

_____

_____

_____

_____

Write down a focus question, cluster questions, and passages that you think you or your students will refer to in discussion. If you choose not to develop your own questions, see Suggested Interpretive Questions for Shared Inquiry Discussion on page 134.

CLUSTER QUESTION

_____

_____

_____

CLUSTER QUESTION

_____

_____

_____

FOCUS QUESTION FOR DISCUSSION

_____

_____

_____

RELATED PASSAGE   page _____

_____

_____

_____

RELATED PASSAGE   page _____

_____

_____

_____

In this Shared Inquiry discussion, look for opportunities to help your students explain their ideas.

FOLLOW-UP QUESTIONS: EXPLAINING IDEAS

◆ What do you mean when you say that?

◆ Where in the story does it show you that's what is happening?

◆ How does that idea help us to answer the focus question?

SUGGESTED INTERPRETIVE QUESTIONS FOR SHARED INQUIRY DISCUSSION

OPTION 1 **Why does Juanito describe himself as the upside-down boy?**

- Why does Juanito's tongue feel like a rock when Mrs. Sampson asks him what his painting is?

- Why does Juanito say that his feet float through the clouds, when all he wants is "to touch the earth"?

- Why does Juanito wait to tell his father that at first he felt "funny, upside down" at school?

- Why is Juanito able to sing in front of the class, even though he finds it difficult to talk?

PASSAGE FOR DISCUSSION In the student anthology, from "The school bell rings and shakes me," on page 61, to "I am the upside-down boy," on page 62

OPTION 2 **Why is Juanito able to direct the choir at the end of the story?**

- Why does Juanito take his painting home to show his family after Mrs. Sampson asks, "What is that?"

- After Mrs. Sampson tells Juanito that he has a beautiful voice, why does he go home and tell everyone?

- After Juanito gets an A on his poem, why does he go home and sing it to the baby chicks?

- Why does Juanito use both English and Spanish when he begins to conduct the choir, saying "*Uno, dos*, and three"?

PASSAGE FOR DISCUSSION In the student anthology, from "Mrs. Sampson invites me to the front," on page 64, to "Let's see if your *buñuelos* come out beautiful too," on page 65

OVERHEARD IN THE CLASSROOM

LEADER Why is Juanito able to direct the choir at the end of the story?

WESLEY Because he learns.

TAMALA And he got an A on his poem.

AMIR He's really a friendly person.

LEADER Tamala, how does getting an A on his poem help him direct the choir?

TAMALA I think he's a smart person who can do all sorts of stuff. He can draw, and sing, and write poetry, so he figures it out.

LEADER What does he figure out?

TAMALA How to eat lunch at lunch, and play at recess, and direct the choir.

LEADER Wesley, is that what you meant when you said he learns?

WESLEY I meant school stuff.

TAMALA I was talking about school stuff.

WESLEY But not recess and lunch, I mean he learns letters and words.

LEADER And how does that help him?

SALVADOR His tongue's not a rock anymore, so he doesn't feel stupid. He learns that he can do things, like sing and write poems.

LEADER How does learning he can do things help Juanito direct the choir?

SALVADOR He feels more comfortable about trying things, like directing the choir.

TAMALA I agree. He can be himself because he learns he can do things.

EXTENDED EXAMPLES OF DISCUSSION

By now, you should be feeling more comfortable using the seating chart to map your discussions and record students' participation, and you may already be thinking about how to take your discussions to the next level. To help you do this, the rest of the units in this book provide an expanded sample discussion with short annotations in the margins, instead of a sample seating chart.

COAXING ANSWERS OUT OF IDEAS

In this discussion, the students offer a lot of fragmented ideas. Here the leader patiently follows up with questions to help them develop those ideas into complete answers to the focus question.

Expository Writing: Feeling Upside Down (45 minutes)

Students explain how imagery helps them understand a character.

> **STUDENT LEARNING OBJECTIVE**
>
> **WRITING: To write an essay about imagery in the story**

TEACHING LITERARY CONCEPTS: IMAGERY

1. Ask students what they know about imagery in a story. Then write the following definition on the board:

   Imagery is language that creates a picture in the reader's mind.

2. Give students examples of imagery in "The Upside-Down Boy"— such as, "Will my tongue turn into a rock?" (page 58); "The school bell rings and shakes me" (page 61); and "Crazy tomato cars and cucumber sombreros" (page 60). For every example, have students share what the image is and what it tells them about Juanito.

PREWRITING

3. Inform students that they will find and write about imagery in the story that helps them understand Juanito's character, thoughts, and feelings. Lead the class in describing Juanito's experiences and feelings as he starts at a new school. Encourage students to review the story to help them think of ideas. List the ideas on the board.

4. Help students connect these ideas to imagery in the story. Write "My tongue is a rock" on the board and draw lines connecting it to ideas about Juanito's experiences and feelings, such as "Juanito feels shy" or "He is afraid he won't learn English."

5. Have students find three examples of imagery in the story that help them understand Juanito's character, thoughts, or feelings. Ask students to complete page 41 of the Reader's Journal with a partner, using the list on the board and the story as references.

WRITING A DRAFT

6. Have students draft their essays on page 42 of the Reader's Journal.

Creative Writing: You're a Poet! (45 minutes)

Students write a poem using metaphors.

> **STUDENT LEARNING OBJECTIVE**
>
> **WRITING:** To use metaphor in a poem

PREWRITING

1. Tell students that poets express what they see and feel in new and different ways. One way that they do this is by using metaphors.

2. On the board, create a list of nouns related to school, and one of nouns related to nature, or create your own categories. Ask for suggestions and list words in each column. For example:

At School	In Nature
Eraser	Turtle
Pencil	Rainstorm
Clock	Forest
Playground	Fire

3. Model how to create an interesting noun/noun combination by thinking about how two nouns could be alike. For example, a clock and a turtle might be related because both sometimes go slowly. Use this sentence structure as the first line of a poem:

    The _____ is a _____ .

4. Now tell students that they will add a second line, which uses a verb (an action word) to explain their metaphor. For example:

    The clock is a turtle.   My eraser is a rainstorm.
    The minutes crawl slowly by. It washes away my mistakes.

5. Have students create a metaphor, using one noun from each list in the Reader's Journal (page 44). Have them create their own second lines that support and extend their metaphors.

WRITING A DRAFT

6. Ask students to write their poems in the Reader's Journal (page 45).

METAPHORS DEFINED

Metaphors are statements or sentences that compare two things without using the words *like* or *as*. Examples from the story include:

♦ "My tongue is a rock" (page 60).

♦ "Ms are sea waves. They crash over my table" (page 67).

♦ "The hard round clock above my head clicks and aims its strange arrows at me." (page 59).

Curriculum Connections

Below are resources related to "The Upside-Down Boy" for further reading and investigation in a number of subject areas.

 Appropriate for classroom read-alouds; above-grade reading and interest levels

 Appropriate for independent reading; at- or near-grade reading and interest levels

OTHER WORKS BY THE AUTHOR

 Herrera, Juan Felipe. *Super Cilantro Girl.* San Francisco: Children's Book Press, 2003.

Eight-year-old Esmeralda is transformed into a superhero and flies off to rescue her mother, who visited Mexico without her green card and is not being permitted to return to the United States.

SPANISH LANGUAGE

 Bertrand, Diane Gonzales. *Upside Down and Backwards/De cabeza y al reves.* Houston: Pinata Books, 2004.

A collection of short stories about children's relationships with friends, parents, teachers, and others.

 Lomba, Ana, and Marcella Summerville. *Play and Learn Spanish.* New York: McGraw-Hill, 2005.

Teaches Spanish to English-speaking children.

 First Spanish Picture Dictionary: 500 Brightly Illustrated Words to Start Speaking Spanish. New York: McGraw-Hill, 2004.

Pictures labeled in English and Spanish are grouped in such familiar categories as "Good morning!" "In the bathroom," "At the grocery store," "Christmas," and "Colors." Includes bilingual indexes with pronunciation guide.

POETRY

 Wonderful Words: Poems about Reading, Writing, Speaking, and Listening.
New York: Simon & Schuster, 2004.

Presents an illustrated collection of poems that celebrate words, featuring selections by Emily Dickinson, Nikki Grimes, Carl Sandburg, and others.

EMOTIONS

 Amos, Janine. *Moving.* Milwaukee: Gareth Stevens, 2002.

Uses letters, stories, and informational text to help children cope with moving to a new home.

FOR THE TEACHER

Holmes, Vicki L., and Margaret R. Moulton. *Writing Simple Poems: Pattern Poetry for Language Acquisition.* Cambridge: Cambridge University, 2001.

Explains how teachers can use poetry writing as a medium to teach and reinforce structure, vocabulary, parts of speech, and punctuation, as well as improve grammar and writing skills.

Routman, Regie. *Kids' Poems: Teaching Third and Fourth Graders to Love Writing Poetry.* New York: Scholastic, 2000.

Discusses how third- and fourth-grade teachers may help their students appreciate poetry and gain confidence to write their own poems.

Ruurs, Margriet. *The Power of Poems: Teaching the Joy of Writing Poetry.* Gainesville, FL: Maupin House, 2001.

Provides teachers with instructions and activities for how to introduce children in grades 3 through 8 to reading and writing poetry, focusing on the components of content and craft.

Highlighted words are the suggested target words in the vocabulary activity. Underlined words can be briefly explained as you read the story aloud, using the definitions provided.

LEADER'S NOTES AND QUESTIONS

"Time to start school," Mama tells me.

THE UPSIDE-DOWN BOY

Juan Felipe Herrera

Mama, who loves words, sings out the name on the
street sign—Juniper. "Who-nee-purr! Who-nee-purr!"

Papi parks our old army truck on Juniper Street
in front of Mrs. Andasola's tiny pink house.
"We found it at last," Papi shouts, "Who-nee-purr!"

"Time to start school," Mama tells me with music in
   her voice.
"My Who-nee-purr Street!" I yell to the chickens in
   the yard.

57

...

"Don't worry, *chico*,"
Papi says as he walks me to school.
"Everything changes. A new place has new leaves
on the trees and blows fresh air into your body."

I pinch my ear. Am I really here?
Maybe the street lamp is really a golden cornstalk
with a dusty gray coat.

People speed by alone in their fancy melting cars.
In the valleys, *campesinos* sang "*Buenos días*,
Juanito."

I make a clown face, half funny,
half scared. "I don't speak English," I say to Papi.
"Will my tongue turn into a rock?"

I slow step into school.
My *burrito de papas*, my potato burrito, in a
brown bag.
Empty playground,
fences locked. One cloud up high.

Think-Aloud

"Papi's words tell me that they
have just made a big move to
a new place. This is important
because I know that moving can
involve a lot of changes."

**LEADER'S NOTES
AND QUESTIONS**

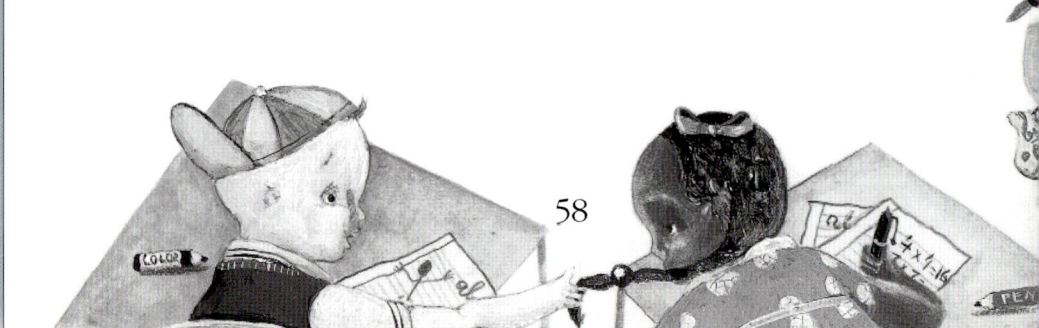

58

chico: Spanish for *boy*

campesinos: Spanish for *people who live in the country*

...

No one
in the halls. Open a door with a blue number 27.
"*¿Dónde estoy?*" Where am I?
My question in Spanish fades
as the thick door slams behind me.

Mrs. Sampson, the teacher, shows me my desk.
Kids laugh when I poke my nose into
    my lunch bag.

The hard round clock above my head
clicks and aims its strange
    arrows at me.

LEADER'S NOTES
AND QUESTIONS

Think-Aloud

"Juanito describes himself as
'the upside-down boy.' I think
that is an important idea because
it is the title of the story."

•••

The high bell
roars again.

This time everyone eats their sandwiches,
while I play in the breezy baseball diamond
by myself.

"Is this recess?" I ask again.

When I jump up,
everyone sits.
When I sit,
all the kids swing through the air.
My feet float through the clouds,
when all I want is to touch the earth.
I am the upside-down boy.

62

...

Papi comes home to Mrs. Andasola's pink house.
I show him my finger painting.
"What a spicy sun," he sings out.
"It reminds me of hot summer days in the
    San Joaquin Valley,"
he says, brushing his dark hair with his hands.

"Look, Mama!
 See my painting?"

"Those are flying tomatoes
 ready for salsa," Mama sings.
 She shows my painting to Mrs. Andasola,
 who shows it to Gabino, her canary.

"Gabino, Gabino, see?" Mrs. Andasola yells.
"What do you think?"
 Gabino nods his head back and forth.
 "*Pío, pío, piiiii!*"

63

···

Mrs. Sampson invites me
to the front of the class.
   "Sing, Juanito,
sing a song we have been
   practicing."

I pop up shaking. I am
   alone facing the class.

"Ready to sing?" Mrs. Sampson
   asks me.
I am frozen, then a deep
   breath fills me,
"Three blind mice, three
   blind mice," I sing.

My eyes open as big as the ceiling, and
my hands spread out as if catching
raindrops from the sky.

"You have a very beautiful voice, Juanito,"
   Mrs. Sampson says.
"What is beautiful?" I ask Amanda after school.

At home, I help Mama and Mrs. Andasola
make *buñuelos*—fried sweet cinnamon tortilla chips.

"Piiiiicho, come heeeere," I sing out,
calling my dog as I stretch a dough ball.

"Listen to meeeee," I sing to Picho with his ears
curled up into fuzzy triangles. "My voice is
beauuuuutiful!"

"What is he singing?" Mrs. Andasola asks my mom,
as she gently lays a *buñuelo* into the frying pan.

"My teacher says my voice is beauuuuutiful," I sing,
dancing with a tiny dough ball stuck on my nose.

"*Sí, sí,*" Mama laughs.
"Let's see if your *buñuelos* come out beautiful, too."

65

•••

"I only made it to the third grade, Juanito,"
Mama tells me as I get ready for bed.

"When we lived in El Paso, Texas,
my mother needed help at home. We were
very poor
and she was tired from cleaning people's houses."

"That year your mama won a spelling medal,"
Papi says as he shaves in the bathroom.

"Your Papi learned English without a school,"
Mama says.
"When he worked the railroads, he would pay
his buddies a penny for each word they taught him."

Papi says softly, "Each word,
each language has its own magic."

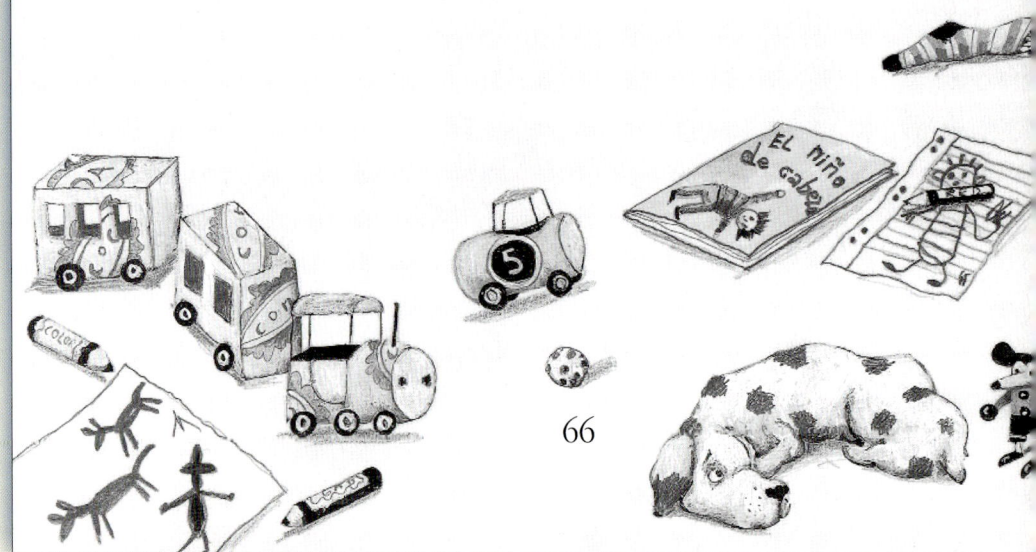

66

...

After a week of reading a new poem aloud to
   us every day,
Mrs. Sampson says, "Write a poem,"
as she plays <mark>symphony</mark> music on the old red
   phonograph.

I think of Mama, squeeze my pencil,
pour letters from the shiny tip like a skinny river.

The waves tumble onto the page
Ls curl at the bottom.
Fs tip their hats from their heads.
Ms are sea waves. They crash over my table.

symphony: a long piece of music played by many different
musical instruments

LEADER'S NOTES AND QUESTIONS

...

JUANITO'S POEM

Papi Felipe with a mustache of words.
Mama Lucha with strawberries in her hair.
I see magic salsa in my house
and everywhere!

68

...

"I got an A on my poem!" I yell to everyone
in the front yard where Mama gives Papi a
    haircut.

I show Gabino my paper
as I fly through the kitchen to the backyard.

"Listen," I sing to the baby chicks,
with my hands up as if I am a famous music
    conductor.

I sprinkle corn kernels and sing out my poem.
Each fuzzy chick gets a name:
"Beethoven! You are the one with the bushy
    head!
Mozart! You jumpy black-spotted hen!
Johann Sebastian! Tiny red rooster, dance,
    dance!"

69

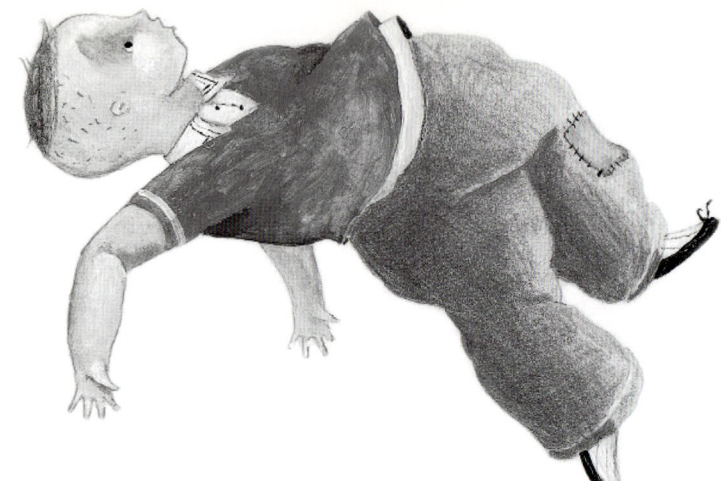

In the morning, as we walk to school,
Papi turns and says, "You do have a nice voice,
   Juanito.
I never heard you sing until yesterday
when you fed the chickens.
At first, when we moved here,
you looked sad, and I didn't know what to do."

"I felt funny, upside down," I say to him.
"The city streets aren't soft with flowers.
   Buildings don't have faces. You know, Papi,
   in the *campo* I knew all the names, even of
      those bugs
   with little wild eyes and shiny noses!"

"Here," he says. "Here's my harmonica.
   It has many voices, many beautiful songs
   just like you. Sing them!"

70

campo: Spanish for *countryside*

On Open House Day,
Mama and Papi sit in the front row.
Mrs. Andasola admires our drawings on the walls,
Gabino on her shoulder.

"Our paintings look like the flowery fields back
in the Valley," I tell Amanda.

"I have a surprise," I whisper to Mama.
"I am *El Maestro* Juanito, the choir conductor!"
Mrs. Sampson smiles wearing a chile sombrero
and puts on the music.

I blow a C with my harmonica—"La la la laaaaah!
Ready to sing out your poems?" I ask my choir.
"*Uno . . . dos . . .* and three!"

admires: looks at with pleasure and likes

The Green Man

Gail E. Haley

STORY LENGTH: 12 pages   READ-ALOUD TIME: About 11 minutes

◆ ABOUT THE STORY

Haughty Claude thinks the neighboring villagers are foolish for believing in the Green Man legend about a keeper of the forest who helps children and cares for animals. One day, Claude goes into the forest to hunt, but gets lost. In order to survive Claude clothes himself in green foliage and lives in a cave. He comes to enjoy his new life, and he changes in unexpected ways.

◆ ABOUT THE AUTHOR

Born in Charlotte, North Carolina, in 1939, Gail E. Haley has written and illustrated numerous children's books. She was awarded the Caldecott Medal for *A Story, a Story* in 1971, and the Kate Greenaway Medal for *The Post Office Cat* in 1976. Haley spent several years living in England, where she researched the myth that is the basis for "The Green Man."

The story starts on page 176 of the Leader's Edition, and on page 72 of the student anthology.

Unit Overview

★ Core activity

Prereading (5–10 minutes)

Students share their ideas about what it would be like to live in a forest for a year.

1. Tell students that you are going to read a story about a young man who lives in the forest for a year.

2. Ask students what they know about forests. To get them started, ask questions such as:
   - Who has been in a forest?
   - What is the light like in the forest?
   - What does a forest smell like?
   - What sounds do you hear?

3. Have students imagine what it would be like to live in a forest. Help them by asking questions such as:
   - What might you eat?
   - Where could you sleep?
   - How could you find or make clothes?
   - What might be unpleasant or scary about the experience?
   - What might be fun?

First Reading (15–20 minutes)

Students note important ideas in the story as the leader reads it aloud.

> **STUDENT LEARNING OBJECTIVE**
>
> **READING COMPREHENSION: To determine important ideas in the story**

BEFORE READING

MORE ON DETERMINING IMPORTANT IDEAS

Rich literature presents a variety of concepts and ideas. The point of teaching students to determine important ideas is not to steer them toward one main idea or set of ideas, but to encourage them to make decisions about what they consider important and to explain their reasoning.

1. Have students follow along in their books as they listen to you read "The Green Man," a story about a rich young man who learns to live in a forest.

2. Explain to students that in a story, some of the information is important to understanding the story's meaning, and other information, while enjoyable or interesting, is not as important. Figuring out what is important in a story helps readers discover the main ideas or themes.

3. Ask students to mark with an **!** places where they think something is **important** in the story, and to mark with a **?** places where they have a **question** about the story. After listening to the story, they will have a chance to share important passages and questions.

DURING READING

4. Read the story aloud with expression.

5. Pause several times while reading to model how you determine whether something is important. Look away from the book to share why something in the story seems important to you, explaining how you arrived at your decision. Use your own ideas or the Think-Alouds provided in the margins of the story.

AFTER READING

6. Ask students to review the story to find passages they marked as important.

7. Have students take a few minutes to share with a partner a passage that they think is important and why. If time allows, have a few students share their ideas with the class.

8. Tell students to review the story to find the passages they marked with a **?** and to think about questions they would like to share with the class.

Sharing Questions (25–35 minutes)

Students share their questions about the story, concentrating on interpretive questions.

STUDENT LEARNING OBJECTIVE

READING COMPREHENSION: To identify interpretive questions that address important issues in the story

LOOK FOR STUDENTS TO

Ask questions about the story

Recognize interpretive questions about the story

Identify interpretive questions about important issues in the story

---

ASKING DEEPER QUESTIONS

One good indication that students are not only asking questions but relishing the opportunity to do so is spontaneity. When they no longer need prompting, you know they are enjoying expressing their curiosity. While you will always need to spend some time on basic comprehension questions—readers cannot go deeper if they do not understand the basics—it is also a positive sign when they move beyond asking literal questions and instead go straight to questions about the story's deeper meaning. All this practice will help your students learn to ask meaningful questions in other areas of their lives.

1. Record questions on the board with students' names, or have students write out their questions on strips of paper to post around the room.

2. Encourage students to answer factual and vocabulary questions by using the text, the Reader's Journal glossary, a dictionary, or classmates for help.

3. Identify any evaluative, speculative, or background questions. Help the class revise, answer, or skip them as appropriate.

4. Have students identify a few questions that they think might be interpretive.

5. Test one of the questions by asking students to offer possible answers that can be supported with evidence from the story.

6. If students are able to find support for two different answers, do not explore the question in detail. Tell students that they have identified an interpretive question.

7. Repeat the process for as many questions as time allows.

8. Tell students to choose their keeper question. As they choose, ask them to think about what makes a good keeper question. Ask them to consider:

♦ Whether the question has two or more possible answers

♦ How the question will help them understand the story as they reread it

9. Have students spend a few minutes locating parts of the story that relate to their keeper question. Have them write their keeper question and related parts of the story on page 48 of the Reader's Journal.

10. Use your Leader Discussion Planner (page 169) to jot down posted questions that you will want to remember later for Shared Inquiry discussion.

11. Have students turn to page 49 in the Reader's Journal to practice determining important ideas as a reading strategy. This can also serve as homework.

THE KEEPER QUESTION AND THE SECOND READING

Keeper questions are just another tool to help students have a purpose in mind as they reread. If your students are having trouble both thinking about their keeper question and taking notes during the second reading, there is no reason for them to juggle both. Select one or the other for the class to concentrate on, depending on students' needs and interests, or have students make their own choice.

Second Reading with Directed Notes (45 minutes)

Students mark passages that address an important concept in the story.

STUDENT LEARNING OBJECTIVE

READING COMPREHENSION: To reread with a purpose and articulate ideas about the story

LOOK FOR STUDENTS TO

Explain why a passage means one thing and not another

Explain marked passages by pointing to words and phrases in those passages

Explain the significance of words and phrases in marked passages

SPOTLIGHT
on Follow-Up Questions

For this unit, the spotlight is on **asking follow-up questions to encourage students to provide more precise evidence to support their ideas.** By now, students should be ready to offer supporting evidence more readily and to notice deeper character motivation. Asking students to point to the words, phrases, or sentences within a passage that support their conclusions gives students practice explaining their evidence. Your follow-up questions can also help students find information in other parts of the story to lend support to their ideas.

FOLLOW-UP QUESTIONS: PROVIDING PRECISE EVIDENCE

◆ Which words or phrases in this passage help you understand that about Claude?

◆ Are there certain words or phrases that tell you how Claude is changing?

◆ What else does Claude do or say to lead you to think that?

BEFORE READING

1. Explain to students that during the second reading, they will be taking notes. Write the following on the board:

    C = Claude **changes** in some way.

2. Tell students that as they reread the story, they should mark with a **C** places where Claude **changes** in some way.

3. Ask students to think about why they are choosing those places, as they make their notes.

DURING READING

4. Tell students to read the story on their own or with a partner, or have them listen to the story read aloud (by you or on the CD), making notes as they go.

AFTER READING

5. Have students read aloud passages they marked with a **C**, and ask them to explain why they chose those passages.

6. Ask follow-up questions to help students provide more precise evidence to explain how their notes support their ideas about the story. Remember to ask if anyone sees a passage differently. Examine as many passages and notations as time allows.

7. Use your Leader Discussion Planner (page 169) to jot down questions or ideas to explore later.

8. Have students turn to Head in the Clouds on page 52 of the Reader's Journal and choose a topic for writing or drawing.

FLUENCY TIP

Tell students to think about how they can read a passage aloud so as to help listeners understand why they chose that passage to support their answer. Remind students that their tone of voice or facial expressions can help convey what is happening in a passage or emphasize important words or phrases that support their ideas.

Vocabulary (20 minutes)

Students practice using new vocabulary words.

> **STUDENT LEARNING OBJECTIVE**
>
> **READING COMPREHENSION: To understand and use new words in a variety of contexts**

SUGGESTED TARGET WORDS: arrogant, disgraced, hospitable

Choose the target words you want your class to learn, or use the suggested target words above. As you present a word, have students say it with you. Work on one word at a time, using these steps as a guide:

1. **Place the word** in context. Review how the word is used in the story.

2. **Define the word.** Use active language in your definition. Include a few examples of how to use the word in situations students will understand. For example:

   ◆ An **arrogant** person thinks he or she is better than other people and often acts rude or snobby. There is an **arrogant** girl in my class who never listens to the teacher and thinks she is smarter than the other students. If you behave in an **arrogant** way, people might think you are stuck-up.

   ◆ You are **disgraced** if you do something that causes people to look down on you or lose respect for you. The students were **disgraced** when the teacher caught them cheating on a test. He was **disgraced** at the game by fighting with a player on the other team.

   ◆ To be **hospitable** is to treat visitors or guests in a friendly and welcoming way. You would be **hospitable** if you invited your new neighbors over for dinner. The server at our favorite restaurant is very **hospitable** and always greets us with a big smile.

3. **Use the word.** Encourage students to make the word their own by asking a few of them to use it in a sentence or to apply it to real-life situations.

4. Ask a question about the story, using the word. Have several students apply their knowledge of the word to answer the question.

5. Optional: Have students turn to Curious Words on page 157 of the Reader's Journal to write down some of their favorite words from the story.

OVERHEARD IN THE CLASSROOM

TARGET WORD: arrogant

PLACE THE WORD IN CONTEXT
"Claude was the only son of Squire Archibald. He was **arrogant**, vain, and selfish." (Refer students to page 72 in the student anthology.)

DEFINE THE WORD
An **arrogant** person thinks he or she is better than other people and often acts rude or snobby. There is an **arrogant** girl in my class who never listens to the teacher and thinks she is smarter than the other students. If you behave in an **arrogant** manner, people might think that you are stuck-up. Say the word with me.

USE THE WORD
Which of these things might an **arrogant** person do? Say "**arrogant**" or "not **arrogant**."

♦ Say "I knew that" a lot
♦ Say "thanks for your help" and mean it
♦ Laugh at people
♦ Like to hear what others think
♦ Interrupt when others speak

ASK A QUESTION ABOUT THE STORY
Why does Claude become less **arrogant** after living in the forest?

Shared Inquiry Discussion (45 minutes)

Students discover meaning in the story by discussing an interpretive question.

STUDENT LEARNING OBJECTIVE

CRITICAL THINKING: To answer an interpretive question with specific evidence from the story

LOOK FOR STUDENTS TO

Point to relevant passages to support an answer

Explain how a passage supports an answer

Explain the significance of specific words and phrases to support an answer

EXPLORING A PASSAGE IN DETAIL

To help students analyze important passages in a story, try discussing a short passage line by line, or even word by word. Choose a passage that is significant or difficult in some way—one that signals a crisis or change in the story, or contains language that the author uses in a special way. To help students delve into the meanings of particular words or phrases, ask questions such as, Why do you think the author picked that word to use here?

Use the Leader Discussion Planner on the facing page to prepare yourself for Shared Inquiry discussion. To prepare your group, have everyone sit in a circle or a square; remind them of the five discussion guidelines and any behavioral guidelines you want to share. Then follow these steps to conduct the discussion:

1. Write the focus question on the board and have students copy it on the Building Your Answer page of the Reader's Journal (page 53).

2. Give students a few minutes to review the story and to write down an answer.

3. Begin the discussion by asking the focus question. On your seating chart, keep track of students' participation and ideas.

4. Lead the discussion by asking follow-up questions to help students clarify their ideas, provide evidence (see sample questions in your Leader Discussion Planner, page 169), and respond to one another. Aim to have the discussion last 20 to 30 minutes.

5. As the discussion winds down, have students finish the Building Your Answer page. Then ask volunteers to share what they wrote.

6. Spend a few minutes talking about the discussion. Ask students what they liked about it, what was hard about it, what they think makes a good discussion, and what might go better next time.

LEADER DISCUSSION PLANNER

After the first and second readings, use this section to keep track of:

◆ Questions that you and your students have about the story

◆ Characters, incidents, and ideas that interest you

◆ Passages that interest you

NOTES AND QUESTIONS

_____

_____

_____

_____

_____

Write down a focus question, cluster questions, and passages that you think you or your students will refer to in discussion. If you choose not to develop your own questions, see Suggested Interpretive Questions for Shared Inquiry Discussion on page 170.

CLUSTER QUESTION

_____

_____

_____

_____

CLUSTER QUESTION

_____

_____

_____

_____

FOCUS QUESTION FOR DISCUSSION

_____

_____

_____

RELATED PASSAGE   page _____

_____

_____

_____

_____

RELATED PASSAGE   page _____

_____

_____

_____

_____

In this Shared Inquiry discussion, look for opportunities to encourage your students to provide more precise evidence to support their answers.

FOLLOW-UP QUESTIONS: PROVIDING PRECISE EVIDENCE

◆ How does that passage support your answer?

◆ Which words in the passage support your answer?

◆ What are some other passages that are connected to your idea?

SUGGESTED INTERPRETIVE QUESTIONS FOR SHARED INQUIRY DISCUSSION

OPTION 1 Why doesn't Claude realize right away that he has become the Green Man?

◆ Why does Claude start taking care of the animals before he feeds himself?

◆ When his father's men come looking for him, why is Claude more worried about being disgraced than about being left in the forest?

◆ Why doesn't Claude know he is the Green Man until the little girl asks him if he is?

◆ Why does Claude choose the next Green Man in the same way he was chosen?

PASSAGE FOR DISCUSSION In the student anthology, from "One day when Claude was out," on page 80, to "safely to the edge of the forest," on page 81

OPTION 2 Why does being the Green Man make Claude a better person?

◆ Why doesn't Claude believe in the Green Man at the beginning of the story?

◆ Why does Claude almost forget that he is "Claude, the squire's son"?

◆ Why does Claude remain in the forest for only one year?

◆ Why does Claude tell his parents that it was the Green Man who saved his life?

PASSAGE FOR DISCUSSION In the student anthology, from "Winter passed and spring was on its way," on page 82, to "set out food and drink for the Green Man," on page 83

OVERHEARD IN THE CLASSROOM

LEADER   Why does being the Green Man make Claude a better person?

SALVADOR   Because he was selfish and mean and then went through all of that stuff in the forest.

LEADER   Like what?

DENISE   He had to milk the goats, and clean the fields, and save the children and the cow.

LEADER   How does saving the children make him a better person?

DENISE   I'm not really sure. The boar was going to kill them.

LEADER   Let's all look at that part of the story. Fred, would you read on page 80, beginning from "One day when Claude was out gathering acorns"?

FRED   (*Reads aloud.*)

LEADER   So does this help us understand why being the Green Man made him a better person?

JOAN   Not really. It shows that he already is a better person.

SALVADOR   I think he learns not to be mean like the boar.

WHEN TO ASK FOR EVIDENCE

Leaders cannot ask students to back up everything they say; they must pick and choose. Even though Salvador's assertion that Claude was "mean" is important to the focus question, this leader decides not to ask him for evidence; instead, she thinks it is better to let more students' ideas naturally arise as the discussion progresses. She also decides not to pursue Denise's misreading that Claude had to "clean" the fields. Instead she chooses to follow up on the passage where he saves the two children, because it raises interesting possibilities for answering the focus question.

Expository Writing: Story Setting (45 minutes)

Students write an essay about story setting.

> **STUDENT LEARNING OBJECTIVE**
>
> **WRITING: To demonstrate understanding of setting and character in an essay**

TEACHING LITERARY CONCEPTS: SETTING

1. Ask students what they know about the setting of a story before putting this definition on the board:

   The **setting** is the time and place of a story.

PREWRITING

2. Have the class identify some settings in "The Green Man," and list them on the board. Help students notice setting changes such as changes in season or location.

3. Tell students to list some settings from "The Green Man" in the left-hand column on page 54 of the Reader's Journal, using settings from the board and adding their own if they wish.

4. Point out that while there are different settings in the story, almost all are somewhere in the forest. Write the following essay question on the board:

   How does living in the forest change Claude?

5. Have students complete the right-hand column of their chart in pairs. Remind them that reviewing the story will help them notice how Claude behaves and feels in different settings.

WRITING A DRAFT

6. After students complete the chart, have them draft their essay on page 55 of the Reader's Journal.

Creative Writing:
How to be a Green Man (45 minutes)

Students write a set of instructions from a character's point of view.

> **STUDENT LEARNING OBJECTIVE**
>
> **WRITING: To develop a set of instructions**

PREWRITING

1. Remind students that Claude had to figure out how to live in the forest on his own, using his imagination and things that the last Green Man left behind. Tell students that they will now pretend to be Claude and will write instructions to help the next Green Man.

2. Have students review the story and brainstorm about tasks Claude does as he becomes the Green Man. List the tasks on the board.

3. Select a task from the list and create a chart on the board like the one below. Lead students in listing steps the new Green Man should take to complete the task. Ask them to find details from the story first, then to use their imaginations to invent additional details, using the imperative.

4. Lead students in determining the order in which the steps should appear in a set of instructions. Number the steps accordingly.

Rescues a calf from the river	Order
Wade across the river.	2
Pick up the calf and carry it to its mother.	4
Check the river every day to see if any animals are stuck.	1
Do not slip and fall on the rocks.	3

5. Have students select another task from the board and record it above the chart on page 57 in the Reader's Journal. Then have them complete the chart the same way you did on the board.

WRITING A DRAFT

6. Have students write the instructions on page 58 of the Reader's Journal. Optional: Make a class "Green Man Guidebook."

Curriculum Connections

Below are resources related to "The Green Man" for further reading and investigation in a number of subject areas.

 Appropriate for classroom read-alouds; above-grade reading and interest levels

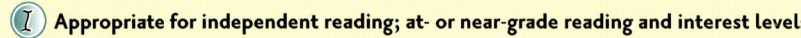 Appropriate for independent reading; at- or near-grade reading and interest levels

OTHER WORKS BY THE AUTHOR

Haley, Gail E. *Kokopelli, Drum in Belly*. Palmer Lake, CO: Filter Press, 2003.
Kokopelli the Cicada leads the Ant People from the Dark World up to various other worlds and finally to the Green World, teaching them along the way what they will need to know to survive and thrive there as the First People.

Haley, Gail E. *A Story, a Story: An African Tale*. New York: Atheneum, 1970.
Recounts how most African folktales came to be called "spider stories."

FOLKLORE

Van Allsburg, Chris. *The Stranger*. Boston: Houghton Mifflin, 1986.
The enigmatic origins of the stranger that Farmer Bailey hits with his truck and brings home to recuperate seem to have a mysterious relation to the changing season.

Wilde, Oscar. *The Selfish Giant*. New York: Putnam, 1995.
A once-selfish giant welcomes children to his previously forbidden garden and is eventually rewarded by an unusual little child.

RECREATION/SPORTS

Calder, Kate. *Horseback Riding in Action*. New York: Crabtree, 2001.
Presents an illustrated introduction to the techniques, equipment, and safety requirements of horseback riding, and includes information on how to care for horses.

Gruber, Beth. *Horseback Riding for Fun!* Minneapolis: Compass Point Books, 2004.
Introduces horseback riding, discussing a horse's anatomy, how to care for a horse, riding equipment and techniques, and various equestrian events.

SCIENCE

(I) Galko, Francine. *Forest Animals.* Chicago: Heinemann Library, 2003.
Explores the animals that live in the forest.

(R) Gibbons, Gail. *Caves and Caverns.* San Diego: Harcourt Brace, 1996.
Text and labeled illustrations describe the formation and physical features of various kinds of caves, with a brief section on spelunking.

(I) Gibbons, Gail. *The Reason for Seasons.* New York: Holiday House, 1995.
Explains how the position of the earth causes seasons and describes the wonderful things that each season brings.

(I) Heligman, Deborah. *Honeybees.* Washington, D.C.: National Geographic, 2002.
Illustrations and simple text teach young readers about honeybees, and the different jobs they perform within the hive.

(R) Johansson, Philip. *The Temperate Forest: A Web of Life.* Berkeley Heights, NJ: Enslow, 2004.
Explores the temperate forest biome and the plant and animal life that survives there.

(R) Kalman, Bobbie. *Forest Food Chains.* New York: Crabtree, 2005.
Introduces forests and the food chain cycle within such an environment.

(I) Murray, Julie. *Chickens.* Edina, MN: Abdo, 2002.
An introduction to the physical characteristics, behavior, and different breeds of chickens.

(I) Murray, Julie. *Goats.* Edina, MN: Abdo, 2002.
An introduction to the physical characteristics, behavior, and care of goats.

Highlighted words are the suggested target words in the vocabulary activity. Underlined words can be briefly explained as you read the story aloud, using the definitions provided.

LEADER'S NOTES AND QUESTIONS

_____
_____
_____
_____
_____
_____
_____
_____
_____
_____
_____

Think-Aloud

"The author describes Claude as 'arrogant, vain, and selfish.' Maybe Claude's character traits are important, since this is the first thing the author says about him."

THE GREEN MAN

Gail E. Haley

The story you are about to read may have happened just this way—or perhaps it came about in a different manner in some other place entirely. . . .

Claude was the only son of Squire Archibald. He was arrogant, vain, and selfish. He spent most of his time hunting, hawking, and riding about the countryside in his fine clothes.

One evening Claude rode into the village, and after ordering a lavish meal at the Mermaid and Bush, he sat watching the bustle of village life.

72

squire: an English country gentleman

arrogant: thinking you are better than other people; snobby

hawking: using trained hawks for hunting

lavish: grand and expensive

• • •

"Look at those ignorant peasants putting food out for the Green Man when they can barely feed their own children."

"They are grateful, Master Claude," replied the landlord. "For the Green Man keeps their animals healthy. He protects their children if they stray into the forest. Without him, the crops would not grow, nor the seasons turn in their course."

"Rubbish! Those are just silly tales. There is no Green Man!"

"Mind your tongue, sir," chided the landlord. "Terrible things can happen to those who make fun of old beliefs."

Some days afterward, Claude set out for a day's hunting. He never hunted on foot; he preferred to shoot from horseback. His men and dogs had gone ahead as beaters to drive the game toward him, but nothing was happening, and Claude grew tired of waiting. He rode deeper into the forest.

73

beaters: people who hit the bushes so that the animals will come out into the open

...

"Those beaters are <u>incompetent</u>. I haven't seen an animal all day!" he grumbled.

Soon Claude was hopelessly lost. It was hot, and his clothes felt heavy, when through the trees he saw a shady pond. Tethering his horse to a tree, he stripped off his clothes and dived into the cool water. He did not see a thin bony hand reaching out of the bushes.

Claude came out of the water refreshed and hungry, but on the bank he found nothing but a coil of rope.

Claude tied some leafy branches around his waist with the rope. Then he ate some of the strawberries that were growing on the bank. Feeling better, he chose a stout branch as a walking stick and set off to find his way home. But as the day drew to a close, Claude realized that he would have to spend the night in the forest.

Peering about in the gloom, he saw before him the entrance to a large cave and felt his way inside. As he grew accustomed to the dark, Claude realized that he was not alone. There seemed to be something with glittering eyes and sharp horns near the mouth of the cave.

74

incompetent: not able to do something well

"Stay back! I'm armed!" Claude shouted. But the creature came no closer. Then something moved near the back of the cave. Claude clutched his stick for protection and drew his legs up onto a ledge. He lay there until, exhausted, he fell asleep.

When Claude woke it was morning and a little nanny goat was standing before him, tossing her head. He laughed with relief. It must have been she who had been at the back of the cave in the night.

75

...

Claude looked around. A young rooster was pecking busily near a nest full of eggs. A clay jug and a stone ax hung on the wall above Claude's head. Several rough baskets stood on the floor, and there was ash from a recent fire.

"'This is someone's home," thought Claude. "Perhaps I should feed the animals." He gave the hens some grain which he found in a bowl and picked some fresh grass for the goat as a special treat. Then he helped himself to goat's milk and eggs.

The goat nuzzled his hand, and he scratched her behind the ears. She frisked about and followed him when he set off to explore.

Not far away, Claude found a bees' nest in a tree, its honeycomb shining from inside the hollow trunk. Covering his body with mud to protect himself from stings, he climbed up to collect some honey.

Just then, a party of his father's men broke through the trees, blowing their horns and hallooing for him.

"They'll think I've gone mad, if they see me sitting in a tree covered with mud," thought Claude. "I can't let them see me without my clothes and my boots. I would be disgraced!"

76

disgraced: doing something that causes people to look down on you or lose respect for you

So he let the party pass without revealing himself. Then he climbed down from the tree and crept back to the cave, followed all the time by the goat.

"I'll borrow something to cover myself from the owner of the cave when he returns, and then I'll set off for home again," Claude said to his new friend, the goat. But time passed, and no one came. Claude lived on in the cave, growing leaner and stronger every day.

77

Think-Aloud

"When Claude has a chance to be found, he doesn't take it. He doesn't want to be disgraced. I think maybe it shows something important about him."

•••

As the warm days went by, Claude forgot altogether about clothes. He nearly forgot that he was Claude, the Squire's son. He became Milker-of-the-Goat, Feeder-of-the-Hens, Friend-of-All-Wild-Animals. The forest creatures were not afraid of him. He fed them, talked to them, and spent hours watching them hunt and play.

As the berries, fruits, and nuts ripened, Claude became Gatherer-and-Preserver. When the grain was harvested in distant fields, he became Gleaner, venturing out at night to gather the leftovers for himself and his animals.

Claude was enjoying his new life. Even the sun and the moon seemed to smile upon him.

One morning, after a heavy rainstorm, Claude heard a frantic bellow coming from the direction of the river. He hurried there to see what was wrong, and found a cow who had been separated from her calf. They had taken shelter from the rain in a hilltop thicket, and as the water rose the river had surrounded them,

78

gleaner: someone who picks up grain left in a field after crops have been gathered

...

turning the hillock into an island. The terrified calf would not follow its mother through the swirling current, and the cow was mooing loudly for help.

Claude waded across the water, picked up the calf, and carried it to its mother. Gratefully, the cow licked his hand and then led her calf away through the forest toward the safety of the farmyard.

Think-Aloud

"Wow, Claude helps, feeds, and cares for animals. I think how he is changing is important."

As the days grew colder, Claude added more ivy leaves to his costume. He tucked strips of moss and lichen between them to keep out the cold. He pounded birch bark to make it soft and sewed pieces together to make a curtain for the mouth of the cave. After several attempts he even succeeded in making himself some birch-bark boots.

LEADER'S NOTES AND QUESTIONS

He built a fireplace near the entrance. He had found stones the right size and shape to make a mortar and a pestle, and each day he ground grain or nuts or acorns into flour. The smell of baking bread filled the air. A family of hedgehogs moved in.

The cave was now well stocked with food. Strings of mushrooms, parsnips, wild onions, and herbs hung on drying poles. Claude made slings

79

hillock: a small hill

mortar: a deep bowl in which grains and nuts can be crushed

pestle: a small rounded tool used to crush things in a mortar

· · ·

for the fruit and vegetables he had gathered. He formed barrels out of bark to hold apples and roots. Baskets of nuts, grain, and seeds were stored on a shelf above his mossy bed.

One day when Claude was out gathering acorns, he encountered a fierce wild boar threatening two small children from the village.

"Don't be such a selfish swine!" Claude spoke firmly to the boar. "There are enough acorns for everyone. Go away and let the children have their share."

The boar snorted defiantly but turned and trotted back into the forest.

80

"There, there, don't cry. The old boar is gone now," Claude comforted the children.

The girl looked up through her tears at the tall, sunburned man. He seemed as ancient, green, and moss-covered as the oak tree that towered above them.

"Are you the Green Man?" she asked in a whisper.

Claude looked down in surprise. Warm sunshine caressed his hair. A gentle breeze rippled his leafy costume. His feet felt as if they were rooted in the earth.

"Yes," Claude answered her at last, "I am the Green Man."

He helped the children to gather up their acorns and filled their basket to the brim. Then he led them safely to the edge of the forest.

81

LEADER'S NOTES AND QUESTIONS

• • •

When winter came, at night Claude visited the nearby sleeping villages. He helped himself to some of the food put out for him but always left some for hungry, prowling animals. At times he felt lonely as he walked through the deserted streets, looking into the windows of the cozy houses. He was homesick for his own village and his family. But he returned each night to his cave and his animals. He was needed now in the forest.

Winter passed and spring was on its way. The smell of budding leaves, warm earth, and growing things filled the air. The days went by, and when he knew that the strawberries would be ripening by the pond, Claude went to pick them.

A man was splashing in the water. A fine suit of clothing lay on the bank and a handsome horse was tethered nearby.

Claude quietly took off his leaves and put on the clothes. He found shears and a glass in the horse's saddlebag, so he cut his long hair and trimmed his beard. Then he rode through the forest until he found his own home.

82

•••

His mother and father were amazed and delighted to see him. Everyone thought that he had been killed long ago by robbers or eaten by wild animals.

"It was the Green Man who saved my life," was all that Claude would say.

His year away had changed the arrogant young man. Now he was <mark>hospitable</mark> to travelers. He cared for his animals. And each night Claude set out food and drink for the Green Man.

83

hospitable: treating visitors in a friendly and welcoming way

The Ugly Duckling

Hans Christian Andersen

STORY LENGTH: 23 pages   READ-ALOUD TIME: About 28 minutes

◆ ABOUT THE STORY

A duckling is harassed for being bigger and uglier than his siblings, so he leaves his family and the familiar world of the barnyard. After a year of adventures, hardships, and loneliness, the ugly ducklng comes upon a group of swans in a lake and gains a new understanding of himself.

◆ ABOUT THE AUTHOR

Born in Odense, Denmark, in 1805, Hans Christian Andersen developed an interest in literature and theater as a child. At the age of fourteen, he left home for Copenhagen. He is best known today for the more than 150 fairy stories he wrote. Some of them are derived from folktales he heard; others he invented. Among the best known are "The Little Mermaid," "The Princess and the Pea," and "The Emperor's New Clothes." Andersen died in 1875.

The story starts on page 209 of the Leader's Edition, and on page 85 of the student anthology.

Unit Overview

❖ **SESSION I:** PAGE 191

PREREADING Students think about places where they feel comfortable being themselves.

★ **FIRST READING** Students note important ideas in the story as the leader reads it aloud.

★ **SHARING QUESTIONS** Students share their questions about the story, concentrating on interpretive questions.

SESSION 2: PAGE 196

★ **SECOND READING WITH DIRECTED NOTES** Students mark passages that address an important concept in the story.

SPOTLIGHT ON FOLLOW-UP QUESTIONS The leader asks follow-up questions to highlight connections between different students' ideas.

SESSION 3: PAGE 198

VOCABULARY Students practice using new vocabulary words. Suggested target words: *adversity*, *downhearted*, and *persecuted*

SESSION 4: PAGE 200

★ **SHARED INQUIRY DISCUSSION** Students discover meaning in the story by discussing an interpretive question.

SESSION 5 OPTIONS: PAGE 204

❖ **EXPOSITORY WRITING** Students sequence story events orally and in writing.

CREATIVE WRITING Students write a letter from a character's point of view, then write a reply to a partner's letter.

CURRICULUM CONNECTIONS The leader can use these resources to link the story to other subject areas.

❖ May require two class periods

★ Core activity

Prereading (5–10 minutes)

Students think about places where they feel comfortable being themselves.

1. Tell students that you are going to read a story about a character who spends a long time searching for a place where he feels comfortable with himself.

2. Ask students to think about a place where they feel comfortable being themselves.

3. Have a few students briefly describe their chosen places and explain why they feel comfortable there. Help them by asking questions such as:
   - What does this place look like? Sound like? Smell like?
   - What is it about this place that makes you feel comfortable?
   - How do you feel when you are in this place? Why do you feel this way?

4. Now ask students to think of a place where they feel uncomfortable. Ask them to consider how this place makes them feel and what makes them feel uncomfortable.

5. Ask students to share their uncomfortable places with the class, but only if they wish to; otherwise they can consider these places in silence.

First Reading (50–65 minutes)

Students note important ideas in the story as the leader reads it aloud.

> **STUDENT LEARNING OBJECTIVE**
>
> **READING COMPREHENSION: To determine important ideas in the story**

WORKING WITH LONGER STORIES

Due to this story's length, you may wish to spread the activities in Session 1 over two class periods. Here are some suggestions for how to break up the activities:

CLASS PERIOD 1

- Complete the prereading activity (page 191) and steps 1 to 3 of this activity.

- Read the story aloud, pausing now and then to model how you determine importance (steps 4 and 5). Break at a point that takes into account time needed for other session activities and the attention span of your students. A suggested stopping point for this story is after the paragraph ending "slip into the room through the opening, and that is what he did," on page 96 of the student anthology.

- Complete steps 6 and 7. Collect students' questions, but do not review them until you have finished reading the story.

CLASS PERIOD 2

- Ask students to briefly recap the main characters, setting, and important events thus far. Take a few minutes to review the story's reading comprehension strategy, determining important ideas.

- Finish reading the story aloud, pausing now and then to model how you determine importance.

- Collect new questions and see whether any of the questions from class period 1 have been answered. Move on to the sharing questions activity (page 194).

Note: If necessary, skip or shorten the prereading, vocabulary, and writing activities to allow time for core activities.

BEFORE READING

1. Have students follow along in their books as they listen to you read "The Ugly Duckling," a story about a duckling who doesn't fit in.

2. Explain to students that in a story, some of the information is important to understanding the story's meaning, and other information, while enjoyable or interesting, is not as important. Figuring out what is important in a story helps readers discover the main ideas or themes.

3. Ask students to mark with an **!** places where they think something is **important** in the story, and to mark with a **?** places where they have a **question** about the story. After listening to the story, they will have a chance to share their important passages and questions.

DURING READING

4. Read the story aloud with expression.

5. Pause several times while reading to model how you determine whether something is important. Look away from the book to share why something in the story seems important to you, explaining how you arrived at your decision. Use your own ideas or the Think-Alouds provided in the margins of the story.

AFTER READING

6. Ask students to review the story to find passages they marked as important.

7. Have students take a few minutes to share with a partner something in the story that they think is important and why. If time allows, have a few students share their ideas with the class.

8. Tell students to review the story to find the passages they marked with a **?** and to think about questions they would like to share with the class.

READING FOR DIFFERENT PURPOSES

How a reader determines important ideas depends on the reader's purpose and on the text itself. Point out to your students that important ideas in fiction and narrative nonfiction can be signaled by change (of a character's perspective, actions, feelings, or beliefs) or by repetition of words, phrases, symbols, or concepts. In textbooks, important ideas in expository or informational writing can be signaled by how the text is organized—for example, headings, inset boxes, and numbered lists. Graphic elements such as boldface words and highlighting can also point to important ideas.

Sharing Questions (25–35 minutes)

Students share their questions about the story, concentrating on interpretive questions.

STUDENT LEARNING OBJECTIVE

READING COMPREHENSION: To identify interpretive questions that address important issues in the story

LOOK FOR STUDENTS TO

Ask questions about the story

Recognize interpretive questions about the story

Identify interpretive questions about important issues in the story

IDENTIFYING IMPORTANT ISSUES

As students test interpretive questions, ask them whether their answers are based on one small section of the story or from two or three different sections. Point out that if passages from several different sections of the story inspire answers to the question, then the question probably addresses an important issue about the story's meaning. An interpretive question based on just one section of the story is not a bad keeper question, as long as it reflects the student's genuine curiosity. But when you encourage students to look through the whole story for meaningful passages, they are more likely to identify questions that address the story's main issues, rather than relatively minor ones.

1. Record questions on the board with students' names, or have students write their questions on strips of paper to post around the room.

2. Encourage students to answer factual and vocabulary questions by using the text, the Reader's Journal glossary, a dictionary, or classmates for help.

3. Identify any evaluative, speculative, or background questions. Help the class revise, answer, or skip them as appropriate.

4. Have students identify a few questions that they think might be interpretive.

5. Ask students to take a few minutes with a partner to test each question, reminding them to look for two different answers that can be supported with evidence from the story. (If your students are struggling with this independent work, continue identifying and testing interpretive questions as a class.)

6. Tell students to choose a keeper question from among the interpretive questions they have identified.

7. Have students locate parts of the story that relate to their keeper question. Have them write their keeper question and related parts of the story on page 60 of the Reader's Journal.

8. Ask volunteers to share with the class their keeper questions and related parts of the story.

9. Use your Leader Discussion Planner (page 201) to jot down the questions and passages that seem to come up most often. Consider whether you can use any of these later, during the discussion.

10. Have students turn to page 61 in the Reader's Journal to practice determining important ideas as a reading strategy. This can also serve as homework.

Second Reading With Directed Notes (45 minutes)

Students mark passages that address an important concept in the story.

STUDENT LEARNING OBJECTIVE

READING COMPREHENSION: To reread with a purpose and articulate ideas about the story

LOOK FOR STUDENTS TO

Agree or disagree with other students' ideas

Give reasons for agreement or disagreement

Refer to other students' ideas when agreeing or disagreeing

SPOTLIGHT
on Follow-Up Questions

For this unit, the spotlight is on **asking follow-up questions to highlight connections between different students' ideas.** With your help, students will become more adept at hearing and considering useful insights in their classmates' comments. Eventually students will recognize that considering the ideas of others—whether they agree with them or not—can help them develop their own perspective.

FOLLOW-UP QUESTIONS: CONNECTING STUDENTS' IDEAS

◆ Why do you agree with the way Jason marked that passage?

◆ Did you mark it that way for the same reason Deborah did?

◆ Can you ask Cai to explain the part of her idea that you don't understand?

BEFORE READING

1. Explain to students that during the second reading they will be taking notes. Write the following on the board:

   U = Something **unexpected** happens (something that you didn't think would happen).

2. Tell students that as they reread the story, they should mark with a **U** places where something unexpected happens.

3. Ask students to think about why they are choosing those places, as they make their notes.

DURING READING

4. Tell students to read the story on their own or with a partner, or have them listen to the story read aloud (by you or on the CD), making notes as they go.

AFTER READING

5. Have students read aloud the passages they marked with a **U**, and ask them to explain why they chose those passages.

6. Ask follow-up questions to highlight connections between students' ideas. Remember to ask if anyone sees a passage differently. Examine as many passages and notations as time allows.

7. Use your Leader Discussion Planner (page 201) to jot down questions or ideas to explore later.

8. Have students turn to Head in the Clouds on page 63 of the Reader's Journal and choose a topic for writing or drawing.

FLUENCY TIP

Have students practice reading the expressive narrative of this story in small groups. Point out that dashes, question marks, exclamation points, italics, indents, and capitalized words all affect pronunciation and inflection. Have groups of students perform choral readings of passages from the story, first deciding which lines should be read as a group, and which by individual students in order to emphasize certain words or phrases.

Vocabulary (20 minutes)

Students practice using new vocabulary words.

SUGGESTED TARGET WORDS: **adversity, downhearted, persecuted**

Choose the target words you want your class to learn, or use the suggested target words above. As you present a word, have students say it with you. Work on one word at a time, using these steps as a guide:

CREATIVE OPTIONS FOR TARGET WORDS

Follow up vocabulary lessons with practice using target words in various ways. Creative applications of target words include drawing pictures to interpret a word, writing dialogue that uses the words, performing a short skit interpreting a word, or creating a comic strip using the words. These activities need not take long but provide essential reinforcement.

I. Place the word in context. Review how the word is used in the story.

2. Define the word. Use active language in your definition. Include a few examples of how to use the word in situations students will understand. For example:

   ♦ **Adversity** is great difficulty or suffering. Someone who survived a bad accident might say he made it through much **adversity**. It is often said that we become stronger when we face **adversity**.

   ♦ If you are **downhearted** you feel sad or gloomy. You might be **downhearted** if your best friend moved away. A cold, rainy day always makes me feel a little **downhearted**.

   ♦ If you are **persecuted**, you are treated very badly and unfairly, over and over. I was **persecuted** by the neighborhood bully, who called me names every time I walked by him. The man was so **persecuted** by his nasty neighbors that he decided to move to another part of town.

3. Use the word. Encourage students to make the word their own by asking a few of them to use it in a sentence or to apply it to real-life situations.

4. Ask a question about the story, using the word. Have several students apply their knowledge of the word to answer the question.

5. Optional: Have students turn to Curious Words on page 158 of the Reader's Journal to write down some of their favorite words from the story.

OVERHEARD IN THE CLASSROOM

TARGET WORD: persecuted

PLACE THE WORD IN CONTEXT
"He remembered how once he had been despised and **persecuted**; and now he heard everyone saying that he was the most beautiful of all beautiful birds." (Refer students to pages 106–107 in the student anthology.)

DEFINE THE WORD
If you are **persecuted**, you are treated very badly and unfairly, over and over. I was **persecuted** by the neighborhood bully, who called me names every time I walked by him. The man was so **persecuted** by his nasty neighbors that he decided to move to another part of town. Let's say the word together.

USE THE WORD
Have students draw a picture of how they would look if they felt **persecuted**.

ASK A QUESTION ABOUT THE STORY
Why is the ugly duckling **persecuted** by the animals in the barnyard?

SUGGESTED INTERPRETIVE QUESTIONS FOR SHARED INQUIRY DISCUSSION

OPTION 1 **Why does the duckling think there is something wrong with him, instead of becoming angry at the animals who pick on him?**

♦ Why does the duckling try to explain to the cat and the hen what it feels like to swim?

♦ When he first sees the swans, why does the duckling love them but "not envy them in the least"?

♦ Why doesn't the duckling understand that the farmer's children only want to play with him?

♦ Why does the duckling expect the swans to peck him to death?

PASSAGE FOR DISCUSSION In the student anthology, from "One evening, when the sun was setting," on page 100, to "the poor ugly creature!" on page 101

OPTION 2 **At the end of the story, why does the duckling still have a good heart despite everything that has happened?**

♦ Why doesn't the duckling's treatment in the barnyard make him angry?

♦ Why does the duckling tell the cat and hen that he'd "better go out into the wide world"?

♦ Why doesn't the duckling envy the swans' beauty?

♦ Why does the duckling think it "doesn't matter in the least" as long as he is killed by the royal swans?

PASSAGE FOR DISCUSSION In the student anthology, from "I will fly near those royal birds," on page 104, to "for a good heart never becomes proud," on page 106

OVERHEARD IN THE CLASSROOM

LEADER   Why does the duckling think there is something wrong with him, instead of becoming angry at the animals who pick on him?

VALENTINA   It's not their fault. For a duck, he really is ugly.

ELLEN   Of course it's their fault. They made him feel bad.

LEADER   Ellen, did you want to say something to Valentina?

ELLEN   I was just saying that I don't agree with Valentina.

LEADER   Can you speak right to Valentina?

ELLEN   Okay. Valentina, I think that you're—I mean, I think if they didn't say he was too big and odd and stuff, then he wouldn't feel so bad.

LEADER   Valentina, do you want to respond?

VALENTINA   I kind of agree with Ellen that if they didn't say that stuff he wouldn't feel bad.

WILLIS   I agree with Valentina. You can't blame them for telling the truth. For a duck he is too tall and strange.

DEBORAH   No. Willis and Valentina don't get how mean they are.

LEADER   Deborah, can you turn to Willis and Valentina and explain what you mean?

DEBORAH   Okay. Willis and Valentina, don't you think the other animals are mean to the duckling?

VALENTINA   I think they are mean. But that's not the problem. The problem is that everybody thinks he's a duck when he's not.

LEARNING TO TALK TO ONE ANOTHER

Asking students to respond directly to their classmates might seem risky, but it often encourages them to respect one another. It challenges them to confront classmates' ideas more directly and give real consideration to differing points of view. After some practice, differences and similarities between students' interpretations will emerge constructively.

Expository Writing: Retelling the Story (60–75 minutes; may require two class periods)

Students sequence story events orally and in writing.

> ### STUDENT LEARNING OBJECTIVE
>
> **WRITING: To retell story events in writing in the correct sequence**

STAGE 5 ASSESSMENT

In the Reflect and Connect activity following this unit, students will have an opportunity to revise a piece of their writing from Stage 5, which you may then choose to assess.

SEQUENCING EVENTS

Sequencing, or presenting events in chronological order, helps students build a foundation for developing an effective story summary. In the next unit, students will move beyond communicating a sequence of events (retelling) to summarizing— communicating an interpretation of important ideas in the story.

TEACHING LITERARY CONCEPTS: SEQUENCE OF EVENTS

1. Ask students what they know about the sequence of events in a story before writing the following definition on the board:

   > The **sequence of events** is the order in which things happen.

PREWRITING

2. Lead the class in listing on the board the sequence of important events in "The Ugly Duckling," up to the point where the duckling leaves the cat, hen, and old woman (page 99). Encourage students to review the story to verify the order in which things happen.

3. Have students work in pairs to identify the sequence of important events after the duckling leaves the cat, hen, and old woman. They should write down the sequence in the left-hand column of the chart in the Reader's Journal (page 66).

4. Ask students to work together to complete the setting and character columns on page 67 of the Reader's Journal, reviewing the story for accuracy.

5. Have students retell the second half of the story out loud to a partner, using the chart to help them remember the order of events in the story. In their retelling, students may include story details they have not listed, as they remember them.

WRITING A DRAFT

6. Have students retell "The Ugly Duckling" in writing, using their own words, on page 68 of the Reader's Journal. This can also serve as homework.

7. Optional: Have students create a storyboard for "The Ugly Duckling," with illustrations, descriptions, and dialogue bubbles.

Creative Writing:
Advice for the Ugly Duckling (45–60 minutes)

Students write a letter from a character's point of view, then write a reply to a partner's letter.

> **STUDENT LEARNING OBJECTIVE**
>
> **WRITING: To write and respond to letters**

PREWRITING

1. Discuss with students the concept of a letter of advice. You may want to share an advice column from a newspaper. Tell students that they will write a letter to a partner as if they were the ugly duckling, asking for advice about a problem he has in the story. Then students will answer a partner's letter with advice about how to solve the problem.

2. Lead students in listing on the board some specific problems that the ugly duckling has in the story. For example:
   - He is bitten and made fun of by another duck (pages 92–93).
   - He gets frozen in the ice (page 102).
   - He is chased by the children and the farmer's wife (page 103).

3. Have students choose a problem on the board (or one of the duckling's other problems) and answer the questions on page 70 of the Reader's Journal.

WRITING A DRAFT

4. In the Reader's Journal (page 71), have students draft a letter from the ugly duckling's point of view, asking for advice.

5. Have partners trade Reader's Journals, read their partners' letters, and discuss what advice they could give to solve the problem.

6. Have each student write a letter to their partner on page 72, giving advice about how to solve the problem.

7. Have students return Reader's Journals to their owners and read the advice they received from their partner.

RESPONDING IN WRITING

Your students have a natural audience in their classmates. Writing to one another makes writing more authentic and gives students an incentive to put forth their best effort. The students' task in this activity is not to provide feedback to one another for improvement and revisions, as in peer editing, but rather to listen to, understand, and consider experiences and ideas that differ from their own.

Curriculum Connections

Below are resources related to "The Ugly Duckling" for further reading and investigation in a number of subject areas.

 Appropriate for classroom read-alouds; above-grade reading and interest levels

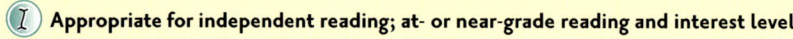 Appropriate for independent reading; at- or near-grade reading and interest levels

OTHER WORKS BY THE AUTHOR

ⓡ Andersen, Hans Christian. *Tales of Hans Christian Andersen*. Trans., Naomi Lewis. Cambridge, MA: Candlewick Press, 2004.

> Presents illustrated retellings of thirteen fairy tales by Hans Christian Andersen, including "The Little Mermaid," "The Ugly Duckling," and "The Snow Queen."

ⓡ Andersen, Hans Christian. *Andersen's Fairy Tales*. Trans., E. V. Lucas and H. B. Paull. New York: Grosset & Dunlap, 1984.

> Twenty-nine fairy tales by Hans Christian Andersen.

BIOGRAPHY

ⓘ Langley, Andrew. *Hans Christian Andersen: The Dreamer of Fairy Tales*. New York: Oxford University Press, 1998.

> Chronicles the life of Hans Christian Andersen in an easy-to-read format for children.

ⓡ Yolen, Jane. *The Perfect Wizard: Hans Christian Andersen*. New York: Dutton's Children's Books, 2004.

> A biography of the famous Danish writer of fairy tales, interspersed with excerpts from his stories.

FOLKLORE

ⓘ Setterington, Ken. *The Wild Swans: An Adventure in Six Parts*. Plattsburgh, NY: Tundra Books, 2003.

> A young princess places her life in peril as she works in silence to weave eleven shirts from the yarn of stinging nettles, in order to free her brothers from an evil spell that has turned them into swans.

SCIENCE

(R) Boring, Mel. *Birds, Nests, and Eggs.* Minocqua, WI: NorthWord Press, 1996.
Groups birds according to whether they are found in city and town, farm
country, field and meadow, or woodland and then describes the birds, their
nests, and their eggs.

(I) Cooper, Jason. *Geese.* Vero Beach, FL: Rourke, 1995.
Photographs and text provide information about the lives, appearance,
behavior, and uses of geese on the farm.

(I) Gibbons, Gail. *Ducks!* New York: Holiday House, 2001.
Text and illustrations provide information about ducks, examining
their physical characteristics, and discussing how they swim, eat, dive,
communicate, build nests, and raise their ducklings.

(I) Jenkins, Priscilla. *A Nest Full of Eggs.* New York: HarperCollins, 2005.
Explains how four blue eggs develop into robins and shows feathers from
many different types of birds.

(I) Morgan, Sally. *Ducks and Other Birds.* North Mankato, MN: Thameside Press,
2001.
Photographs and simple text introduce young readers to ducks and
other birds.

(I) Pascoe, Elaine. *Animals Hatch from Eggs.* Milwaukee: Gareth Stevens, 2002.
Explains how animals protect their eggs and why some animals lay their
eggs in special places.

(R) Wexo, John Bonnett. *Ducks, Geese and Swans,* Zoobooks Series. Poway, CA:
Wildlife Education, 2001.
An introduction to the physical characteristics, habits, and natural
environment of ducks, geese, and swans.

SOCIAL STUDIES

(I) Murphy, Patricia J. *Denmark.* Mankato, MN: Bridgestone Books, 2003.
Introduces the geography, food, and culture of Denmark, including
information about the capital, Copenhagen, and Hans Christian Andersen.

...

could stand upright under the biggest of them. The place was as much of a wilderness as the densest wood, and there sat a duck on her nest; she was busy hatching her ducklings, but she was almost tired of it, because sitting is such a tedious business, and she had very few callers. The other ducks thought it more fun to swim about in the moat than to come and have a gossip with her under a wild rhubarb leaf.

At last one eggshell after another began to crack open. "Cheep, cheep!" All the yolks had come to life and were sticking out their heads.

"Quack, quack," said the duck, and all her ducklings came scurrying out as fast as they could, looking about under the green leaves, and their mother let them look as much as they liked, because green is good for the eyes.

"How big the world is!" said all the ducklings, for they felt much more comfortable now than when they were lying in the egg.

"Do you imagine this is the whole of the world?" asked their mother. "It goes far beyond the other side of the garden, right into the Rector's field, but I've never been there yet. I hope you're all here," she went on, and hoisted herself up. "No, I haven't got all of you even now; the biggest egg is still there. I wonder how much longer it will take! I'm getting rather bored with the whole thing." And she squatted down again on the nest.

"Well, how are you getting on?" asked an old duck who came to call on her.

"That last egg is taking an awfully long time," said the brooding duck. "It won't break; but let me show you the others, they're the sweetest ducklings I've ever seen. They are all exactly like their father; the scamp—he never comes to see me!"

"Let me look at the egg that won't break," said the old duck. "You may be sure it's a turkey's egg. I was fooled like that once, and the trouble and bother I had with those youngsters, because

87

Think-Aloud

"All the others have hatched, and this egg looks different. I think this egg may have an important part in the story."

LEADER'S NOTES AND QUESTIONS

they were actually afraid of the water! I simply couldn't get them to go in! I quacked at them and I snapped at them, but it was no use. Let me see the egg—of course it's a turkey's egg. Leave it alone, and teach the other children to swim."

"Oh, well, if I've taken so much trouble I may just as well sit a little longer," said the duck.

"Please yourself," said the old duck, and she waddled off.

At last the big egg cracked. "Cheep, cheep!" said the youngster, scrambling out; he was so big and ugly! The duck looked at him: "What a frightfully big duckling that one is," she said. "None of the others looked like that! Could he possibly be a turkey chick? We'll soon find out; he'll have to go into the water, even if I have to kick him in myself!"

The next day the weather was simply glorious; the sun shone on all the wild rhubarb plants. Mother Duck appeared with her family down by the moat. Splash! There she was in the water!

Think-Aloud

"The story keeps saying the ugly duckling is bigger than the other ducklings. Even the mother duck says the ugly duckling is 'frightfully big.' I wonder if this will be important."

...

"Quack, quack," she said, and one duckling after another plumped in. The water closed over their heads, but they were up again in a second and floated beautifully. Their legs worked of their own accord; they were all out in the water now, and even the ugly gray creature was swimming along with them.

"That's no turkey!" she said. "Look how nicely he uses his legs, and how straight he holds himself! He's my own flesh and blood, I tell you. He isn't really so bad when you take a good look at him. Quack, quack—come along with me, I'll bring you out into the world and introduce you to the duckyard, but keep close to me or you may get stepped on, and look out for the cat!"

So they made their entrance into the duckyard. What a pandemonium there was! Two families were quarreling over an eel's head; but in the end the cat got it.

LEADER'S NOTES AND QUESTIONS

89

pandemonium: noisy confusion

•••

"There you are, that's the way of the world!" said Mother Duck, licking her lips, for she did so want the eel's head herself. "Now use your legs," she said. "Move about briskly and curtsey with your necks to the old duck over there; she is the most aristocratic person here, and of Spanish blood, that's why she is so stout; and be sure to observe that red rag round her leg. It's a great distinction, and the highest honor that can be bestowed upon a duck; it means that her owner wishes to keep her, and that she is to be specially noticed by man and beast. Now hurry! Don't turn your toes in; a well-brought-up duckling turns his toes out just as father and mother do—like that. That's right! Now make a deep curtsey with your necks and say, 'Quack, quack!' "

And they did as they were told; but the other ducks all round about looked at them and said out loud, "There now! Have we got to have that crowd too? As if there weren't enough of us already; and ugh, what a dreadful-looking creature that duckling is! We won't put up

90

aristocratic: very important because of family background

with him." And immediately a duck rushed at him and bit him in the neck.

"Leave him alone," said the mother. "He's not bothering any of you."

"I know," said the duck who had bitten him, "but he's too big and odd. What he wants is a good smacking."

"Those are pretty children you've got, Mother," said the old duck with the rag round her leg. "They are all nice-looking except that one—he didn't turn out so well. I wish he could be made all over again!"

"That can't be done, Your Grace," said Mother Duck. "He's not handsome, but he's as good as gold, and he swims as well as any of the others, I daresay even a little better. I expect his looks will improve, or perhaps in time his size won't be so noticeable. He was in the egg too long, that's why he isn't properly shaped." And she pecked his neck and brushed up the little man. "As it happens he's a drake," she added, "so it doesn't matter quite so much.

91

drake: a male duck

So he lay there for two whole days, and then came two wild geese, or rather ganders, for they were two young men; they had not been out of the egg very long, and that was why they were so cocky.

"Listen, young fellow," they said, "you're so ugly that we quite like you. Will you join us and be a bird of passage? Close by, in another marsh, there are some lovely wild geese, all nice young girls, and they can all say 'Quack.' You're so ugly that you might appeal to them."

Two shots rang out—bang! bang!—both ganders fell dead among the reeds, and the water was reddened with their blood. Bang! bang! was heard again, and whole flocks of wild geese flew up from the reeds, and—bang! bang! bang! again and again. A great shoot was going on. The men

94

were lying under cover all round the marsh, and some of them were even up in the trees whose branches stretched out above the reeds. Blue smoke drifted in among the dark trees and was carried far out over the water. Through the mud came the gun-dogs—splash! splash!—bending down the reeds and rushes on every side. The poor duckling was scared out of his wits, and tried to hide his head under his wing, when suddenly a fierce-looking dog came close to him, with his tongue hanging far out of his mouth and his wild eyes gleaming horribly. He opened his jaws wide, showed his sharp teeth, and—splash! splash!—off he went without touching the duckling.

"Thank heaven!" he sighed. "I'm so ugly that even the dog won't bother to bite me!"

And so he lay perfectly still, while the shots rattled through the reeds as gun after gun was fired.

It was toward evening when everything quieted down, but the poor duckling dared not

95

LEADER'S NOTES AND QUESTIONS

···

stir yet. He waited several hours before he looked about him, and then hurried away from the marsh as fast as he could. He ran over field and meadow, hardly able to fight against the strong wind.

Late that night he reached a wretched little hut, so wretched, in fact, that it did not know which way to fall, and that is why it remained standing upright. The wind whistled so fiercely round the duckling that the poor thing simply had to sit down on his little tail to resist it.

The storm grew worse and worse. Then he noticed that the door had come off one of its hinges and hung so crooked that he could slip into the room through the opening, and that is what he did.

An old woman lived here with her tomcat and her hen. The cat, whom she called "Sonny," knew how to arch his back and purr; in fact he could even give out sparks, but for that you had to rub his fur the wrong way. The hen had little short legs and was called "Stumpy."

96

···

She was an excellent layer and the old woman loved her as her own child.

Next morning they at once noticed the strange duckling; the cat began to purr and the hen to cluck.

"What's the matter?" asked the old woman, looking about her; but her eyes were not very good, and so she mistook the duckling for a fat duck that had lost her way. "What a windfall!" she said. "Now I shall have duck's eggs—if it doesn't happen to be a drake. We must make sure of that." So the duckling was taken on trial for three weeks, but not a single egg came along.

Now the cat was master of the house, and the hen was mistress, and they always said, "We, and the world"; for they imagined themselves to be not only half the world, but by far the better half. The duckling thought that other people might be allowed to have an opinion too, but the hen could not see that at all.

"Can you lay eggs?" she asked.

"No."

"Well, then, you'd better keep your mouth shut!"

97

_____

_____

_____

_____

_____

_____

_____

_____

⋯

And the cat said, "Can you arch your back, purr, and give out sparks?"

"No."

"Well, then, you can't have any opinion worth offering when sensible people are speaking."

The duckling sat in a corner, feeling very gloomy and depressed. Then he suddenly thought of the fresh air and the bright sunshine, and such a longing came over him to swim in the water that he could not help telling the hen about it.

"What's the matter with you?" asked the hen. "You haven't got anything to do, that's why you get these silly ideas. Either lay eggs or purr and you'll soon be all right."

"But it's so delightful to swim in the water," said the duckling, "so delightful to get it over your head and dive down to the bottom!"

98

Think-Aloud

"I think it is important that when the duckling feels really sad, he thinks of how delightful it would be to swim in the water. Sometimes when I am sad, thinking of something I love to do helps me feel better."

···

"Yes, it must be delightful!" said the hen. "You've gone crazy, I think. Ask the cat, the cleverest creature I know, if he likes swimming or diving. I say nothing of myself. Ask our mistress, the old woman, as well; no one in the world is wiser than she. Do you think she would like to swim or to get the water over her head?"

"You don't understand me," said the duckling.

"Well, if we don't understand you, then who would? You surely don't imagine you're wiser than the cat or the old woman?—not to mention myself, of course. Don't give yourself such airs, child, but be grateful to your Maker for all the kindness you have received. Didn't you get into a warm room, and haven't you fallen in with people who can teach you a thing or two? But you talk such nonsense, it's no fun at all to have you about. Believe me, I wish you well. I tell you unpleasant things, but that's the way to know one's real friends. Come on, hurry up, see that you lay eggs, and do learn how to purr or to give out sparks!"

"I think I had better go out into the wide world," said the duckling.

"Please yourself," said the hen.

99

Think-Aloud

"I think it is important that the duckling decides to go away from a place where he is misunderstood. I think the duckling realizes that he won't be happy there."

•••

So the duckling went away: he swam in the water and dived down into it, but he was still snubbed by every creature because of his ugliness.

Autumn set in. The leaves in the woods turned yellow and brown: the wind caught them and whirled them about; up in the air it looked very cold. The clouds hung low, heavy with hail and snowflakes, and on the fence perched the raven, trembling with the cold and croaking, "Caw! Caw!" The mere thought of it was enough to make anybody shiver. The poor duckling was certainly to be pitied!

One evening, when the sun was setting in all its splendor, a large flock of big handsome birds came out of the bushes. The duckling had never before seen anything quite so beautiful as these birds. They were dazzlingly white, with long supple necks—they were swans! They uttered a most uncanny cry and spread their splendid great wings to fly away from the cold regions, away to warmer countries, to open lakes. They rose so high, so very high in the air, that a strange feeling came over the ugly little duckling as he watched them. He turned round

100

supple: bending and moving easily

uncanny: mysterious or strange

and round in
the water like a wheel, craned his
neck to follow their flight, and uttered a cry
so loud and strange that it frightened him.

He could not forget those noble birds, those
happy birds, and when they were lost to sight
he dived down to the bottom of the water; then
when he came up again he was quite beside
himself. He did not know what the birds were
called, nor where they were flying to, and yet he
loved them more than he had ever loved
anything. He did not envy them in the least; it
would never have occurred to him to want such
beauty for himself. He would have been quite
content if only the ducks would have put up
with him—the poor ugly creature!

101

Think-Aloud

"He says 'he loved them more
than he had ever loved anything.'
Those are strong words, so
I think this experience is an
important one."

•••

And the winter grew so cold, so bitterly cold. The duckling was forced to swim about in the water to keep it from freezing altogether, but every night the opening became smaller and smaller; at last it froze so hard that the ice made cracking noises, and the duckling had to keep on paddling to prevent the opening from closing up. In the end he was exhausted and lay quite still, caught in the ice.

Early next morning a farmer came by, and when he saw him he went onto the ice, broke it with his wooden shoe, and carried him home to his wife. There the duckling revived.

The children wanted to play with him, but he thought they meant to do him harm, so he fluttered, terrified, into the milk pail, splashing the milk all over the room. The woman screamed and threw up her hands in fright. Then he flew into the butter tub, and from that into the flour barrel and out again. What a sight he was! The woman shrieked and struck at him with the tongs. Laughing and shouting, the children fell over each other trying to catch him. Fortunately the door was open, so the duckling dashed out into the bushes and lay there in the newly fallen snow, as if in a daze.

It would be too sad, however, to tell all the trouble and misery he had to suffer during that cruel winter. . . . When the sun began to shine warmly he found himself once more in the marsh among the reeds. The larks were singing—it was spring, beautiful spring!

Then suddenly he spread his wings; the sound of their whirring made him realize how much stronger they had grown, and they carried him powerfully along. Before he knew it, he found himself in a great garden where the apple trees stood in bloom, and the lilac filled the air with

103

•••

its fragrance, bending down the long green branches over the <u>meandering</u> streams.

It was so lovely here, so full of the freshness of spring. And look! From out of the thicket in front of him came three beautiful white swans. They ruffled their feathers proudly and floated so lightly on the water. The duckling recognized the glorious creatures and felt a strange sadness come over him.

"I will fly near those royal birds, and they will peck me to death for daring to bring my ugly self near them. But that doesn't matter in the least! Better to be killed by them than to be bitten by the ducks, pecked by the hens, kicked by the girl in charge of the hen-run, and suffer untold agony in winter."

104

meandering: following a twisting and turning path

Then he flew into the water and swam toward the beautiful swans. They saw him and dashed at him with outspread rustling feathers. "Kill me," said the poor creature, and he bowed his head down upon the surface of the stream, expecting death. But what was this he saw mirrored in the clear water? He saw beneath him his own image, but it was no longer the image of an awkward dirty gray bird, ugly and repulsive—he himself was a swan!

It does not matter being born in a duckyard, if only one has lain in a swan's egg.

105

...

He felt quite glad to have been through so much trouble and <mark>adversity,</mark> for now he could fully appreciate not only his own good fortune, but also all the beauty that greeted him. The great swans swam round him and stroked him with their beaks.

Some little children came to the garden to throw bread and corn into the water, and the youngest exclaimed, "There's a new one!" And the other children chimed in, "Yes, there's a new one!" They clapped their hands, danced about, and ran to fetch their father and mother.

Bread and cake were thrown into the water, and everyone said, "The new one is the most beautiful of all! He's so young and handsome!" And the old swans bowed to him.

That made him feel quite embarrassed, and he put his head under his wing, not knowing what it was all about. An overwhelming happiness filled him, and yet he was not at all proud, for a good heart never becomes proud.

He remembered how once he had been despised and <mark>persecuted;</mark> and now he heard

106

⏀ **adversity:** great difficulty or suffering

⏀ **persecuted:** treated very badly or unfairly, over and over

•••

everyone saying that he was the most beautiful of all beautiful birds.

And the lilac bushes dipped their branches into the water before him; and the sun shone warm and mild. He rustled his feathers and held his graceful neck high, and from the depths of his heart he joyfully exclaimed, "I never dreamt that so much happiness was possible when I was the ugly duckling."

LEADER'S NOTES AND QUESTIONS

STUDENT LEARNING OBJECTIVES IN STAGE 5

The following is a collection of the student learning objectives from all activities in units 4 through 6 (Stage 5).

READING COMPREHENSION

◆ To recall experience with and knowledge about a concept in the story

◆ To determine important ideas in the story

◆ To identify interpretive questions that address important issues in the story

◆ To reread with a purpose and articulate ideas about the story

◆ To understand and use new words in a variety of contexts

CRITICAL THINKING

◆ To answer an interpretive question with clear and specific ideas

◆ To answer an interpretive question with specific evidence from the story

◆ To consider other students' ideas when answering an interpretive question

WRITING

◆ To write an essay about imagery in the story

◆ To use metaphor in a poem

◆ To demonstrate understanding of setting and character in an essay

◆ To develop a set of instructions

◆ To retell story events in writing in the correct sequence

◆ To write and respond to letters

STAGE 5: REFLECT AND CONNECT

Each of the activities below will give your students an opportunity to reflect on their learning process in relation to the student learning objectives in Stage 5. Students will also review the concepts and strategies they learned in this stage and make connections between the stories. Choose any or all of the following topics: reading comprehension strategies, Shared Inquiry discussion, story-to-story comparison, and writing revision.

Reading Comprehension Strategies (30–45 minutes)

Briefly review with students the reading strategy of determining important ideas. Choose a story from Stage 5; have students review their notes from the first and second readings, and the Into Reading and Building Your Answer pages of the Reader's Journal to share ideas they think are important in the story. Write a few of the ideas on the board.

Have students complete their own lists, writing down on a piece of paper five important ideas from the story.

After students complete their lists, have them share their ideas with a partner, placing a check mark (✓) next to any important ideas that are on both lists.

Distribute five index cards to each pair of students and tell them to write one important idea from the story on each card. Point out that if partners wrote down the same idea, that might mean it is a good choice for an index card. Tell partners to number their index cards from one to five, with one being the most important idea, two being the second-most important idea, and so on. Partners will need to reach agreement about the order of importance for their cards.

Have students present their important ideas to the class and explain why they ordered them the way they did.

If time permits, students can display their numbered cards in the classroom in different ways. For example, you could have students glue cards onto construction paper in a shape of their choice (e.g., pyramid, line, circle), or punch a top and bottom hole in each card and attach cards in numerical order with string to hang from the ceiling.

Shared Inquiry Discussion (30–45 minutes)

Before class, make a copy of the web on page 430 of appendix C for each student.

Review with students that a discussion question can have more than one right answer. Draw a diagram on the board similar to the one you copied.

Remind students that a Junior Great Books discussion begins with a focus question that can have more than one right answer. Inform students that they will fill in a diagram like the one on the board, recording a focus question the class discussed for that story, two possible answers that were given during the discussion, and two parts of the story that support each answer.

Help students get started by asking them to volunteer a focus question they liked from Stage 5. Give students a few minutes to review the corresponding Building Your Answer page to help them remember the discussion. Then ask them for one possible answer that came from the discussion and one passage that supports it. Diagram the question, its answer, and the piece of evidence on the board. If time permits and you feel your students would benefit from continued work, complete the diagram on the board.

Hand out the diagram that you photocopied earlier. Choose a new focus question or have students continue to work with the one you diagrammed on the board. In pairs or small groups, have students complete their own diagrams. Encourage them to review the story and the Reader's Journal to help them.

If time permits, have pairs or groups of students make displays for the classroom based on their discussion diagrams. For example, they may record each diagram piece (question, answer, evidence) on different colored construction paper and experiment with how to present the discussion diagram as a mobile or poster to put up around the room.

Story-to-Story Comparison (30 minutes)

Before class, make a copy of the Venn diagram on page 431 of appendix C for each student.

Begin class by taking a few minutes to review with students what they know about setting in a story. Tell them you will be comparing and contrasting two stories' settings.

On the board, write the story titles from Stage 5. Have students name or briefly describe some of the settings in each story. Record their responses on the board under the appropriate title.

Choose settings from two of the stories to compare and contrast as a class. Make a Venn diagram on the board similar to the one you photocopied. Help students think of similarities and differences by asking questions such as:

◆ What is the time period of each story?

◆ Where does the story take place—in the country or the city, in a faraway land or somewhere nearby?

◆ What words would you use to describe each setting?

◆ Does the setting make things easier or harder for the main character of each story?

◆ How does the main character feel in the setting?

Distribute the Venn diagrams you photocopied before class. Have students choose two new settings and complete their diagrams with a partner. When they finish, have students share their diagrams with the class.

Writing Revision (45 minutes)

Have your students turn to page 144 in the Reader's Journal to revise one of their expository writing pieces from Stage 5. Review the revision steps on page 139 of the Reader's Journal with students.

ASSESSMENT KIT

When your class completes a stage, you may want to assess your students' progress and evaluate your own progress as a leader. In appendix A, you will find an assessment kit with the story comprehension tests (page 401), rubrics and instructions for grading students' participation in Shared Inquiry discussion (page 410) and their writing (page 412), and leader reflection forms (page 418). In appendix C, you will find a form called Our Collaboration (page 427). Distribute this form to your students to guide them in reflecting on the group's discussion habits and to create a record of their progress.

White Wave

Chinese folktale as told by Diane Wolkstein

The beautiful snail that farmer Kuo Ming takes home and feeds turns out to be the moon goddess White Wave. She cares for his house, prepares his dinners, and helps him feel less lonely. When she leaves him, she promises to help him if he is ever in great need.

The Mousewife

Rumer Godden

The inquisitive mousewife works hard to take care of her family, yet finds time to befriend a caged dove, who teaches her about the world until she decides to free him.

How the Tortoise Became

Ted Hughes

The much disliked but very speedy Torto likes not having a skin, but asks God to make him one that he can put on and take off so he will be allowed to participate in the other animals' races. However, Torto gets stuck in his skin and becomes the slowest creature of all.

Two Wise Children

Robert Graves

Having lost his own magical powers, Bill warns his close friend Avis to keep her magical ability a secret. In the end, though, he makes a mistake, exposing her powers to others.

STAGE 6: PUTTING THE PUZZLE TOGETHER

Stage 6 contains four units. In this stage, students explore their interpretations of a story thoroughly, establishing discussion and independent thinking skills. Due to longer stories and more advanced activities, some sessions require more time than a traditional class period. Suggested time allotments and tips on how to handle longer sessions appear in the relevant activities.

	Student Learning Objectives			**Leader Learning Objectives**
	READING COMPREHENSION	**CRITICAL THINKING**	**EXPOSITORY AND CREATIVE WRITING**	**SPOTLIGHT ON FOLLOW-UP QUESTIONS**
STAGE 4: CONSIDERING INTERPRETATIONS	• To recognize and make inferences while reading • To reread with a purpose and articulate ideas about the story • To identify different types of questions about the story	To recognize multiple interpretations of the story	• To practice prewriting strategies and drafting methods • To integrate literary terms and concepts into writing	To ask follow-up questions that help students recognize differing ideas
STAGE 5: EXPLORING IDEAS	• To determine important ideas in the story • To reread with a purpose and articulate ideas about the story • To identify interpretive questions about important issues in the story	To consider multiple interpretations of the story	• To develop prewriting strategies and drafting methods • To integrate literary terms and concepts into writing	To ask questions that help students explore ideas
STAGE 6: PUTTING THE PUZZLE TOGETHER	• To begin to synthesize information in the story • To reread with a purpose and articulate ideas about a story • To explore interpretive questions about the story	To discuss multiple interpretations of the story	• To hone drafting methods • To integrate literary terms and concepts into writing	• To ask questions that help students add depth to their reasoning • To choose a target area for follow-up questions

Reading Comprehension

Students learn to synthesize as they read in Stage 6, a strategy in which they summarize and respond to parts of the story and then recombine them to shed light on the story's overall meaning. In the first reading, you will model synthesizing and students will have an opportunity to practice this strategy themselves. In the sharing questions activity, students identify and explore interpretive questions, finding relevant passages in the story. In the second reading in Stage 6, you and your students will have opportunities to select a note-taking activity, based on your students' interests and your assessment of their needs.

Critical Thinking

In Stage 6, students combine and hone the critical-thinking skills they have acquired across all three stages, as they answer interpretive questions using evidence from the story and considering classmates' ideas. In Shared Inquiry discussion, as well as in second reading, you will have the opportunity to consider your students' strengths and weaknesses, and to target your follow-up questions toward particular critical-thinking skills.

Expository and Creative Writing

The expository writing activities in Stage 6 help students develop strong persuasive essays, identifying and explaining a story theme. Creative writing options in this stage provide additional practice with narrative structure and descriptive detail, as well as an opportunity to write a folktale.

Spotlight on Follow-Up Questions

In Unit 7 of Stage 6, you will practice asking follow-up questions that help students add depth to their reasoning. In units 8, 9, and 10 you reflect on your students' strengths and weaknesses in the three key areas of critical thinking and tailor your follow-up questions accordingly.

Curriculum Connections

Use Curriculum Connections to find books by the authors of the Stage 6 stories, as well as resources linking the stories to art, folklore, science, social studies, and other subjects. Icons designate whether books are appropriate for classroom read-alouds or independent reading, according to each book's reading and interest level.

Reflect and Connect

Reflect and Connect allows your students to compare concepts across stories and reinforces what they have learned in Stage 6. It also contains guidelines to help you evaluate your students' progress in meeting the learning objectives thus far.

Unit Overview

❖ **Session 1:** PAGE 243

   PREREADING   Students imagine what it would be like to have a magical helper.

   ★ **FIRST READING**   Students learn about synthesizing and listen as the leader reads the story aloud.

   ★ **SHARING QUESTIONS**   Students identify interpretive questions and recall related parts of the story.

Session 2: PAGE 248

   ★ **SECOND READING WITH DIRECTED NOTES**   Students mark passages to note contrasting ideas in the story.

   SPOTLIGHT ON FOLLOW-UP QUESTIONS   The leader asks follow-up questions to help students add depth to their reasoning.

Session 3: PAGE 250

   VOCABULARY   Students practice using new vocabulary words. Suggested target words: *eager*, *flourished*, and *longing*

Session 4: PAGE 252

   ★ **SHARED INQUIRY DISCUSSION**   Students discover meaning in the story by discussing an interpretive question.

Session 5 Options: PAGE 256

   EXPOSITORY WRITING   Students write a summary of the story's plot.

   CREATIVE WRITING   Students develop oral and written descriptions of a shrine for an important person.

   CURRICULUM CONNECTIONS   The leader can use these resources to link the story to other subject areas.

❖ May require two class periods

★ Core activity

Prereading (5–10 minutes)

Students imagine what it would be like to have a magical helper.

> **STUDENT LEARNING OBJECTIVE**
>
> **READING COMPREHENSION: To become familiar with a concept in the story**

1. Tell students that you are going to read a story about a person who discovers that he has a magical helper that he is not allowed to see.

2. Ask students to imagine what it would be like to have a helper like this. Lead them in briefly sharing what the helper might do for them.

3. Have students describe how they would feel about having a magical helper. Ask questions such as:
   - What might you wonder about when you discover you have a magical helper?
   - How might you feel about having a helper? Why?

4. Ask students how they would feel if their helper decided it was time to leave.

First Reading (25–30 minutes)

Students learn about synthesizing and listen as the leader reads the story aloud.

> **STUDENT LEARNING OBJECTIVE**
>
> **READING COMPREHENSION:** To begin to synthesize by summarizing and responding to parts of the story

BEFORE READING

1. Have students follow along in their books as they listen to you read "White Wave," a story about a farmer who discovers he has a magical helper.

2. Explain to students that when strong readers try to discover the overall meaning or theme of the story, they use a strategy called synthesizing. The first step in synthesis is to summarize and respond to parts of the story. To do this, the reader stops now and then to review what has happened so far and to think of a question, connection, inference, opinion, or other response to the story. This helps the reader follow the story and keep track of ideas about it.

3. Ask students to mark with an **S** places where you stop to **summarize** and respond to the story. They should also mark with a **?** places where they have a **question** about the story. After listening to the story, they will have a chance to summarize part of the story and to share their thoughts about its meaning.

SYNTHESIZING: A READING COMPREHENSION STRATEGY

Synthesizing encompasses many other reading comprehension strategies and is the most complex of all the strategies highlighted in Junior Great Books. The highest level of synthesis involves critical and creative thinking—analyzing the parts of a story and combining them with one's own knowledge and perspective to form new insights about the meaning of the story. At its most basic level, synthesizing involves summarizing. A good way for students to begin is to periodically stop reading, mentally summarize the portion they have just read, and then respond with a question, connection, inference, opinion, or other response.

DURING READING

4. Read the story aloud with expression.

5. Pause several times while reading to model how you briefly summarize what just happened in the story and to share your response to those events. Use your own examples or the Think-Alouds provided in the margins of the story. If you wish, after you have modeled the process several times, stop at an appropriate spot and ask students to briefly summarize and respond to the part you just read. Have them mark these places with an **S**.

AFTER READING

6. Help students sequence the story events after White Wave leaves Kuo Ming, listing the events on the board. Then ask volunteers to summarize this part of the story.

7. Have students share with the class their thoughts about this part of the story. Explain that when readers synthesize, they start to put parts of the story together the way they would start to connect pieces of a puzzle. Then they try to come up with the main ideas and themes of the story. Ask students how the part of the story they summarized and discussed might help them reach conclusions about the story's themes or its overall meaning.

8. Tell students to review the story to find the passages they marked with a **?** and to think about questions they would like to share with the class.

Sharing Questions (25–35 minutes)

Students identify interpretive questions and recall related parts of the story.

TAKING THE TIME YOU NEED

Sharing questions is essential preparation for Shared Inquiry discussion. However, since students are identifying and exploring many types of questions and time can run short, you can and should tailor this activity to suit your class. Here are some options:

- Assign steps 2 and 3 as homework.
- Finish the activity in your next class period.
- Complete steps 4 and 5 after the second reading (especially if your students would benefit from rereading before identifying interpretive or keeper questions).
- Forgo steps 4, 5, and 6 and concentrate on earlier steps (especially if your students are still learning to identify different types of questions).

1. Record questions on the board with students' names, or have students write their questions on strips of paper to post around the room.

2. Encourage students to answer factual and vocabulary questions by using the text, the Reader's Journal glossary, a dictionary, or classmates for help.

3. Identify any evaluative, speculative, or background questions. Help the class revise, answer, or skip them as appropriate.

4. Ask students to identify a few questions that they think might be interpretive.

5. Have students work individually, in small groups, or as a class to test each question. Remind students to look for two different answers that can be supported with evidence from the story.

6. Tell students to choose their keeper question from among the interpretive questions they have identified, and ask them to write it down on page 75 in the Reader's Journal. Then have students complete the page, noting two possible answers to the question and locating parts of the story to support each answer.

7. Ask volunteers to share some of their keeper questions and related parts of the story.

8. Use your Leader Discussion Planner (page 253) to jot down the questions and passages that seem to come up most often. Consider whether you can use any of these later, during the discussion.

9. Have students turn to page 76 in the Reader's Journal to practice synthesizing as a reading strategy. This can also serve as homework.

OPTIONS FOR THE KEEPER QUESTION

The goal for the sharing questions activity in Stage 6 is for your students to develop some understanding of how Shared Inquiry discussion questions are identified. As the stage progresses, you might try to use students' keeper questions as guides for your own discussion preparation. Alternately, you may find that your students are sufficiently challenged by steps 1 through 5, and you may choose to forgo exploring keeper questions.

Vocabulary (20 minutes)

Students practice using new vocabulary words.

SUGGESTED TARGET WORDS: eager, flourished, longing

Choose the target words you want your class to learn, or use the suggested target words above. As you present a word, have students say it with you. Work on one word at a time, using these steps as a guide:

1. Place the word in context. Review how the word is used in the story.

2. Define the word. Use active language in your definition. Include a few examples of how to use the word in situations students will understand. For example:

   ◆ You are **eager** if you are very interested in and excited about something. You might be **eager** to go to the store if they have a new game that you really want to look at. I was not **eager** to go outside because it was pouring rain.

   ◆ To **flourish** is to grow well and become strong. Plants will **flourish** if you give them the sunlight and water they need. The shopkeeper's business **flourished** once he started advertising in the newspaper.

   ◆ To have a **longing** is to want or wish for something very much. If you are very thirsty, you might have a **longing** for a huge glass of lemonade. All her life, the woman has had a **longing** to visit a far-away country.

3. Use the word. Encourage students to make the word their own by asking a few of them to use it in a sentence or to apply it to real-life situations.

4. Ask a question about the story, using the word. Have several students apply their knowledge of the word to answer the question.

5. Optional: Have students turn to Curious Words on page 159 of the Reader's Journal to write down some of their favorite words from the story.

OVERHEARD IN THE CLASSROOM

TARGET WORD: eager

PLACE THE WORD IN CONTEXT

"Long ago, in the time of mysteries, a young farmer was walking home from the fields in the evening. He walked slowly, for he was not **eager** to return to his house." (Refer students to page 109 in the student anthology.)

DEFINE THE WORD

You are **eager** if you are very interested in and excited about something. You might be **eager** to go to the store if they have a new game that you really want to look at. I was not **eager** to go outside because it was pouring rain. Let's say the word together.

USE THE WORD

Have students share something they're **eager** about, and something they feel the opposite about. Begin by providing an example, such as "I'm **eager** to go to the park on Saturday, but I'm not **eager** to do the laundry tonight."

ASK A QUESTION ABOUT THE STORY

Why was Kuo Ming **eager** to meet White Wave?

Shared Inquiry Discussion (45 minutes)

Students discover meaning in the story by discussing an interpretive question.

DRAWING ON STUDENTS' QUESTIONS

While your own curiosity about the story is key in choosing an appropriate focus question for discussion, you can also draw on your students' questions to help you prepare. What ideas or themes from the story have they expressed an interest in? Did students raise issues during the sharing questions activity that you can explore during the discussion?

Use the Leader Discussion Planner on the facing page to prepare yourself for Shared Inquiry discussion. To prepare your group, have everyone sit in a circle or a square; remind them of the five discussion guidelines and any behavioral guidelines you want to share. Then follow these steps to conduct the discussion:

1. Write the focus question on the board and have students copy it on the Building Your Answer page of the Reader's Journal (page 79).

2. Give students a few minutes to review the story and to write down an answer.

3. Begin the discussion by asking the focus question. On your seating chart, keep track of students' participation and ideas.

4. Lead the discussion by asking follow-up questions to help students clarify their ideas, provide evidence, and respond to one another. Aim to have the discussion last 20 to 30 minutes.

5. As the discussion winds down, have students finish the Building Your Answer page. Then ask volunteers to share what they wrote.

6. Spend a few minutes talking about the discussion. Ask students what they liked about it, what was hard about it, what they think makes a good discussion, and what might go better next time.

LEADER DISCUSSION PLANNER

NOTES AND QUESTIONS

After the first and second readings, use this section to keep track of:

◆ Questions that you and your students have about the story

◆ Characters, incidents, and ideas that interest you

◆ Passages that interest you

_____

_____

_____

_____

_____

Write down a focus question, cluster questions, and passages that you think you or your students will refer to in discussion. If you choose not to develop your own questions, see Suggested Interpretive Questions for Shared Inquiry Discussion on page 254.

CLUSTER QUESTION

_____

_____

_____

CLUSTER QUESTION

_____

_____

_____

FOCUS QUESTION FOR DISCUSSION

_____

_____

_____

RELATED PASSAGE   page _____

_____

_____

_____

RELATED PASSAGE   page _____

_____

_____

_____

In this Shared Inquiry discussion, look for opportunities to help your students add depth to their reasoning.

FOLLOW-UP QUESTIONS: ADDING DEPTH TO REASONING

◆ How does that idea help us answer the question?

◆ Does this passage here support your idea?

◆ Does your comment mean you agree or disagree with Donald? Why?

SUGGESTED INTERPRETIVE QUESTIONS
FOR SHARED INQUIRY DISCUSSION

OPTION 1 **Why does White Wave grant Kuo Ming the gift of her shell even though he has done what he knew he should not do?**

- Why does Kuo Ming take the snail home?

- Why does White Wave, a goddess, do Kuo Ming's chores?

- Why does White Wave have to leave once Kuo Ming has "forgotten what [he] knew"?

- Why does Kuo Ming speak each number a little louder as he counts?

PASSAGE FOR DISCUSSION In the student anthology, from "Do not move," on page 114, to "No living creature was inside," on page 115

OPTION 2 **According to the story, was it wise of Kuo Ming to build the shrine instead of taking care of his farm?**

- Why does Kuo Ming build the shrine instead of taking care of his farm?

- Why does White Wave never come to the shrine?

- Why does White Wave give Kuo Ming the rice?

- Why doesn't Kuo Ming remain lonely for White Wave after she sends him the rice?

PASSAGE FOR DISCUSSION In the student anthology, from "As he was wandering over the hills," on page 115, to "but he did not forget White Wave," on page 117

KEEPING QUESTIONS FOCUSED ON THE STORY

You may be thinking, why can't I just ask, *Was it wise of Kuo Ming to build the shrine instead of taking care of the farm?* Adding the phrase *according to the story* to a focus question ensures that your discussion will be based on the story. Your students can easily offer a personal opinion on whether they think it was, or was not, wise of Kuo Ming to build the shrine. Asking students to figure out whether the story conveys a certain idea engages them more deeply. Now they must make an effort to understand the facts, consider how they are presented (the author's choice of language, detail, and structure), and offer a more thoughtful opinion.

SCIENCE

(I) Bredeson, Carmen. *The Moon.* New York: Childrens Press, 2003.

A simple introduction to the physical features, orbit, and efforts to explore Earth's moon.

(R) Morgan, Sally. *Slugs and Snails.* Mankato, MN: Thameside Press, 2000.

Describes slugs and snails in their natural habitats, with information on how to observe these creatures without harming them or their environment.

SOCIAL STUDIES

(I) Beatty, Theresa M. *Food and Recipes of China.* New York: PowerKids Press, 1999.

Describes some of the foods enjoyed in China and provides recipes for several popular Chinese dishes.

(R) Fisher, Leonard Everett. *The Gods and Goddesses of Ancient China.* New York: Holiday House, 2003.

Presents color-illustrated profiles of seventeen gods and goddesses of ancient China, describing their origins, powers, and roles in ancient Chinese society.

(R) Lilly, Melinda. *Rice.* Vero Beach, FL: Rourke, 2002.

Provides historical and scientific information about rice, and includes a glossary, maps, and photographs.

(R) Llewellyn, Claire. *Silk.* New York: Franklin Watts, 2002.

An introduction to the production, characteristics, and uses of silk.

(R) Minnis, Ivan. *You Are in Ancient China.* Chicago: Raintree, 2005.

Describes everyday life in the towns and countryside of ancient China during the Han dynasty, covering such aspects as food and drink, reading and writing, art, science and technology, entertainment, religion, and the life of children.

Highlighted words are the suggested target words in the vocabulary activity. Underlined words can be briefly explained as you read the story aloud, using the definitions provided.

LEADER'S NOTES AND QUESTIONS

• *He knew she was a moon goddess.* •

WHITE WAVE

*Chinese folktale
as told by Diane Wolkstein*

*In the hills of southern China, there once stood a
shrine. It was made of stones—beautiful white,
pink, and gray stones—and was built as a house
for a goddess.*

*Now the stones lie scattered on the hillside. If
you should happen to find one, remember this
story . . . of the stones, the shrine, and the goddess
White Wave.*

Long ago, in the time of mysteries, a young
farmer was walking home from the fields in the
evening. He walked slowly, for he was not eager

109

---

eager: very interested in and excited about something

LEADER'S NOTES
AND QUESTIONS

...

to return to his house. He lived alone. His parents had died two years before. He was too poor to marry and too shy to speak with any of the young women in his village.

As he passed through a small forest, he saw a stone, a beautiful white stone, gleaming in the moonlight.

The young man, whose name was Kuo Ming, bent over to look at the stone. It wasn't white. It was every color in the rainbow. And when he held it in his hands, he saw it wasn't a stone at all but a snail, a moon snail. And what was the most wonderful good fortune—it was alive!

The farmer gently carried the snail home and placed it in an earthenware jar. Then, before fixing his own dinner, he went out again and gathered fresh leaves for the snail.

The first thing he did the next morning was to look in the jar. The leaves were gone. The

LEADER'S NOTES AND QUESTIONS

earthenware: a type of clay pottery

snail had eaten them. Kuo Ming picked four
more leaves and went off to the fields to work.

When he came home that evening, the farmer
found his dinner waiting for him on the table—a
bowl of cooked rice, steamed vegetables, and a
cup of hot tea.

He looked around the room. No one was
there. He went to the door and looked out into
the night. No one. He left the door open, hoping
that whoever had prepared his dinner might
join him.

The next evening, his dinner was again
waiting for him—and this time there was a
branch of wild peach set in a vase on the table.
The farmer made a special trip to the village to
ask if strangers had arrived. No one knew of any.

111

...

Think-Aloud

"Kuo Ming has a strong feeling that he should never try to touch the moon goddess, but one day he tries to touch her hair. White Wave stops him and leaves him. I wonder why she reacts like that."

LEADER'S NOTES
AND QUESTIONS

"Do not move," she said.

"Who are you?" he asked.

"I am White Wave, the moon goddess. But now I must leave you, for you have forgotten what you knew."

"No!" he cried.

"Good farmer," she said, "if you can hold yourself still and count for me, I will leave you a gift. Let me hear you count. Count to five."

"One," he whispered.

She crossed in front of him and walked toward the open door.

"Two," he said softly.

"I leave you my shell."

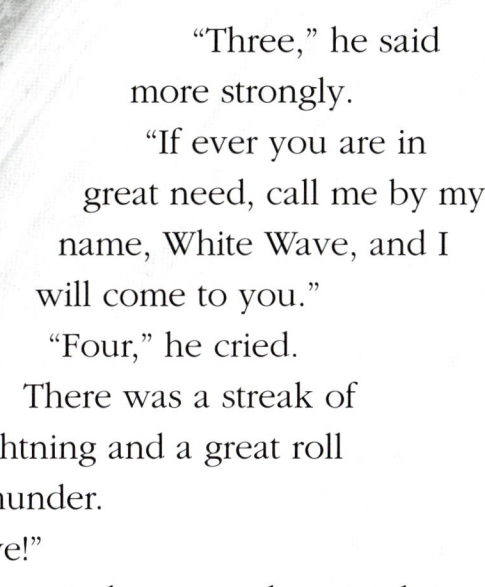

"Three," he said more strongly.

"If ever you are in great need, call me by my name, White Wave, and I will come to you."

"Four," he cried.

There was a streak of lightning and a great roll of thunder.

"Five!"

A huge wind came and swept the goddess into the air. He ran outside, but the rain poured down so fast that he could not see her.

He stood in the pouring rain a long time. Then he went back into the house. The snail shell was there. He picked it up. No living creature was inside.

Kuo Ming went to the fields, but he did not think of his work. He thought only of White Wave and how to bring her back.

As he was wandering over the hills, his foot struck a stone. He bent over to look at it. At that moment, he decided he would build a shrine for White Wave—a beautiful stone house where she

115

LEADER'S NOTES AND QUESTIONS

LEADER'S NOTES AND QUESTIONS

...

might live peacefully. He spent more time choosing the stones—beautiful white, pink, and gray stones—than working in the fields. When the harvest came, it was very small. He ate the little there was. He ate the supplies he had stored, and after that he lived on berries and wild grass.

At last, one evening, the shrine was complete. But that evening the farmer was so weak with hunger, he could barely walk. He stumbled into his house and tripped over the earthenware jar. The shell fell out.

Quickly he picked it up, and as he held it, he remembered the words of the goddess: "If ever you are in great need, call me by my name, White Wave . . ."

The farmer held the shell in front of him. Then he raised it in the air, and with his last strength he cried: *"White Wave, I need you."*

Slowly he turned the shell toward him. A wave of gleaming white rice cascaded out of the shell and onto the floor. He dipped his hands into it. The rice was solid and firm. It was enough to last him until the next harvest.

He never called her name again. With the flowing of the rice, a new strength had come to

116

Think-Aloud

"Kuo Ming was terribly sad when the moon goddess left. He worked so hard building her a shrine that he ignored his farm. But when he called out for White Wave's help, she gave him enough rice to last a year. Maybe he is being rewarded."

···

him. Kuo Ming worked hard in the fields. The rice grew. The vegetables flourished. He married and had children. But he did not forget White Wave.

He told his wife about her, and when his children were old enough, he took them on his knee and told them the story of White Wave. The children liked to hold the shell in their hands as they listened to the story.

The shrine stood on the hill above their house. The children often went there in the early morning and evening, hoping to see White Wave. They never did.

When the old man died, the shell was lost. In time the shrine, too, disappeared. All that remained was the story.

But that is how it is with all of us: when we die, all that remains is the story.

LEADER'S NOTES AND QUESTIONS

flourished: grew well and became strong

The Mousewife

Rumer Godden

STORY LENGTH: 19 pages   READ-ALOUD TIME: About 22 minutes

◆ ABOUT THE STORY

When the husband of an inquisitive house mouse becomes ill and she is forced to find food for the family, she begins taking peas from a captured and caged dove who refuses to eat. The mousewife learns about the world outside of her house from the dove. The more she learns, the more she understands that the dove is not happy living in a cage, and she decides to help him.

◆ ABOUT THE AUTHOR

Rumer Godden was born in Sussex, England, in 1907; her family moved to India—the setting for many of her novels—nine months later. Godden wrote numerous books for adults and children, as well as poetry, autobiographies, and a biography of Hans Christian Andersen. Several of her novels were made into films, including *Black Narcissus*. Her children's books often have dolls as protagonists, such as *The Doll's House* and *Impunity Jane*. She based "The Mousewife" on a story in a journal of Dorothy Wordsworth, the sister of poet William Wordsworth. Godden died in 1998.

The story starts on page 291 of the Leader's Edition, and on page 119 of the student anthology.

Unit Overview

❖ **SESSION 1:** PAGE 273

PREREADING Students imagine the lives of the main characters.

☆ **FIRST READING** Students learn about synthesizing and listen as the leader reads the story aloud.

☆ **SHARING QUESTIONS** Students identify interpretive questions and recall related parts of the story.

SESSION 2: PAGE 278

☆ **SECOND READING WITH DIRECTED NOTES** Students mark passages that address an important concept in the story.

SPOTLIGHT ON FOLLOW-UP QUESTIONS The leader chooses a target area for follow-up questions.

SESSION 3: PAGE 280

VOCABULARY Students practice using new vocabulary words. Suggested target words: *elegant*, *ignorant*, and *seldom*

SESSION 4: PAGE 282

☆ **SHARED INQUIRY DISCUSSION** Students discover meaning in the story by discussing an interpretive question.

SESSION 5 OPTIONS: PAGE 286

EXPOSITORY WRITING Students write about a theme in the story.

CREATIVE WRITING Students write postcards from the perspective of a character in the story.

CURRICULUM CONNECTIONS The leader can use these resources to link the story to other subject areas.

❖ May require two class periods

☆ Core activity

Prereading (5–10 minutes)

Students imagine the lives of the main characters.

> **STUDENT LEARNING OBJECTIVE**
>
> **READING COMPREHENSION: To become familiar with a concept in the story**

1. Tell students that you are going to read a story about a house mouse and a caged wild bird.

2. Have students each choose one of these characters and imagine what it would be like to be that character. Have students briefly share their ideas with a partner.

3. Ask students to consider the experiences each character might have, and how the character might feel about these experiences. Help students by asking questions such as:

   ◆ Where might that character spend time?
   ◆ What might the character do to stay safe, to eat, or to play?
   ◆ What would the character feel or think about?
   ◆ What might the character enjoy or not enjoy about life?

First Reading (30–40 minutes)

Students learn about synthesizing and listen as the leader reads the story aloud.

> **STUDENT LEARNING OBJECTIVE**
>
> **READING COMPREHENSION: To begin to synthesize by summarizing and responding to parts of the story**

BEFORE READING

MORE ABOUT SYNTHESIZING

Synthesizing is an intricate process in which readers integrate many different reading strategies to discover a story's overall meaning or themes. When introducing your students to synthesis, you may want to help them understand it by briefly reviewing all of the reading strategies they have learned thus far and then offering them an analogy such as putting a puzzle together or combining ingredients in cooking.

1. Ask students to follow along in their books as they listen to you read "The Mousewife," a story about a house mouse who visits a caged bird.

2. Explain to students that when strong readers try to discover the overall meaning or theme of the story, they use a strategy called synthesizing. The first step in synthesis is to summarize and respond to parts of the story. To do this, the reader stops now and then to review what has happened so far and to think of a question, connection, inference, opinion, or other response to the story. This helps the reader follow the story and keep track of ideas about it.

3. Ask students to mark with an **S** places where you stop to **summarize** and respond to the story or where you ask them to summarize and respond. They should also mark with a **?** places where they have a **question** about the story. After listening to the story, they will have a chance to summarize more of the story and to share their thoughts about its meaning.

DURING READING

4. Read the story aloud with expression.

5. Pause several times while reading to model how you briefly summarize what just happened in the story and to share your response to those events. After you have modeled the process several times, stop at an appropriate spot and ask students to summarize and respond to the part you just read. Use your own prompts or the Think-Alouds provided in the margins of the story.

AFTER READING

6. Help students sequence the story events after the mousewife goes to see the dove for the last time (page 132), listing the events on the board. Then ask volunteers to summarize this part of the story.

7. Have students share with the class their thoughts about this part of the story. Explain that when readers synthesize, they start to put parts of the story together the way they would start to connect pieces of a puzzle. Then they try to come up with the main ideas and themes of the story. Ask students how the part of the story they summarized and discussed might help them reach conclusions about the story's themes or its overall meaning.

8. Tell students to review the story to find the passages they marked with a **?** and to think about questions they would like to share with the class.

SHARING QUESTIONS AT A DIFFERENT TIME

Due to the length of this story and of the sharing questions activity for this unit, you may wish to wait until the next class meeting to move on to sharing questions. In that case, be sure to collect your students' questions (step 1 of the sharing questions activity on page 276) at the end of this class period, when their questions and curiosity are fresh. The next time you meet, you can briefly review the story before addressing students' questions. Note: You can skip or shorten the prereading, vocabulary, or writing activities in order to devote more time to the first reading and sharing questions activities.

Sharing Questions (25–35 minutes)

Students identify interpretive questions and recall related parts of the story.

STUDENT LEARNING OBJECTIVE

READING COMPREHENSION: To explore interpretive questions about the story

LOOK FOR STUDENTS TO

Recognize interpretive questions about the story

Identify interpretive questions about important issues in the story

Find evidence in the story related to interpretive questions

I. Record questions on the board with students' names, or have students write their questions on strips of paper to post around the room.

2. Encourage students to answer factual and vocabulary questions by using the text, the Reader's Journal glossary, a dictionary, or classmates for help.

3. Identify evaluative, speculative, or background questions. Help the class revise, answer, or skip them as appropriate.

4. Ask students to identify a few questions that they think might be interpretive.

5. Have students work individually, in small groups, or as a class to test each question. Remind students to look for two different answers that can be supported with evidence from the story.

6. Tell students to choose a keeper question from among the interpretive questions they have identified, and ask them to write it down on page 90 of the Reader's Journal. Then have students complete the page, noting two possible answers to the question and locating evidence in the story to support each answer.

7. Ask volunteers to share with the class their keeper questions and related evidence.

8. Use your Leader Discussion Planner (page 283) to jot down the questions and passages that seem to come up most often. Consider whether you can use any of these later, during the discussion.

9. Have students turn to page 91 in the Reader's Journal to practice synthesizing as a reading strategy. This can also serve as homework.

THE KEEPER QUESTION AND THE SECOND READING

Remember that while students' keeper questions can help you prepare for Shared Inquiry discussion, they are ultimately just another tool to help students reread with a purpose. You can determine the extent to which your class works with keeper questions, according to students' needs and interests.

Second Reading with Directed Notes (45 minutes)

Students mark passages that address an important concept in the story.

STUDENT LEARNING OBJECTIVE

READING COMPREHENSION: To reread with a purpose and articulate ideas about the story

LOOK FOR STUDENTS TO

Offer ideas about passages in the story

Support ideas with evidence from the story

Consider other students' ideas about passages in the story

SPOTLIGHT
on Follow-Up Questions

For the last three units of Stage 6, **you decide which area of critical thinking to target with your follow-up questions:** developing meaningful ideas, supporting ideas with evidence, or responding to the ideas of other students. In making your choice, consider your students' strengths and weaknesses, as well as what might best fit the story. Once you have chosen a target area for your follow-up questions, turn to appendix C (page 434), where you will find a list of follow-up questions from this book, collected under the three critical-thinking areas (idea, evidence, and response). The questions from Unit 7 (adding depth to reasoning) are also included. Choose questions, modify them as needed, and write them below.

FOLLOW-UP QUESTIONS: IDEA, EVIDENCE, OR RESPONSE?

- ◆ _____
  _____

- ◆ _____
  _____

- ◆ _____
  _____

BEFORE READING

1. Explain to students that during the second reading they will be taking notes. Write **both** of the following options on the board:

A = The mousewife does something for **another**.　　**H** = The mousewife does something for **herself**.

AND

L = A character **learns** something new.

2. Discuss with students which option they would choose, asking follow-up questions to help them clarify and develop the reasons for their choice. Discuss for no more than five minutes.

3. Either decide which option the class will use and explain your decision to students, or have students vote on which option the class will use. Erase the other option.

4. Tell students that as they reread the story, they should mark places as indicated on the board. Ask them to think about why they are choosing those places, as they make their notes.

DURING READING

5. Ask students to read the story on their own or with a partner, or have them listen to the story read aloud (by you or on the CD), making notes as they go.

AFTER READING

6. Have students read their marked passages aloud, and ask them to explain why they chose those passages.

7. Ask follow-up questions such as those that you recorded on page 278. Remember to ask if anyone sees a passage differently. Examine as many passages as time allows.

8. Use your Leader Discussion Planner (page 283) to jot down questions or ideas to explore later.

9. Have students turn to Head in the Clouds on page 93 of the Reader's Journal and choose a topic for writing or drawing.

ASKING STUDENTS TO DECIDE

If you feel your students are ready, asking them to make a decision about how to approach the second reading helps them take another step toward independent use of the skills and concepts they are learning in Junior Great Books. If students are having difficulty articulating their opinions, explain the features or strengths of each note and ask which they prefer.

FLUENCY TIP

Often, clues about a sentence's meaning become evident only as students reach the end of the sentence. Important syntax, structure, or punctuation may be missed (or unstressed) the first time they read the sentence aloud. Ask students to try to scan ahead as they read aloud so that the end of the sentence does not surprise them. If it is necessary to slow down in order to scan, all the better; many students become adept at reading quickly but lack comprehension. Slowing down will help them listen to themselves as they read.

Shared Inquiry Discussion (45 minutes)

Students discover meaning in the story by discussing an interpretive question.

STUDENT LEARNING OBJECTIVE

CRITICAL THINKING: To answer an interpretive question using evidence from the story and considering other students' ideas

LOOK FOR STUDENTS TO

Explain how their ideas answer an interpretive question

Explain how evidence supports their answer to an interpretive question

Consider other students' ideas when answering an interpretive question

---

KEEPING THE DISCUSSION ON TRACK

Are your students responding more spontaneously and taking ownership of the discussion? That is a positive sign. Remember, though, that your students still need you to maintain a thoughtful environment for learning. Set a steady pace early on by giving students ample time to gather their evidence and compose a response on the Building Your Answer page. This will help them value reflection and understand that writing is a tool that helps them share their best thinking in discussion.

Use the Leader Discussion Planner on the facing page to prepare yourself for Shared Inquiry discussion. To prepare your group, have everyone sit in a circle or a square; remind them of the five discussion guidelines and any behavioral guidelines you want to share. Then follow these steps to conduct the discussion:

1. Write the focus question on the board and have students copy it on the Building Your Answer page of the Reader's Journal (page 95).

2. Give students a few minutes to review the story and to write down an answer.

3. Begin the discussion by asking the focus question. On your seating chart, keep track of students' participation and ideas.

4. Lead the discussion by asking follow-up questions to help students clarify their ideas, provide evidence, and respond to one another. Aim to have the discussion last 20 to 30 minutes.

5. As the discussion winds down, have students finish the Building Your Answer page. Then ask volunteers to share what they wrote.

6. Spend a few minutes talking about the discussion. Ask students what they liked about it, what was hard about it, what they think makes a good discussion, and what might go better next time.

LEADER DISCUSSION PLANNER

NOTES AND QUESTIONS

After the first and second readings, use this section to keep track of:

- Questions that you and your students have about the story
- Characters, incidents, and ideas that interest you
- Passages that interest you

_____
_____
_____
_____
_____

Write down a focus question, cluster questions, and passages that you think you or your students will refer to in discussion. If you choose not to develop your own questions, see Suggested Interpretive Questions for Shared Inquiry Discussion on page 284.

CLUSTER QUESTION

_____
_____
_____
_____

CLUSTER QUESTION

_____
_____
_____
_____

FOCUS QUESTION FOR DISCUSSION

_____
_____
_____

RELATED PASSAGE   page _____

_____
_____
_____
_____

RELATED PASSAGE   page _____

_____
_____
_____
_____

Take a step back and consider how your discussions are going as a whole. Where are they weakest? Where are they strongest? Use the follow-up questions suggested here as a springboard to your own follow-up questions, based on the target area you chose in the second reading.

FOLLOW-UP QUESTIONS: SOME EXAMPLES

- Idea: How does your idea help answer the question?
- Evidence: Can you show us where it says that in the story?
- Response: How is your answer similar to Valentina's?

SUGGESTED INTERPRETIVE QUESTIONS FOR SHARED INQUIRY DISCUSSION

OPTION 1 **At the beginning of the story, why does the mousewife want more than she already has?**

◆ Why doesn't the mousewife just "think about cheese," like her husband?

◆ Why does the mousewife want the dove to tell her about the outside world?

◆ Why could the mousewife "feel as the dove could feel"?

◆ Why does the mousewife realize that the dove should be "in the trees and the garden and the wood"?

PASSAGE FOR DISCUSSION In the student anthology, from "He told her of roofs," on page 127, to "She looked far away," on page 128

OPTION 2 **Why does the mousewife only notice the stars after she lets the dove out of his cage?**

◆ Why does the mousewife let the dove out of the cage?

◆ Why does the mousewife cry after the dove flies away?

◆ At the end of the story, why does the mousewife walk back to bed "proudly"?

◆ What does the mousewife know that the other mice don't know?

PASSAGE FOR DISCUSSION In the student anthology, from "The mousewife picked herself up," on page 135, to "she walked back to bed," on page 136

OVERHEARD IN THE CLASSROOM

LEADER At the beginning of the story, why does the mousewife want more than she already has?

JASON She wants more than she has because she is not an ordinary mouse. Her life is dull and busy. On page 123 it says "She had no time for thinking." She's too smart to be just doing mouse things.

JOAN I think she wants more than she already has because she needs a friend. She needs someone to talk to and have fun with.

LEADER Denise, your answer was different from Joan's or Jason's, wasn't it?

DENISE Yes.

LEADER How is it different?

DENISE I think the mousewife just thinks she wants more than she already has. What she needs is to find out more about what is in the world. That way, she can decide if she has everything she wants.

WANDA I bet Mrs. Wilkinson is sad because her bird flew out the window. Maybe she'll get a new bird.

LEADER We need to stop here. Thank you all for such a good discussion! I would like you to review your Building Your Answer page. Take a few minutes to complete the page by writing down what you now think is the best answer to the focus question.

WHEN IS THE DISCUSSION OVER?

While inquiry into the story's meaning may go on, the discussion must, at some point, come to an end. Sometimes the discussion must end simply because there is not enough time to continue. When you begin the discussion, it is a good idea to note the time at which you must stop, even if things are really interesting. But the discussion should also end when it has run its course. These signs may indicate that this is the case:

- Students have considered all the relevant evidence.
- Students are repeating answers.
- Students are spontaneously changing the topic.

If these things occur, it is time to consider bringing the discussion to a close—but only if you are satisfied that students have considered the focus question thoroughly and have each developed an understanding of the story.

Expository Writing: Writing About Theme (45–60 minutes)

Students write about a theme in the story.

> **STUDENT LEARNING OBJECTIVE**
>
> **WRITING: To identify and explain a story's theme in an essay**

STORY THEMES

In order to determine and write about a story's theme, students must refer to story elements such as conflict/resolution and character development. Writing about the theme is therefore a good way to practice synthesizing, which is the featured reading comprehension strategy in Stage 6.

TEACHING LITERARY CONCEPTS: THEME

1. Ask students what they know about theme in relation to a story before writing the following definition on the board:

   A **theme** is a major idea in a story. A theme goes beyond the characters and events in the story. It has to do with the story's overall meaning or with something important the author is trying to say.

2. Present a list of possible themes for other stories. Have students suggest stories with each theme. For example:
   - Your generosity will be rewarded. ("White Wave")
   - Follow your dreams. ("The Dream Weaver")
   - It's okay to be different, even though it can be hard. ("The Dream Weaver" or "The Ugly Duckling")

   Stress that many stories have more than one theme and several stories can share the same theme.

PREWRITING

3. Brainstorm with students about possible themes in "The Mousewife," writing ideas on the board. Encourage students to review their discussion notes and the story for ideas.

4. Have each student choose a theme to explain in an essay. Have students work independently or in pairs to fill in the web in the Reader's Journal (pages 96–97), noting evidence from the story that supports the theme.

WRITING A DRAFT

5. Have students draft their essay in the Reader's Journal (page 98).

Creative Writing:
Wish You Were Here (45 minutes)

Students write postcards from the perspective of a character in the story.

PREWRITING

1. Review with students the concept of a story's setting. Remind students that even though "The Mousewife" takes place in one setting (the house), the dove describes other settings to the mousewife in a way that makes her able to imagine them.

2. Tell students that they will write postcards to the mousewife as if they are the dove after he escapes from the cage. They will describe a place the dove might visit and how he feels there.

3. On the board, start a setting web like the one below. Ask students to suggest vivid details about that setting, using all five senses.

THE IMPORTANCE OF SETTING

Setting often takes a back seat to plot and character development when students create or retell a story. However, setting serves a number of important purposes—establishing mood, illuminating character, creating obstacles, and accentuating conflict (as it does in "The Mousewife"). Capturing the details of a setting can also help students choose precise imagery and practice using other types of figurative language.

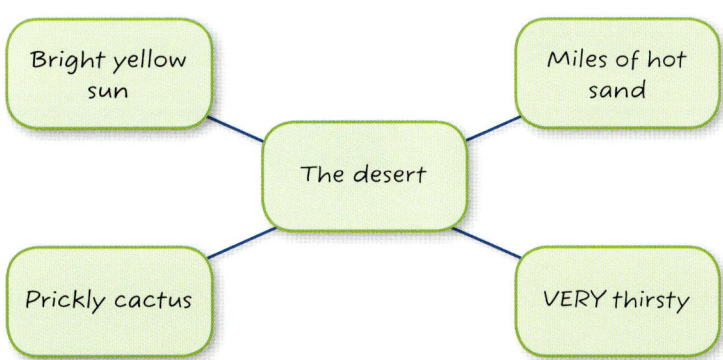

4. Have students complete the web on page 100 of the Reader's Journal. Have them select a few of their favorite details to turn into full sentences for their postcards. Remind students to describe both the setting and how it makes the dove feel.

WRITING A DRAFT

5. Have students draft their postcards in the Reader's Journal on page 101 and illustrate the front of the postcards on page 102.

Curriculum Connections

Below are resources related to "The Mousewife" for further reading and investigation in a number of subject areas.

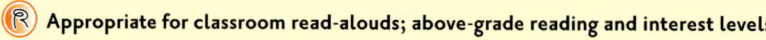 Appropriate for classroom read-alouds; above-grade reading and interest levels

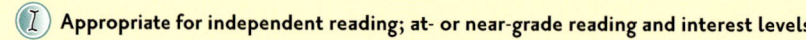 Appropriate for independent reading; at- or near-grade reading and interest levels

OTHER WORKS BY THE AUTHOR

Godden, Rumer. *The Dolls' House.* New York: Puffin Books, 1976.

The activities, sorrows, and joys of a family of dolls living in an old doll house are related from the dolls' point of view.

Godden, Rumer. *Miss Happiness and Miss Flower.* New York: HarperCollins, 2002.

After she leaves India to live with her cousins in England, eight-year-old Nona is overcome with homesickness until her great-aunt sends two Japanese dolls that need love and care.

Godden, Rumer. *The Story of Holly and Ivy.* New York: Puffin Books, 1987.

Orphaned Ivy finds her Christmas wish fulfilled with the help of a lonely couple and a doll named Holly.

POETRY

Wings on the Wind: Bird Poems. Collected by Kate Kiesler. New York: Clarion Books, 2002.

A collection of serious and humorous poems about birds, by such authors as Eleanor Farjeon, Edward Lear, and Carl Sandburg.

SCIENCE

Ⓘ Branley, Franklyn M. *The Sky Is Full of Stars*. New York: HarperCollins, 1983.
Explains how to view stars and ways to locate star pictures, known as constellations, throughout the year.

Ⓡ Coupe, Robert. *Feathers and Flight*. Broomall, PA: Mason Crest, 2003.
Discusses how birds fly and the role their individual body parts play in this ability.

Ⓘ Hewitt, Sally. *Air and Flight*. New York: Childrens Press, 2000.
Discusses the properties of air, its necessity for life, environmental issues, and aerodynamics.

Ⓘ Kalz, Jill. *Doves*. Mankato, MN: Smart Apple Media, 2003.
Describes the physical characteristics, behavior, and habitat of doves.

Ⓘ Miles, Elizabeth. *Dew and Frost*. Chicago: Heinemann Library, 2005.
Explains what dew and frost are and how they form, some of the dangers caused by frost, and the importance of dew and frost to plants and animals.

Ⓘ Rosinsky, Natalie M. *Wind*. Minneapolis: Compass Point Books, 2004.
A brief introduction to wind and its causes and effects.

Ⓘ Sjonger, Rebecca, and Bobbie Kalman. *Mice*. New York: Crabtree, 2004.
Discusses the selection, care and handling, and safety of having mice as pets.

Ⓘ Taylor, Barbara. *Birds and Other Flying Animals*. Columbus, OH: Peter Bedrick Books, 2003.
Briefly describes some of the physical characteristics and behaviors of such flying animals as hummingbirds, swans, fruit bats, and butterflies.

SOCIAL SCIENCE

Ⓘ Rondeau, Amanda. *Freedom*. Edina, MN: Abdo, 2003.
Describes the many kinds of freedom we have in the United States, including the freedom to vote, freedom of religion, and freedom of speech.

Highlighted words are the suggested target words in the vocabulary activity. Underlined words can be briefly explained as you read the story aloud, using the definitions provided.

LEADER'S NOTES AND QUESTIONS

"What is fly?" asked the mousewife.

THE MOUSEWIFE

Rumer Godden

Wherever there is an old house with wooden floors and beams and rafters and wooden stairs and wainscots and skirting boards and larders, there are mice. They creep out on the carpets for crumbs, they whisk in and out of their holes, they run in the wainscot and between the ceiling and the floors. There are no signposts because they know the way, and no milestones because no one is there to see how they run.

In the old nursery rhyme, when the cat went to see the queen, he caught a little mouse under her chair; that was long long ago and

119

wainscots: panels made of wood that are used to decorate the walls in a house

skirting boards: long pieces of wood placed along the bottom edge of the walls in a house

...

that queen was different from our queen, but the mouse was the same.

Mice have always been the same. There are no fashions in mice, they do not change. If a mouse could have a portrait painted of his great-great-grandfather, and *his* great-grandfather, it would be the portrait of a mouse today.

But once there was a little mousewife who was different from the rest.

She looked the same; she had the same ears and prick nose and whiskers and dewdrop eyes; the same little bones and grey fur; the same skinny paws and long skinny tail.

120

…

She did all the things a mousewife does: she made a nest for the mouse babies she hoped to have one day; she collected crumbs of food for her husband and herself; once she bit the tops off a whole bowl of crocuses; and she played with the other mice at midnight on the attic floor.

"What more do you want?" asked her husband.

She did not know what it was she wanted, but she wanted more.

The house where these mice lived belonged to a spinster lady called Miss Barbara Wilkinson. The mice thought the house was the whole world. The garden and the wood that lay round it were as far away to them as the stars are to you, but the mousewife used sometimes to creep up on the windowsill and press her whiskers close against the pane.

In spring she saw snowdrops and appleblossom in the garden and bluebells in the wood; in summer there were roses; in autumn all the trees changed colour; and in winter they were bare until the snow came and they were white with snow.

The mousewife saw all these through the windowpane, but she did not know what they were.

121

spinster: an old-fashioned word used to describe an older woman who has never been married

LEADER'S NOTES AND QUESTIONS

Think-Aloud

"The mousewife does things like other mice, but is different in some way. Looking out the window is important to her, and she feels she wants more in her life. It would be hard for me to only see the seasons change through a window."

She was a house mouse, not a garden mouse or a field mouse; she could not go outside.

"I think about cheese," said her husband. "Why don't you think about cheese?"

Then, at Christmas, he had an attack of indigestion through eating rich crumbs of Christmas cake. "There were currants in those crumbs," said the mousewife. "They have upset you. You must go to bed and be kept warm." She decided to move the mousehole to a space behind the <u>fender</u> where it was warm. She lined the new hole with tufts of carpet wool and

122

fender: a metal screen placed in front of a fireplace to keep sparks from flying into the room

put her husband to bed wrapped in a pattern of grey flannel that Miss Wilkinson's lazy maid, Flora, had left in the dustpan. "But I am grateful to Flora," said the mousewife's husband as he settled himself comfortably in bed.

Now the mousewife had to find all the food for the family in addition to keeping the hole swept and clean.

She had no time for thinking.

While she was busy, a boy brought a dove to Miss Wilkinson. He had caught it in the wood. It was a pretty thing, a turtledove. Miss Wilkinson put it in a cage on the ledge of her sitting room window.

The cage was an elegant one; it had gilt bars and a door that opened if its catch were pressed down; there were small gilt trays for water and peas. Miss Wilkinson hung up a lump of sugar and a piece of fat. "There, you have everything you want," said Miss Barbara Wilkinson.

For a day or two the dove pecked at the bars and opened and shut its wings. Sometimes it called "Roo coo, roo coo," then it was silent.

"Why won't it eat?" asked Miss Barbara Wilkinson. "Those are the very best peas."

123

LEADER'S NOTES
AND QUESTIONS

elegant: beautiful and stylish

gilt: covered with a thin layer of gold or gold-colored paint

**LEADER'S NOTES
AND QUESTIONS**

_____

_____

_____

_____

_____

_____

_____

_____

_____

_____

Think-Aloud

"The woman is given a dove
and she puts him in a cage. The
mousewife takes the food in the
dove's cage but the dove doesn't
mind. She asks a lot of questions
and he tells her about dew and
flying. It sounds like they're
becoming friends."

...

"Then at least take a little water," begged the mousewife, but he said he did not like water. "Only dew, dew, dew," he said.

"What is dew?" asked the mousewife.

He could not tell her what dew was, but he told her how it shines on the leaves and grass in the early morning for doves to drink. That made him think of night in the woods and of how he and his mate would come down with the first light to walk on the wet earth and peck for food, and of how, then, they would fly over the fields to other woods farther away. He told this to the mousewife too.

"What is fly?" asked the ignorant little mousewife.

"Don't you know?" asked the dove in surprise. He stretched out his wings and they hit the cage bars. Still he struggled to spread them, but the bars were too close, and he sank back on his perch and sank his head on his breast.

The mousewife was strangely moved but she did not know why.

Because he would not eat his peas she brought him crumbs of bread and, once, a preserved blackberry that had fallen from

126

ignorant: having very little knowledge or education about things

a tart. (But he would not eat the blackberry.) Every day he talked to her about the world outside the window.

He told her of roofs and the tops of trees and of the rounded shapes of hills and the flat look of fields and of the mountains far away. "But I have never flown as far as that," he said, and he was quiet. He was thinking now he never would.

To cheer him the mousewife asked him to tell her about the wind; she heard it in the house on stormy nights, shaking the doors and windows with more noise than all the mice put together. The dove told her how it blew in the cornfields, making patterns in the corn,

127

LEADER'S NOTES AND QUESTIONS

•••

and of how it made different sounds in the different sorts of trees, and of how it blew up the clouds and sent them across the sky.

He told her these things as a dove would see them, as it flew, and the mousewife, who was used to creeping, felt her head growing dizzy as if she were spinning on her tail, but all she said was, "Tell me more."

Each day the dove told her more. When she came he would lift his head and call to her, "Roo coo, roo coo," in his most gentle voice.

"Why do you spend so much time on the windowsill?" asked her husband. "I do not like it. The proper place for a mousewife is in her hole or coming out for crumbs and frolic with me."

The mousewife did not answer. She looked far away.

Then, on a happy day, she had a nestful of baby mice. They were not as big as half your thumb, and they were pink and hairless, with pink shut eyes and little pink tails like threads. The mousewife loved them very much. The eldest, who was a girl, she called Flannelette, after the pattern of grey flannel.

128

For several days she thought of nothing and no one else. She was also busy with her husband. His digestion was no better.

One afternoon he went over to the opposite wall to see a friend. He was well enough to do that, he said, but certainly not well enough to go out and look for crumbs. The mice-babies were asleep, the hole was quiet, and the mousewife began to think of the dove. Presently she tucked the nest up carefully and went up on the windowsill to see him; also she was hungry and needed some peas.

What a state he was in! He was drooping and nearly exhausted because he had eaten scarcely

129

•••

anything while she had been away. He cowered over her with his wings and kissed her with his beak; she had not known his feathers were so soft or that his breast was so warm. "I thought you had gone, gone, gone," he said over and over again.

"Tut! Tut!" said the mousewife. "A body has other things to do. I can't be always running off to you." But, though she pretended to scold him, she had a tear at the end of her whisker for the poor dove. (Mouse tears look like millet seeds, which are the smallest seeds I know.)

She stayed a long time with the dove. When she went home, I am sorry to say, her husband bit her on the ear.

That night she lay awake thinking of the dove; mice stay up a great part of the night, but, towards dawn, they, too, curl into their beds and sleep. The mousewife could not sleep. She still thought of the dove. "I cannot visit him as much as I could wish," she said. "There is my husband, and he has never bitten me before. There are the children, and it is surprising how quickly crumbs are eaten up. And no one would believe how dirty a hole can get if it is not attended to every

130

day. But that is not the worst of it. The dove should not be in that cage. It is thoughtless of Miss Barbara Wilkinson." She grew angry as she thought of it. "Not to be able to scamper about the floor! Not to be able to run in and out, or climb up the larder to get at the cheese! Not to flick in and out and to whisk and to feel how you run in your tail! To sit in the trap until your little bones are stiff and your whiskers grow stupid because there is nothing for them to smell or hear or see!" The mousewife could only think of it as a mouse, but she could feel as the dove could feel.

Her husband and Flannelette and the other children were breathing and squeaking happily in their sleep, but the mousewife could hear her heart beating; the beats were little, like the tick of a watch, but they felt loud and disturbing to her. "I cannot sleep," said the mousewife, and then, suddenly, she felt she must go then, that minute, to the dove. "It is too late. He will be asleep," she said, but still she felt she should go.

She crept from her bed and out of the hole onto the floor by the fender. It was bright moonlight, so bright that it made her blink.

131

Think-Aloud

"The mousewife has to take care of her chores and can't visit the dove as often as she wants to. She misses him and feels sorry for him because he's locked in a cage. I wonder if he will ever get free."

LEADER'S NOTES AND QUESTIONS

...

It was bright as day, but a strange day, that made her head swim and her tail tremble. Her whiskers quivered this way and that, but there was no one and nothing to be seen; no sound, no movement anywhere.

She crept across the pattern of the carpet, stopping here and there on a rose or a leaf or on the scroll of the border. At last she reached the wall and ran lightly up onto the windowsill and looked into the cage. In the moonlight she could see the dove sleeping in his feathers, which were ruffled up so that he looked plump and peaceful, but, as she watched, he dreamed

132

···

and called "roo coo" in his sleep and shivered
as if he moved. "He is dreaming of scampering
and running free," said the mousewife.
"Poor thing! Poor dove!"

She looked out into the garden. It too was
as bright as day, but the same strange day.
She could see the tops of the trees in the wood,
and she knew, all at once, that was where
the dove should be, in the trees and the garden
and the wood.

He called "roo coo" again in his sleep—and
she saw that the window was open.

Her whiskers grew still and then they
stiffened. She thought of the catch on the cage
door. If the catch were pressed down, the
door opened.

"I shall open it," said the mousewife. "I shall
jump on it and hang from it and swing from it,
and it will be pressed down; the door will
open and the dove can come out. He can whisk
quite out of sight. Miss Barbara Wilkinson will
not be able to catch him."

She jumped at the cage and caught the catch
in her strong little teeth and swung. The door
sprang open, waking the dove.

133

He was startled and lifted his wings and
they hit hard against the cage so that it shivered
and the mousewife was almost shaken off.

"Hurry! Hurry!" she said through her teeth.

In a heavy sidelong way he sidled to the door
and stood there looking. The mousewife would
have given him a push, but she was holding
down the catch.

At the door of the cage the dove stretched his
neck towards the open window. "Why does he
not hurry?" thought the mousewife. "I cannot stay
here much longer. My teeth are cracking."

He did not see her or look towards her;
then—clap—he took her breath away so that she

134

sidled: sneakily moved sideways

...

fell. He had opened his wings and flown straight
out. For a moment he dipped as if he would
fall, his wings were cramped, and then he moved
them and lifted up and up and flew away
across the tops of the trees.

The mousewife picked herself up and shook
out her bones and her fur.

"So that is to fly," she said. "Now I know."
She stood looking out of the window where the
dove had gone.

"He has flown," she said. "Now there is no
one to tell me about the hills and the corn
and the clouds. I shall forget them. How shall
I remember when there is no one to tell me
and there are so many children and crumbs and
bits of fluff to think of?" She had millet tears,
not on her whiskers but in her eyes.

"Tut! tut!" said the mousewife and blinked
them away. She looked out again and saw
the stars.

It has been given to few mice to see the stars;
so rare is it that the mousewife had not even
heard of them, and when she saw them shining
she thought at first they must be new brass
buttons. Then she saw they were very far off,

135

**LEADER'S NOTES
AND QUESTIONS**

farther than the garden or the wood, beyond the farthest trees. "But not too far for me to see," she said. She knew now that they were not buttons but something far and big and strange. "But not so strange to me," she said, "for I have seen them. And I have seen them for myself," said the mousewife, "without the dove. I can see for myself," said the mousewife, and slowly, proudly, she walked back to bed.

She was back in the hole before her husband waked up, and he did not know that she had been away.

Miss Barbara Wilkinson was astonished to find the cage empty next morning and the dove gone. "Who could have let it out?" asked

136

Miss Wilkinson. She suspected Flora and never knew that she was looking at someone too large and that it was a very small person indeed.

The mousewife is a very old lady mouse now. Her whiskers are grey and she cannot scamper anymore; even her running is slow. But her great-great-grandchildren, the children of the children of the children of Flannelette and Flannelette's brothers and sisters, treat her with the utmost respect.

She is a little different from them, though she looks the same. I think she knows something they do not.

137

How the Tortoise Became

Ted Hughes

STORY LENGTH: 16 pages   READ-ALOUD TIME: About 22 minutes

◆ ABOUT THE STORY

God makes Torto and gives him life before he is properly cooled. Torto is so warm that he insists God not give him skin. Without skin to weigh him down, Torto is very fast and wins all the races, but the other animals dislike and ignore him. Torto asks God for a skin he can put on and take off at will. When his wish is granted, Torto's life changes in unexpected ways.

◆ ABOUT THE AUTHOR

Ted Hughes served as England's poet laureate from 1984 until his death in 1998. Born in 1930, in Mytholmroyd, England, Hughes gained a reputation in the 1950s for dark, sometimes violent poems that explore the depths of the natural world. He also wrote many works for children, including plays; a fantasy novel, *The Iron Man*; and several collections of poems and stories, including *How the Whale Became and Other Stories*, from which this story is taken.

The story starts on page 330 of the Leader's Edition, and on page 138 of the student anthology.

Unit Overview

❖ **SESSION 1:** PAGE 313

   PREREADING Students think about the helpful and harmful aspects of pride.

   ☆ **FIRST READING** Students learn about synthesizing and listen as the leader reads the story aloud.

   ☆ **SHARING QUESTIONS** Students identify interpretive questions and locate relevant evidence in the story.

SESSION 2: PAGE 318

   ☆ **SECOND READING WITH DIRECTED NOTES** Students mark passages that address an important concept in the story.

   SPOTLIGHT ON FOLLOW-UP QUESTIONS The leader chooses a target area for follow-up questions.

SESSION 3: PAGE 320

   VOCABULARY Students practice using new vocabulary words. Suggested target words: *agile*, *disadvantage*, and *snobbery*

SESSION 4: PAGE 322

   ☆ **SHARED INQUIRY DISCUSSION** Students discover meaning in the story by discussing an interpretive question.

SESSION 5 OPTIONS: PAGE 326

   EXPOSITORY WRITING Students write about a theme in the story.

   CREATIVE WRITING Students write a folktale.

   CURRICULUM CONNECTIONS The leader can use these resources to link the story to other subject areas.

❖ May require two class periods

☆ Core activity

Prereading (5–10 minutes)

Students think about the helpful and harmful aspects of pride.

> **STUDENT LEARNING OBJECTIVE**
>
> **READING COMPREHENSION: To recall experience with and knowledge about a concept in the story**

1. Tell students that you are going to read a story about a tortoise who is proud of his ability to win races. Have students consider that it is good to be happy with yourself, but being too proud or stuck-up can be bad for you.

2. Make a two-column chart on the board labeled "Pride," with the column headings "Helpful" and "Harmful."

3. Have students share examples of when being proud can be helpful and when it can be harmful. Help them by asking questions such as:

   ◆ How would that help (or harm) you?
   ◆ Might there be a helpful (or harmful) side to that?
   ◆ Can you tell us more about why you think that is?

First Reading (30–40 minutes)

Students learn about synthesizing and listen as the leader reads the story aloud.

> **STUDENT LEARNING OBJECTIVE**
>
> **READING COMPREHENSION: To begin to synthesize by summarizing and responding to parts of the story**

BEFORE READING

PRACTICE WITH SYNTHESIZING

Synthesis involves an evolution of thinking. As a story unfolds, readers revise their thinking to accommodate new information. Every time they reread the story, their thinking about the meaning of the story is likely to change in some way as they notice details and clues they missed in earlier readings. Encourage your students to practice synthesizing during independent reading throughout the school day by telling them to mark with an **S** places where they stop to silently summarize what they have read and think of a response. Have students write a short response next to each **S**.

1. Have students follow along in their books as they listen to you read "How the Tortoise Became," a story about a creature who is proud of his ability to run fast.

2. Explain to students that when strong readers try to discover the overall meaning or theme of the story, they use a strategy called synthesizing. The first step in synthesis is to summarize and respond to parts of the story. To do this, the reader stops now and then to review what has happened so far and to think of a question, connection, inference, opinion, or other response to the story. This helps the reader follow the story and keep track of ideas about it.

3. Ask students to mark with an **S** places where you stop to **summarize** and respond to the story or where you ask them to summarize and respond. They should also mark with a **?** places where they have a **question** about the story. After listening to the story, they will have a chance to summarize more of the story and to share their thoughts about its meaning.

DURING READING

4. Read the story aloud with expression.

5. Pause several times while reading to model how you briefly summarize what just happened in the story and to share your response to those events. After you have modeled the process several times, stop at an appropriate spot and ask students to summarize and respond to the part you just read. Use your own prompts or the Think-Alouds provided in the margins of the story.

AFTER READING

6. Ask a few volunteers to summarize a part of the story they think is important or memorable and to offer a response to it. They can suggest passages that have interesting or surprising language, events, character choices or feelings, or anything else that students find notable. Jot their ideas on the board. Try to elicit summaries of portions from the beginning, middle, and end of the story.

7. Have the class consider a possible theme or the overall meaning of the story. Remind students that coming up with the story's main ideas or themes is an important part of synthesizing. Encourage students to support their ideas with evidence from the passages they summarized.

8. Tell students to review the story to find the passages they marked with a **?** and to think about questions they would like to share with the class.

SHARING QUESTIONS AT A DIFFERENT TIME

As with Unit 8, you may wish to wait until the next class meeting to complete the sharing questions activity. Remember to collect students' questions at the end of this class period and to briefly review the story next time you meet, before addressing students' questions.

Sharing Questions (25–35 minutes)

Students identify interpretive questions and locate relevant evidence in the story.

1. Record questions on the board with students' names, or have students write their questions on strips of paper to post around the room.

2. Encourage students to answer factual and vocabulary questions by using the text, the Reader's Journal glossary, a dictionary, or classmates for help.

3. Identify any evaluative, speculative, or background questions. Help the class revise, answer, or skip them as appropriate.

4. Ask students to identify a few questions that they think might be interpretive.

5. Have students work individually, in small groups, or as a class to test each question. Remind students to look for two different answers that can be supported with evidence from the story.

6. Arrange students in pairs or small groups. Ask them to choose a keeper question from among the interpretive questions and to write it down on page 105 of the Reader's Journal. Let students know that they can work on one question together or they can each work on a different question.

7. Have students locate evidence in the story related to their keeper question and write down the passages and page numbers in the Reader's Journal.

8. As students work on their keeper question pages, assist any students who need help choosing a question or finding passages. Jot down in your Leader Discussion Planner (page 323) any questions you notice that look like good possibilities for Shared Inquiry discussion.

9. Have students turn to page 106 in the Reader's Journal to practice synthesizing as a reading strategy. This can also serve as homework.

IDENTIFYING CLUSTER QUESTIONS

Interpretive questions related to only a small section of the story or a minor issue often feed into a more central interpretive matter. You may find that some of your students' interpretive questions make good cluster questions that can be grouped under a focus question that has emerged. For more on focus and cluster questions, refer to your Shared Inquiry professional development materials.

Second Reading with Directed Notes (45 minutes)

Students mark passages that address an important concept in the story.

STUDENT LEARNING OBJECTIVE

READING COMPREHENSION: To reread with a purpose and articulate ideas about the story

LOOK FOR STUDENTS TO

Offer ideas about passages in the story

Support ideas with evidence from the story

Consider other students' ideas about passages in the story

AN ADVANCED ALTERNATIVE

Have students individually choose which note-taking option they are interested in pursuing for the second reading. Group students according to the note they chose (three to six students per group) and have them share and compare notes after reading. Since you will not be able to lead multiple groups at once, note the following guidelines on the board:

◆ Ask each other questions about why you marked passages as you did.

◆ Ask follow-up questions about details. Which words, phrases, or punctuation led you to mark the passage the way you did?

◆ Find out if other people see the passage differently from you.

◆ Pick a reporter to take notes while you talk. The reporter will present your ideas to the class.

SPOTLIGHT
on Follow-Up Questions

For the last three units of Stage 6, **you decide which area of critical thinking to target with your follow-up questions:** developing meaningful ideas, supporting ideas with evidence, or responding to the ideas of others. In making your choice, consider your students' strengths and weaknesses, as well as what might best fit the story. Once you have chosen a target area for your follow-up questions, turn to appendix C (page 434), where you will find a list of follow-up questions from this book. They are collected under the three critical-thinking areas (idea, evidence, and response). The questions from Unit 7 (adding depth to reasoning) are also included. Choose questions, modify them as needed, and write them below.

FOLLOW-UP QUESTIONS: IDEA, EVIDENCE, OR RESPONSE?

◆ _____

_____

◆ _____

_____

◆ _____

_____

BEFORE READING

1. Explain to students that during the second reading, they will be taking notes. Write **both** of these options on the board.

> **T** = **Torto** is the cause of his own problems.
>
> **O** = **Others** cause Torto's problems.
>
> **AND**
>
> **L** = Torto **likes** being different from the other animals.
>
> **D** = Torto **doesn't like** being different from the other animals.

2. Discuss with students which option they would choose, asking follow-up questions to help them clarify and develop the reasons for their choice. Discuss this for no more than five minutes.

3. Decide which option the class will use and explain your decision to students, or have students vote on which option the class will use. Erase the other option.

4. Tell students that as they reread the story, they should mark places as indicated on the board. Ask them to think about why they are choosing those places, as they make their notes.

DURING READING

5. Ask students to read the story on their own or with a partner, or have them listen to the story read aloud (by you or on the CD), making notes as they go.

AFTER READING

6. Have students read their marked passages aloud, and ask them to explain why they chose those passages.

7. Ask follow-up questions such as those that you recorded on page 318. Remember to ask if anyone sees a passage differently. Examine as many passages as time allows.

8. Use your Leader Discussion Planner (page 323) to jot down questions or ideas to explore later.

9. Have students turn to Head in the Clouds on page 109 of the Reader's Journal and choose a topic for writing or drawing.

HELPING STUDENTS CHOOSE A NOTE

If students are having difficulty articulating their opinions about which directed note they prefer, help them think through the choice aloud by articulating the positive aspects of each note. For example:

We're going to decide which of these notes will help us reread with a purpose. After our first reading, a lot of you asked about Torto's behavior, so the first note might help us answer some of those questions. We've talked a lot in class about being a part of a group and being different from others, though, so the second note would also be interesting. What do you think?

FLUENCY TIP

Before students read their passages aloud, have them take a moment to find words that give them clues about how to read the passage aloud expressively. For instance, verbs such as *roared* or *moaned* and adverbs such as *sadly* or *kindly* can describe how a character is speaking. Encourage students to think about what characters are doing, too. For instance, are characters thinking the words to themselves or speaking directly to others?

Shared Inquiry Discussion (45 minutes)

Students discover meaning in the story by discussing an interpretive question.

STUDENT LEARNING OBJECTIVE

CRITICAL THINKING: To answer an interpretive question using evidence from the story and considering other students' ideas

LOOK FOR STUDENTS TO

Explain how their ideas answer an interpretive question

Explain how evidence supports their answer to an interpretive question

Consider other students' ideas when answering an interpretive question

---

WEIGHING ANSWERS

Remind your students to listen to each other carefully throughout the discussion. Ask questions that help students weigh their original answer to the focus question against other answers they hear during the discussion. Remind students that changing their mind or considering a new idea is an important sign of learning. Also, let them know that a discussion is not a contest to see who has the best answer, but an opportunity to learn from each other and to work together to come away with a personally satisfying understanding of the story's meaning.

Use the Leader Discussion Planner on the facing page to prepare yourself for Shared Inquiry discussion. To prepare your group, have everyone sit in a circle or a square; remind them of the five discussion guidelines and any behavioral guidelines you want to share. Then follow these steps to conduct the discussion:

1. Write the focus question on the board and have students copy it on the Building Your Answer page of the Reader's Journal (page 111).

2. Give students a few minutes to review the story and to write down an answer.

3. Begin the discussion by asking the focus question. On your seating chart, keep track of students' participation and ideas.

4. Lead the discussion by asking follow-up questions to help students clarify their ideas, provide evidence, and respond to one another. Aim to have the discussion last 20 to 30 minutes.

5. As the discussion winds down, have students finish the Building Your Answer page. Then ask volunteers to share what they wrote.

6. Spend a few minutes talking about the discussion. Ask students what they liked about it, what was hard about it, what they think makes a good discussion, and what might go better next time.

LEADER DISCUSSION PLANNER

After the first and second readings, use this
section to keep track of:

◆ Questions that you and your students have
about the story

◆ Characters, incidents, and ideas that
interest you

◆ Passages that interest you

Write down a focus question, cluster questions, and passages that you think you or your students will refer to in
discussion. If you choose not to develop your own questions, see Suggested Interpretive Questions for Shared
Inquiry Discussion on page 324.

CLUSTER QUESTION

CLUSTER QUESTION

FOCUS QUESTION FOR DISCUSSION

RELATED PASSAGE   page _____

RELATED PASSAGE   page _____

Use the follow-up questions here as a
springboard to your own follow-up
questions, based on the target area you
chose in the second reading.

FOLLOW-UP QUESTIONS: SOME EXAMPLES

◆ Idea: Could you tell us more about what you mean by that?

◆ Evidence: Could that part of the story mean anything else?

◆ Response: How is your answer different from Fred's?

SUGGESTED INTERPRETIVE QUESTIONS
FOR SHARED INQUIRY DISCUSSION

OPTION 1 According to the story, who is responsible for Torto's unhappiness?

◆ Why do the other animals decide that the best way to treat Torto is to "leave him to himself"?

◆ Why does Torto tell the other animals, "I was made different"?

◆ Why does God give Torto an "ugly" skin?

◆ According to the story, is Torto right in calling the other animals snobs?

PASSAGE FOR DISCUSSION In the student anthology, from "Except for one thing," on page 143, to "I'll go on winning all the races," on page 146

OPTION 2 Why is winning races so important to Torto?

◆ Why does Torto think that by winning all the races he will "punish" the other animals?

◆ Why does Torto think that winning races will make the other animals respect him?

◆ Why does Torto eventually accept a skin?

◆ Why does Torto become fond of his new skin, even though it makes him slow?

PASSAGE FOR DISCUSSION In the student anthology, from "That night, God came to Torto," on page 146, to "God came up to him," on page 147

OVERHEARD IN THE CLASSROOM

LEADER   Why is winning races so important to Torto?

DENISE   Because the animals are so mean to him.

DONALD   Yeah, they're no fun, so why not at least win the races?

LEADER   Sophia, what do you think?

SOPHIA   They don't like him, so there's really nothing else he can do.

CAI   I agree with Sophia. They ignore him.

LEADER   Let's look at that part of the story. Cai, would you read for us? Start on page 144 where it says, "At first, Torto didn't care at all."

CAI   (*Reads aloud.*)

LEADER   Why does Torto say at the end of that passage, "Wait till it comes to the races"?

TAMALA   Because that's when he gets back at them and makes them feel bad.

WANDA   Because he'll feel better when he gets to run some races.

LEADER   So are the races important to Torto because he can get back at the other animals, or because he feels good when he runs?

BE PATIENT

Sometimes it seems like all your students have the same answer. They may behave as if the answer is obvious, offer little evidence, or simply echo each others' responses. Be patient and let the process work. Explore passages, ask students to compare their ideas, or ask about the implications of certain phrases or details. Eventually, different interpretations will emerge.

Expository Writing: Writing About Theme (45–60 minutes)

Students write about a theme in the story.

> **STUDENT LEARNING OBJECTIVE**
>
> **WRITING: To identify and explain a story's theme in an essay**

TEACHING LITERARY CONCEPTS: THEME

1. Review with students what they know about theme before writing the following definition on the board:

   > A **theme** is a major idea in a story. A theme goes beyond the characters and events in the story. It has to do with the story's meaning, or with something important the author is trying to say.

   If you wish, briefly discuss the themes of other familiar stories.

PREWRITING

2. Remind students that in Unit 8 they wrote about a story theme. Tell them that now they will write an essay about a theme they see in "How the Tortoise Became," and that this time they are going to work on explaining the theme in greater detail.

3. Brainstorm with students about possible themes in "How the Tortoise Became," writing ideas on the board. Encourage students to review their discussion notes and the story for ideas.

4. Ask each student to choose a theme to explain in an essay. Have students work independently or in pairs to fill in the web in the Reader's Journal (pages 112–113), noting evidence from the story and explaining how that evidence supports the theme.

5. After students complete the web, have them explain their theme and supporting evidence to a partner. Encourage students to ask their partner questions about anything that does not seem clear.

WRITING A DRAFT

6. Have students draft their essays in the Reader's Journal (page 114).

Creative Writing: A Folktale (45–60 minutes)

Students write a folktale.

> **STUDENT LEARNING OBJECTIVE**
>
> **WRITING:** To write a narrative with a beginning, middle, and end

PREWRITING

1. Introduce the concept of the *pourquoi* tale (see sidebar) using "How the Tortoise Became," which explains how the tortoise got his name and why he is so slow. Tell students they can each write a tale about an animal that interests them.

2. Brainstorm with students and write on the board a list of animals and corresponding important features, such as:
   - Sharks—have sharp teeth; live in the ocean
   - Worms—don't have legs; live in the dirt

3. Have students write down their choice of animal, some corresponding details, and a *why* or *how* question about it in the Reader's Journal on page 116.

4. Using "How the Tortoise Became" as an example, discuss with students that *pourquoi* tales have a beginning, middle, and end. Use the chart below as an example.

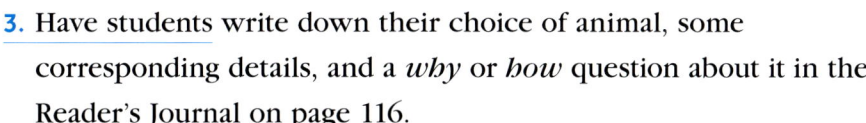

Beginning: How things used to be	Middle: A problem or change and what happened because of it	End: How things are now because of what happened
Torto is the fastest runner because he has no skin.	Torto asks for a skin he can take off and put on whenever he wants.	Torto's shell slows him down. The animals say, "Who's the slowest? Torto is." So now he is called Tortoise.

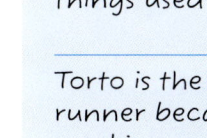

5. Have students work individually or in groups to plan their tales in the Reader's Journal (page 117).

WRITING A DRAFT

6. Have students draft their tales in the Reader's Journal (pages 118–119).

STARTING AT THE END

Folktales that explain how an animal or phenomenon came to be the way it is now, called *pourquoi* tales, are appealing because they are simple, imaginative, and universally entertaining. They also have ready-made conclusions, so young writers are free to invent the beginnings and middles of their narrative while writing toward a clear, simple, and unchangeable end. For this reason, *pourquoi* tales offer an excellent structure for students to learn to write logical cause-effect narratives.

Curriculum Connections

Below are resources related to "How the Tortoise Became" for further reading and investigation in a number of subject areas.

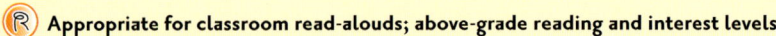 Appropriate for classroom read-alouds; above-grade reading and interest levels

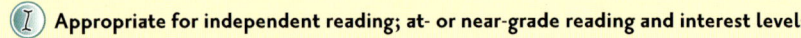 Appropriate for independent reading; at- or near-grade reading and interest levels

OTHER WORKS BY THE AUTHOR

Ⓘ Hughes, Ted. *The Cat and the Cuckoo.* Brookfield, CT: Roaring Brook Press, 2003.

> Illustrated poems about an otter, a dragonfly, a cow, a robin, and many other creatures of the land, sea, and air.

Ⓘ Hughes, Ted. *The Iron Giant: A Story in Five Nights.* New York: Knopf, 1999.

> The fearsome iron giant becomes a hero when he challenges a huge space monster.

Ⓡ Hughes, Ted. *The Mermaid's Purse.* New York: Knopf, 2000.

> A collection of poems about the creatures of the sea, including the limpet, crab, and conger eel.

ART

Ⓡ Arima, Elaine. *The Kids 'N' Clay Ceramics Book: Handbuilding and Wheel-Throwing Projects from the Kids 'N' Clay Pottery Studio.* Berkeley, CA: Tricycle Press, 2000.

> Teaches basic ceramic techniques and provides step-by-step instructions for a variety of projects, including handbuilt items, sculptures, and creations using a potter's wheel.

Ⓘ Firestone, Mary. *Clay.* Mankato, MN: Capstone Press, 2005.

> Explains in simple prose where clay comes from and how it is mined and processed.

Ⓘ Reid, Barbara. *Fun with Modeling Clay.* Toronto: Kids Can Press, 1998.

> Illustrated, step-by-step techniques to help children create many different figures out of modeling clay.

EMOTIONS

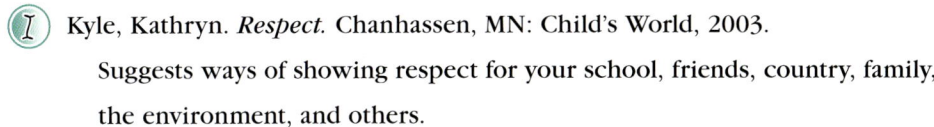 Kyle, Kathryn. *Respect.* Chanhassen, MN: Child's World, 2003.

Suggests ways of showing respect for your school, friends, country, family, the environment, and others.

Loewen, Nancy. *Treat Me Right! Kids Talk about Respect.* Minneapolis: Picture Window Books, 2003.

Information about various ways of showing respect for others, for property, and for oneself is presented in the form of an advice column.

FOLKLORE

McDermott, Gerald. *Jabuti the Tortoise: A Trickster Tale from the Amazon.* San Diego: Harcourt, 2001.

All the birds enjoy the song-like flute music of Jabuti the Tortoise, except Vulture, who is jealous because he cannot sing. Vulture tricks Jabuti into riding his back toward a festival planned by the King of Heaven.

SCIENCE

Gregoire, Elizabeth. *Whose House is This? A Look at Animal Homes—Webs, Nests, and Shells.* Minneapolis: Picture Window Books, 2005.

Contains riddles and facts about the different types of places in which animals live.

Hall, Peg. *Whose Legs Are These? A Look at Animal Legs—Kicking, Running, and Hopping.* Minneapolis: Picture Window Books, 2003.

Examines a variety of animal legs, noting how they look different and function in various ways.

Miles, Elizabeth. *Skin, Scales, and Shells.* Chicago: Heinemann Library, 2003.

Briefly describes how the outer coverings of various animals of the land and sea differ in size, texture, and function, although all provide protection.

Miller, Sara Swan. *Turtles: Life in a Shell.* New York: Franklin Watts, 1999.

An introduction to turtles that includes descriptions of fifteen species and recommendations for finding, identifying, and observing them.

Highlighted words are the suggested target words in the vocabulary activity. Underlined words can be briefly explained as you read the story aloud, using the definitions provided.

LEADER'S NOTES AND QUESTIONS

HOW THE TORTOISE BECAME

Ted Hughes

Long ago when the world was brand new, before animals or birds, the sun rose into the sky and brought the first day.

The flowers jumped up and stared round astonished. Then from every side, from under leaves and from behind rocks, creatures began to appear.

In those days the colours were much better than they are now, much brighter. And the air sparkled because it had never been used.

But don't think everything was so easy.

138

To begin with, all the creatures were pretty much alike—very different from what they are now. They had no idea what they were going to become. Some wanted to become linnets, some wanted to become lions, some wanted to become other things. The ones that wanted to become lions practised at being lions—and by and by, sure enough, they began to turn into lions. So, the ones that wanted to become linnets practised at being linnets, and slowly they turned into linnets. And so on.

But there were other creatures that came about in other ways. . . .

When God made a creature, he first of all shaped it in clay. Then he baked it in the ovens of the sun until it was hard. Then he took it out of the oven and, when it was cool, breathed life into it. Last of all, he pulled its skin onto it like a tight jersey.

All the animals got different skins. If it was a cold day, God would give to the animals he made on that day a dense, woolly skin. Snow was falling heavily when he made the sheep and the bears.

139

_____

_____

_____

_____

_____

_____

_____

_____

_____

linnets: small, brown songbirds

jersey: a sweater or shirt that you pull over your head

•••

If it was a hot day, the new animals got a thin skin. On the day he made greyhounds and dachshunds and boys and girls, the weather was so hot God had to wear a sun hat and was calling endlessly for iced drinks.

Now on the day he made Torto, God was so hot the sweat was running down onto the tips of his fingers.

After baking Torto in the oven, God took him out to cool. Then he flopped back in his chair and ordered Elephant to fan him with its ears. He had made Elephant only a few days before and was very pleased with its big flapping ears. At last he thought that Torto must surely be cool.

"He's had as long as I usually give a little thing like him," he said, and picking up Torto, he breathed life into him. As he did so, he found out his mistake.

Torto was not cool. Far from it. On that hot day, with no cooling breezes, Torto had remained scorching hot. Just as he was when he came out of the oven.

"Ow!" roared God. He dropped Torto and went hopping away on one leg to the other end of his workshop, shaking his burnt fingers.

140

LEADER'S NOTES AND QUESTIONS

···

"Ow, ow, ow!" he roared again, and plunged his hand into a dish of butter to cure the burns.

Torto meanwhile lay on the floor, just alive, groaning with the heat.

"Oh, I'm so hot!" he moaned. "So hot! The heat. Oh, the heat!"

God was alarmed that he had given Torto life before he was properly cooled.

"Just a minute, Torto," he said, "I'll have a nice, thin, cooling skin on you in a jiffy. Then you'll feel better."

141

LEADER'S NOTES AND QUESTIONS

_____
_____
_____
_____
_____
_____
_____
_____

Think-Aloud

"God makes creatures out of clay and bakes them. He makes Torto on a really hot day and brings him to life before he cools down. God wants to make him a skin, but Torto refuses. Why doesn't Torto listen?"

But Torto wanted no skin. He was too hot as it was.

"No, no!" he cried. "I shall stifle. Let me go without a skin for a few days. Let me cool off first."

"That's impossible," said God. "All creatures must have skins."

"No, no!" cried Torto, wiping the sweat from his little brow. "No skin!"

"Yes!" cried God.

"No!" cried Torto.

"Yes!"

"No!"

God made a grab at Torto, who ducked and ran like lightning under a cupboard. Without any skin to cumber his movements, Torto felt very light and agile.

"Come out!" roared God, and got down on his knees to grope under the cupboard for Torto.

In a flash, Torto was out from under the other end of the cupboard, and while God was still struggling to his feet, he ran out through the door and into the world, without a skin.

The first thing he did was to go to a cool pond and plunge straight into it. There he lay,

142

cumber: get in the way; weigh down

agile: able to move very quickly and easily

for several days, just cooling off. Then he came out and began to live among the other creatures. But he was still very hot. Whenever he felt his own heat getting too much for him, he retired to his pond to cool off in the water. In this way, he found life pleasant enough.

Except for one thing. The other creatures didn't approve of Torto.

They all had skins. When they saw Torto without a skin, they were horrified.

"But he has no skin!" cried Porcupine.

"It's disgusting!" cried Yak. "It's indecent!"

143

LEADER'S NOTES AND QUESTIONS

_____

_____

_____

_____

_____

_____

_____

_____

_____

_____

Think-Aloud

"The other animals ignore Torto and say mean things because he doesn't have a skin. Torto brags about his running ability and wins a lot of races. The other animals mistreat him, but it seems that if Torto wants the other animals to like him, he's going about it the wrong way."

"He's not normal. Leave him to himself," said Sloth.

So all the animals began to ignore Torto. But they couldn't ignore him completely, because he was a wonderfully swift runner, and whenever they held a race, he won it. He was so nimble without a skin that none of the other creatures could hope to keep up with him.

"I'm a genius runner," he said. "You should respect me. I am faster than the lot of you put together. I was made different."

But the animals still ignored him. Even when they had to give him the prizes for winning all the races, they still ignored him.

"Torto is a very swift mover," they said. "And perhaps swifter than any of us. But what sort of a creature is he? No skin!"

And they all turned up their noses.

At first, Torto didn't care at all. When the animals collected together, with all their fur brushed and combed and set neatly, he strolled among them, smiling happily, naked.

"When will this disgusting creature learn to behave?" cried Turkey, loudly enough for everyone to hear.

144

"Just take no notice of him," said Alligator, and lumbered round, in his heavy armour, to face in the opposite direction.

All the animals turned round to face in the opposite direction.

When Torto went up to Grizzly Bear to ask what everyone was looking at, Grizzly Bear pretended to have a fly in his ear. When he went to Armadillo, Armadillo gathered up all his sons and daughters and led them off without a word or a look.

"So that's your game, is it?" said Torto to himself. Then aloud, he said, "Never mind. Wait till it comes to the races."

When the races came, later in the afternoon, Torto won them all. But nobody cheered. He collected the prizes and went off to his pond alone.

"They're jealous of me," he said. "That's why they ignore me.

145

Think-Aloud

"Torto keeps winning races,
trying to show them how great
he is. But they dislike him.
Why does Torto keep doing
something that doesn't work?
Maybe he will try something
different."

•••

But I'll punish them: I'll go on winning all
the races."

That night, God came to Torto and begged
him to take a proper skin before it was too late.
Torto shook his head:

"The other animals are snobs," he said.
"Just because they are covered with a skin, they
think everyone else should be covered with
one too. That's snobbery. But I shall teach them
not to be snobs by making them respect me.
I shall go on winning all the races."

And so he did. But still the animals didn't
respect him. In fact, they grew to dislike
him more and more.

One day there was a very important race
meeting, and all the animals collected at the
usual place. But the minute Torto arrived they
simply walked away. Simply got up and
walked away. Torto sat on the racetrack and
stared after them. He felt really left out.

"Perhaps," he thought sadly, "it would be
better if I had a skin. I mightn't be able to run
then, but at least I would have friends. I have
no friends. Besides, after all this practise,
I would still be able to run quite fast."

146

snobbery: thinking you are better than everyone else

But as soon as he said that he felt angry with himself.

"No!" he cried. "They are snobs. I shall go on winning their races in spite of them. I shall teach them a lesson."

And he got up from where he was sitting and followed them. He found them all in one place, under a tree. And the races were being run.

"Hey!" he called as he came up to them. "What about me?"

But at that moment, Tiger held up a sign in front of him. On the sign, Torto read: "Creatures without skins are not allowed to enter."

Torto went home and brooded. God came up to him.

"Well, Torto," said God kindly, "would you like a skin yet?"

Torto thought deeply.

"Yes," he said at last, "I would like a skin. But only a very special sort of skin."

"And what sort of a skin is that?" asked God.

"I would like," said Torto, "a skin that I can put on, or take off, just whenever I please."

God frowned.

"I'm afraid," he said, "I have none like that."

147

...

"Then make one," replied Torto. "You're God."

God went away and came back within an hour.

"Do you want a beautiful skin?" he asked. "Or do you mind if it's very ugly?"

"I don't care what sort of a skin it is," said Torto, "so long as I can take it off and put it back on again just whenever I please."

God went away again, and again came back within an hour.

"Here it is. That's the best I can do."

"What's this!" cried Torto. "But it's horrible!"

"Take it or leave it," said God, and walked away.

148

LEADER'S NOTES
AND QUESTIONS

...

Torto examined the skin. It was tough, rough, and stiff.

"It's like a coconut," he said. "With holes in it."

And so it was. Only it was shiny. When he tried it on, he found it quite snug. It had only one disadvantage. He could move only very slowly in it.

"What's the hurry?" he said to himself then. "When it comes to moving, who can move faster than me?"

And he laughed. Suddenly he felt delighted. Away he went to where the animals were still running their races.

As he came near to them, he began to think that perhaps his skin was a little rough and ready. But he checked himself:

"Why should I dress up for them?" he said. "This rough old thing will do. The races are the important thing."

Tiger lowered his notice and stared in dismay as Torto swaggered past him. All the animals were now turning and staring, nudging each other, and turning, and staring.

"That's a change, anyway," thought Torto.

Then, as usual, he entered for all the races.

149

LEADER'S NOTES AND QUESTIONS

disadvantage: something that causes problems or makes it hard to succeed

rough and ready: useful but not fancy

···

The animals began to talk and laugh among themselves as they pictured Torto trying to run in his heavy new clumsy skin.

"He'll look silly, and then how we'll laugh." And they all laughed.

But when he took his skin off at the starting post, their laughs turned to frowns.

He won all the races, then climbed back into his skin to collect the prizes. He strutted in front of all the animals.

"Now it's my turn to be snobbish," he said to himself.

Then he went home, took off his skin, and slept sweetly. Life was perfect for him.

This went on for many years. But though the animals would now speak to him, they remembered what he had been. That didn't worry Torto, however. He became very fond of his skin. He began to keep it on at night when he came home after the races. He began to do everything in it, except actually race. He crept around slowly, smiling at the leaves, letting the days pass.

There came a time when there were no races for several weeks. During all this time Torto

150

never took his skin off once. Until, when the first race came round at last, he found he could not take his skin off at all, no matter how he pushed and pulled. He was stuck inside it. He strained and squeezed and gasped, but it was no use. He was stuck.

However, he had already entered for all the races, so he had to run.

He lined up, in his skin, at the start, alongside Hare, Greyhound, Cheetah, and Ostrich. They were all great runners, but usually he could beat the lot of them easily. The crowd stood <u>agog</u>.

"Perhaps," Torto was thinking, "my skin won't make much difference. I've never really tried to run my very fastest in it."

151

LEADER'S NOTES AND QUESTIONS

agog: very excited about something

LEADER'S NOTES
AND QUESTIONS

The starter's pistol cracked, and away went Greyhound, Hare, Cheetah, and Ostrich, neck and neck. Where was Torto?

The crowd roared with laughter.

Torto had fallen on his face and had not moved an inch. At his first step, cumbered by his stiff, heavy skin, he had fallen on his face. But he tried. He climbed back onto his feet and made one stride, slowly, then a second stride, and was just about to make a third when the race was over and Cheetah had won. Torto had moved not quite three paces. How the crowd laughed!

And so it was with all the races. In no one race did Torto manage to make more than three steps before it was over.

The crowd was enjoying itself. Torto was weeping with shame.

After the last race, he turned to crawl home. He only wanted to hide. But though the other animals had let him go off alone when he had the prizes, now they came alongside him, in a laughing, mocking crowd.

"Who's the slowest of all the creatures?" they shouted.

152

···

"Torto is!"

"Who's the slowest of all the creatures?"

"Torto is!" all the way home.

After that, Torto tried to keep himself out of sight, but the other animals never let him rest. Whenever any of them chanced to see him, they would shout at the tops of their voices:

"Who's the slowest of all the creatures?"

And every other creature within hearing would answer, at the tops of their voices:

"Torto is!"

And that is how Torto came to be known as "Tortoise."

153

Two Wise Children

Robert Graves

STORY LENGTH: 19 pages   READ-ALOUD TIME: About 19 minutes

◆ ABOUT THE STORY

Bill and Avis become instant friends when Avis's family moves to the New England town where Bill's father is a minister. The children share the same birthday, and a secret—each has experienced extraordinary magical powers. Bill, who lost his ability to "know everything," warns Avis not to let anyone know about her ability to "do anything." But then something happens that makes it difficult for Avis to keep her secret.

◆ ABOUT THE AUTHOR

Robert Graves was born in 1895 in Wimbledon, England. He is best known as a poet, though he also wrote novels, including the historical novel *I, Claudius*, and an autobiography, *Goodbye to All That*, which chronicled his experiences as a British officer at the Western Front during World War I. In his later years, Graves was a professor of poetry at Oxford University and he wrote a number of children's books, including *Two Wise Children*. He died in 1985.

The story starts on page 367 of the Leader's Edition, and on page 155 of the student anthology.

Unit Overview

❖ **SESSION 1:** PAGE 349

PREREADING Students think about how it might feel to possess magic powers that they must keep secret.

★ **FIRST READING** Students learn about synthesizing and listen as the leader reads the story aloud.

★ **SHARING QUESTIONS** Students identify interpretive questions and locate relevant evidence in the story.

SESSION 2: PAGE 354

★ **SECOND READING WITH DIRECTED NOTES** Students mark passages that address an important concept in the story.

SPOTLIGHT ON FOLLOW-UP QUESTIONS The leader chooses a target area for follow-up questions.

SESSION 3: PAGE 356

VOCABULARY Students practice using new vocabulary words. Suggested target words: *boasting*, *jeering*, and *marvelous*

SESSION 4: PAGE 358

★ **SHARED INQUIRY DISCUSSION** Students discover meaning in the story by discussing an interpretive question.

SESSION 5 OPTIONS: PAGE 362

EXPOSITORY WRITING Students identify and explain a theme by referring to other story elements.

CREATIVE WRITING Students write about possessing a secret magic power and having someone find out about it.

CURRICULUM CONNECTIONS The leader can use these resources to link the story to other subject areas.

❖ May require two class periods

★ Core activity

Prereading (5–10 minutes)

Students think about how it might feel to possess magic powers that they must keep secret.

> **STUDENT LEARNING OBJECTIVE**
>
> **READING COMPREHENSION: To become familiar with a concept in the story**

1. Tell students that you are going to read a story about two children who both have experienced magic powers.

2. Ask students to imagine how they might enjoy having magic powers, such as being able to fly or to read people's minds. Have them consider what it would be like if they had to keep their powers a secret.

3. Have students share their ideas. Help them with questions such as:
   - What could you do that would be fun?
   - Why would that be fun?
   - Would it still be fun if others knew about your powers?
   - What would not be fun about having secret magic powers?

First Reading (30–40 minutes)

Students learn about synthesizing and listen as the leader reads the story aloud.

> **STUDENT LEARNING OBJECTIVE**
>
> **READING COMPREHENSION: To begin to synthesize by summarizing and responding to parts of the story**

BEFORE READING

1. Have students follow along in their books as they listen to you read "Two Wise Children," a story about two children who have experienced extraordinary powers.

2. Explain to students that when strong readers try to discover the overall meaning or theme of the story, they use a strategy called synthesizing. The first step in synthesis is to summarize and respond to parts of the story. To do this, the reader stops now and then to review what has happened so far and to think of a question, connection, inference, opinion, or other response to the story. This helps the reader follow the story and keep track of ideas about it.

3. Ask students to mark with an **S** places where you stop to **summarize** and respond to the story or where you ask them to summarize and respond. They should also mark with a **?** places where they have a **question** about the story. After listening to the story, they will have a chance to summarize more of the story and to share their thoughts about its meaning.

MORE PRACTICE WITH SYNTHESIZING

Like putting together a puzzle to create a picture, the reader synthesizes by piecing together thoughts about the information in the story to determine the overall meaning, main ideas, conclusions, or themes. All of the reading strategies come into play while synthesizing. You can help your students practice synthesis throughout the school day by providing opportunities during reading for them to silently review what has happened, think of a response, and consider possible meanings of what they have read. Encourage students to practice during independent reading by telling them to mark with an **S** places where they stopped to synthesize. Have students write a short response next to each **S**.

DURING READING

4. Read the story aloud with expression.

5. Pause several times while reading to model how you briefly summarize what just happened in the story and to share your response to these events. After you have modeled the process several times, stop at an appropriate spot and ask students to summarize and respond to the part you just read. Use your own prompts or the Think-Alouds provided in the margins of the story.

AFTER READING

6. Ask a few volunteers to summarize a part of the story they think is important or memorable and to offer a response to it. They can suggest passages that have interesting or surprising language, events, character choices or feelings, or anything else that students find notable. Jot their ideas on the board. Try to elicit summaries of portions from the beginning, middle, and end of the story.

7. Have the class consider a possible theme or the overall meaning of the story. Remind students that coming up with the story's main ideas or themes is an important part of synthesizing. Encourage students to support their ideas with evidence from the passages they summarized.

8. Tell students to review the story to find the passages they marked with a **?** and to think about questions they would like to share with the class.

SHARING QUESTIONS AT A DIFFERENT TIME

As with units 8 and 9, you may wish to wait until the next class meeting to complete the sharing questions activity. Remember to collect students' questions at the end of this class session and to briefly review the story the next time you meet, before addressing students' questions.

Second Reading with Directed Notes (45 minutes)

Students mark passages that address an important concept in the story.

STUDENT LEARNING OBJECTIVE

READING COMPREHENSION: To reread with a purpose and articulate ideas about the story

LOOK FOR STUDENTS TO

Offer ideas about passages in the story

Support ideas with evidence from the story

Consider other students' ideas about passages in the story

SPOTLIGHT
on Follow-Up Questions

For the last three units of Stage 6, **you decide which area of critical thinking to target with your follow-up questions:** developing meaningful ideas, supporting ideas with evidence, or responding to the ideas of others. In making your choice, consider your students' strengths and weaknesses, as well as what might best fit the story. Once you have chosen a focus for your follow-up questions, turn to appendix C (page 434), where you will find a list of follow-up questions from this book. They are collected under the three critical-thinking areas (idea, evidence, and response). The questions from Unit 7 (adding depth to reasoning) are also included. Choose questions, modify them as needed, and write them below.

FOLLOW-UP QUESTIONS: IDEA, EVIDENCE, OR RESPONSE?

◆ _____

_____

◆ _____

_____

◆ _____

_____

BEFORE READING

1. Explain to students that during the second reading they will be taking notes. Write **both** of the following options on the board.

   H = Having magic powers makes Bill or Avis **happy**.

   U = Having magic powers makes Bill or Avis **unhappy**.

   AND

   C = A character makes an important **choice**.

2. Discuss with students which option they would choose, asking follow-up questions to help them clarify and explain the reasons for their choice. Discuss this for no more than five minutes.

3. Decide which option the class will use and explain your decision to students, or have students vote on which option the class will use. Erase the other option.

4. Tell students that as they reread the story, they should mark places as indicated on the board. Ask them to think about why they are choosing those places, as they make their notes.

DURING READING

5. Ask students to read the story on their own or with a partner, or have them listen to the story read aloud (by you or on the CD), making notes as they go.

AFTER READING

6. Have students read their marked passages aloud, and ask them to explain why they chose those passages.

7. Ask follow-up questions such as those that you recorded on page 354. Remember to ask if anyone sees a passage differently. Examine as many passages as time allows.

8. Use your Leader Discussion Planner (page 359) to jot down questions or ideas to explore later.

9. Have students turn to Head in the Clouds on page 127 of the Reader's Journal and choose a topic for writing or drawing.

ANOTHER ADVANCED ALTERNATIVE

Consider using a question one of your students had during the sharing questions activity as this session's note-taking activity, especially if your students are asking strong, insightful questions that they wish to pursue. Tell students to reread with the chosen question in mind, marking any passage that they feel will **help answer the question** with a **+**. After students have reread the story and made their notes, proceed with steps 6 through 9.

Here are some tips to contribute to the success of this note-taking option:

- Choose a question about the story's meaning that greatly interests students, relates to several passages in the story, and is likely to elicit different responses.

- Remember that the purpose of comparing notes after the second reading is to consider as many passages as possible. This should not become a Shared Inquiry discussion, which would focus on finding answers to the question, rather than finding passages related to the question.

- Keep Shared Inquiry discussion in mind. Will thinking about this question sap interest and enthusiasm for the discussion? Or will working with this question help students prepare to discuss a different question?

Vocabulary (20 minutes)

Students practice using new vocabulary words.

> **STUDENT LEARNING OBJECTIVE**
>
> **READING COMPREHENSION: To understand and use new words in a variety of contexts**

SUGGESTED TARGET WORDS: boasting, jeering, marvelous

Choose the target words you want your class to learn, or use the suggested target words above. As you present a word, have students say it with you. Work on one word at a time, using these steps as a guide:

1. Place the word in context. Review how the word is used in the story.

2. Define the word. Use active language in your definition. Include a few examples of how to use the word in situations students will understand. For example:

   ◆ To **boast** is to talk about yourself with too much pride. I wish you would stop **boasting** about your wonderful grades all the time.

   ◆ **Jeering** is making fun of someone or saying mean things to someone in a rude way. The mean older kids are always **jeering** at us from across the street when we walk to school. Nobody could hear the man give his speech because the crowd was **jeering** so loudly.

   ◆ Something that is **marvelous** causes wonder or amazement. There might be a **marvelous** fireworks display on the Fourth of July. Something **marvelous** can also be excellent. We cooked with **marvelous** food fresh from the garden.

3. Use the word. Encourage students to make the word their own by asking a few of them to use it in a sentence or to apply it to real-life situations.

4. Ask a question about the story, using the word. Have several students apply their knowledge of the word to answer the question.

5. Have students turn to Curious Words on page 162 of the Reader's Journal to write down some of their favorite words from the story.

OVERHEARD IN THE CLASSROOM

TARGET WORD: **marvelous**

PLACE THE WORD IN CONTEXT
"Bill looked her straight in the eyes. He said, 'I saw you riding the horse. I hope you don't mind. And now there's this **marvelous** needlework.' " (Refer students to page 160 in the student anthology.)

DEFINE THE WORD
Something that is **marvelous** causes wonder or amazement. There might be a **marvelous** fireworks display on the Fourth of July. Something **marvelous** can also be excellent. We cooked with **marvelous** food straight from the garden. Say the word with me.

USE THE WORD
Which of these things would be **marvelous**?
◆ An elephant in the middle of the street
◆ A talking robot that can do all of your chores at home
◆ A pencil with toothmarks and a worn eraser
◆ A long day at school
◆ A movie that is so sad it makes you cry

ASK A QUESTION ABOUT THE STORY
Why does Bill want Avis to explain her **marvelous** needlework?

Shared Inquiry Discussion (45 minutes)

Students discover meaning in the story by discussing an interpretive question.

STUDENT-LED DISCUSSIONS

You may wish to ask your students if they are interested in leading the discussion for this unit. If students are up to the challenge, consider:

◆ Pairing students to lead groups of eight to ten students

◆ Having four to five students lead the rest of the class

◆ Rotating leaders in a few short discussions rather than one full-length one

Talk with them about what it is like to lead a discussion (see bullet points below) and explain the nature and purpose of follow-up questions.

Tell students that discussion leaders should:

◆ Choose and pose the focus questions

◆ Only ask questions, not answer them

◆ Use follow-up questions not to argue with answers, but to explore meaning by asking participants to clarify their ideas, find and explain evidence, and respond to one another's ideas.

Remember that your role is to assist student leaders. Ask students to reflect on the experience afterward to take stock and gain insight for future student-led discussions.

STUDENT LEARNING OBJECTIVE

CRITICAL THINKING: To answer an interpretive question using evidence from the story and considering other students' ideas

LOOK FOR STUDENTS TO

Explain how their ideas answer an interpretive question

Explain how evidence supports their answer to an interpretive question

Consider other students' ideas while answering an interpretive question

Use the Leader Discussion Planner on the facing page to prepare yourself for Shared Inquiry discussion. To prepare your group, have everyone sit in a circle or a square; remind them of the five discussion guidelines and any behavioral guidelines you want to share. Then follow these steps to conduct the discussion:

1. Write the focus question on the board and have students copy it on the Building Your Answer page of the Reader's Journal (page 128).

2. Give students a few minutes to review the story and to write down an answer.

3. Begin the discussion by asking the focus question. On your seating chart, keep track of students' participation and ideas.

4. Lead the discussion by asking follow-up questions to help students clarify their ideas, provide evidence, and respond to one another. Aim to have the discussion last 20 to 30 minutes.

5. As discussion winds down, have students finish the Building Your Answer page. Then ask volunteers to share what they wrote.

6. Spend a few minutes talking about the discussion. Since this is the final unit, you may want to share some memories of particularly successful discussions you have had over the course of the program and let your students share some of their own.

LEADER DISCUSSION PLANNER

After the first and second readings, use this section to keep track of:

◆ Questions that you and your students have about the story

◆ Characters, incidents, and ideas that interest you

◆ Passages that interest you

NOTES AND QUESTIONS

_____

_____

_____

_____

_____

Write down a focus question, cluster questions, and passages that you think you or your students will refer to in discussion. If you choose not to develop your own questions, see Suggested Interpretive Questions for Shared Inquiry Discussion on page 360.

CLUSTER QUESTION

_____
_____
_____
_____

CLUSTER QUESTION

_____
_____
_____
_____

FOCUS QUESTION FOR DISCUSSION

_____
_____
_____

RELATED PASSAGE   page _____

_____
_____
_____
_____

RELATED PASSAGE   page _____

_____
_____
_____
_____

Use the follow-up questions here as a springboard to your own follow-up question, based on the target area you chose in the second reading activity.

FOLLOW-UP QUESTIONS: SOME EXAMPLES

◆ Idea: When you say that, what do you mean?

◆ Evidence: Which part of that passage best shows what you are saying?

◆ Response: Do you agree with what Deborah said?

SUGGESTED INTERPRETIVE QUESTIONS FOR SHARED INQUIRY DISCUSSION

OPTION 1 **Why are Bill and Avis able to share their magic with each other, but not with anyone else?**

- Why does the world seem "changed and right" when Bill and Avis get their magic?

- Why isn't Bill surprised by Avis's magic powers?

- Why does Bill think he might be able to get the kind of magic Avis has?

- Why does Avis continue to think of Bill as her favorite friend, even though she blames him for losing her magic?

PASSAGE FOR DISCUSSION In the student anthology, from "A boy called Bill Brain," on page 155, to "tell his mother and father about it at breakfast," on page 156

OPTION 2 **Why does the story call the children "wise" when they lose their special powers?**

- Why do Bill and Avis lose their magic?

- Why does Bill think he might be able to learn Avis's "doing" magic?

- Why does Avis lose her magic when her mother promises the Governor that Avis will perform at the birthday party, but not when the police and the doctors see what she did for Bill?

- At the end of the story, why does Avis find it a relief to be ordinary again, like Bill?

PASSAGE FOR DISCUSSION In the student anthology, from "'Take care not to let anyone'," on page 163, to "Magic and money don't mix," on page 164

OVERHEARD IN THE CLASSROOM

LEADER Why are Bill and Avis able to share their magic with each other, but not with anyone else?

SALVADOR Because they're connected, like twins.

LEADER Can you describe the kind of connection you mean?

SALVADOR They were born on the same day, and they dreamed of each other even before they met. It's like they always knew each other.

LEADER How does that help to explain why they can share their magic with each other and not with anyone else?

SALVADOR They're not sharing it on purpose. It's just always there, like a twin.

LEADER What do others think? Are Bill and Avis like twins?

PATRICK I think so. Even though Bill was shy with girls, he wasn't with Avis. That's like having a sister.

LEADER So do you think Bill and Avis have an ordinary kind of brother-sister relationship?

DENISE I wouldn't give up my magic powers to help my brother.

LEADER Do you have a friend whom you would be willing to lose magic powers for?

DENISE Yes.

WILLIS Without my best friend, I'd be all alone.

LEADER What does that mean, to be all alone?

JASON You can't do anything. And no one understands you.

LEADER Can we find things in the story that show that Bill and Avis understand each other?

LEARNING TOGETHER

As a leader in Shared Inquiry discussion, you are usually concerned with your students—helping them to clarify and support their ideas, consider alternatives, and develop their own interpretations. But Shared Inquiry also gives leaders a unique opportunity to learn along with their students as the whole group inquires into the meaning of the story. When you genuinely seek to understand the story better yourself, your students will learn and explore along with you, and with greater enthusiasm.

Take the time to ask yourself what you have learned from this experience. What is the biggest challenge you face in being a leader? What is the best part about it? Can you recall some amazing moments from discussions? Build on the success you have achieved so far by sharing some of your memories with your students. And continue learning with them—as much from their answers as from their questions.

Expository Writing: Explaining a Theme (45–60 minutes)

Students identify and explain a theme by referring to other story elements.

> **STUDENT LEARNING OBJECTIVE**
>
> **WRITING: To write an essay demonstrating a knowledge of theme and other story elements**

STAGE 6 ASSESSMENT

In the Reflect and Connect activity following this unit, students will have the opportunity to revise a piece of writing from Stage 6, which you may then choose to assess.

LITERARY CONCEPTS

By isolating literary elements and using them in their explanations, students will be able to see how parts of a story work together to create meaning. Character (or character traits), plot, and figurative language (simile, metaphor, and imagery) are some elements covered in this Junior Great Books series that may be helpful when explaining theme.

TEACHING LITERARY CONCEPTS: REVIEW

1. Ask volunteers to define or give examples of literary elements they have learned in Junior Great Books or at another time in class.

PREWRITING

2. Next have students share ideas about themes in "Two Wise Children," listing students' ideas on the board. (For more about theme, see the Unit 8 expository writing activity, page 286).

3. Choose one of the themes on the board and demonstrate how talking about other elements in the story such as character and plot can help explain the theme. For example:

   Theme: There is nothing stronger than friendship.

   Character: Bill and Avis feel an instant connection to each other and can share their thoughts.

   Plot: Avis's powers are exposed and lost because of Bill's actions, but they remain the best of friends.

4. Tell students that they will write an essay about a theme in "Two Wise Children." The essay will explain how one or two other story elements support this theme. If you wish, give students several themes and have them choose one to write about.

5. Ask students to complete pages 129–130 of the Reader's Journal independently, in pairs, or in small groups.

WRITING A DRAFT

6. Have students draft their essays in the Reader's Journal (page 131) in class or as homework. Optional: Have students share the essays.

Creative Writing:
A Secret Power (45 minutes)

Students write about possessing a secret magic power and having someone find out about it.

PREWRITING

1. Tell students to imagine that they could have any magic power in the world and that it would have to be a secret. Explain that students will write a story about their magic power.

2. Brainstorm with students about some of the powers they would like to have, and why. Help them by asking questions such as:

   ◆ What secret power have you always wanted to have?
   ◆ Why do you want that power?
   ◆ What would your power be useful for?

   Write students' examples on the board, if you wish.

3. Have students turn to page 133 of the Reader's Journal to write down a secret power and the reasons why they want that power.

4. Tell students to imagine what would happen if someone found out about their secret power. Ask them to visualize the moment that their power is discovered, what might happen, and how they might feel.

5. Have students take notes about the beginning, middle, and end of their story in the Reader's Journal (page 134).

WRITING A DRAFT

6. Have students draft their stories on page 135 of the Reader's Journal, using their prewriting notes. Encourage them to develop full, detailed sentences from any fragments they have written. Optional: Have students illustrate their stories or render them in comic-strip form.

Curriculum Connections

Below are resources related to "Two Wise Children" for further reading and investigation in a number of subject areas.

 Appropriate for classroom read-alouds; above-grade reading and interest levels

 Appropriate for independent reading; at- or near-grade reading and interest levels

OTHER WORKS BY THE AUTHOR

 Graves, Robert. *The Big Green Book.* New York: Macmillan, 1985.

A little boy finds a big green book in the attic and learns many handy magic spells that he uses with surprising results.

 Graves, Robert. *Greek Gods and Heroes.* New York: Random House Children's Books, 1965.

Discusses the popularity of Greek myths with chapters about the beauty, wit, and aggressiveness of the Greek gods and goddesses.

APPLIED ARTS

 Sadler, Judy Ann. *Embroidery.* Toronto: Kids Can Press, 2004.

An introduction to embroidery for children that includes photographs and step-by-step instructions designed to help beginners learn basic techniques.

 Wilmore, Kathy. *A Day in the Life of a Colonial Blacksmith.* New York: PowerKids Press, 2000.

Describes the life of a blacksmith in colonial Maryland, including his daily work, some of the many things he made, and his importance to the town in which he worked.

COMMUNICATION

(R) Gorman, Jacqueline Laks. *ESP.* Milwaukee: Gareth Stevens, 2002.

Introduces different types of extrasensory perception, with examples of precognition, psychokinesis, and clairvoyance.

(I) Middleton, Don. *Dealing with Secrets.* New York: PowerKids Press, 1999.

Describes secrets, why people have them, when and with whom to share them, and the difference between good and bad secrets.

RECREATION/SPORTS

(I) Bull, Jane. *The Magic Book.* New York: DK, 2002.

Provides illustrated instructions and describes the materials needed for various magic tricks.

(I) Ho, Oliver. *Young Magician: Magic Tricks.* New York: Sterling, 2003.

Provides step-by-step directions for performing simple magic tricks using common household objects.

(I) Jordan, Denise. *Circus Animal Acts.* Chicago: Heinemann Library, 2002.

Introduces circus animals, how they are trained, and the types of tricks different animals can perform.

(I) McLeese, Tex. *Bull Riding and Bullfighting.* Vero Beach, FL: Rourke, 2001.

Text and illustrations describe the rodeo attraction of bull riding, covering its history, rules, scoring, and how it is done, as well as a brief look at American bullfighting.

Highlighted words are the suggested target words in the vocabulary activity. Underlined words can be briefly explained as you read the story aloud, using the definitions provided.

LEADER'S NOTES AND QUESTIONS

"That's just how I felt when I first came to this field."

TWO WISE CHILDREN

Robert Graves

A boy called Bill Brain, a minister's son, lived in New England near the sea. One Tuesday morning in summer he went for a walk through the fields, picking blueberries into a tin can. Half a mile from home he passed a big house which some newcomers to the town had just bought. They were Colonel and Mrs. Deeds and he had first met them on the Sunday before, outside his father's church. Colonel Deeds watched birds, and Mrs. Deeds drove fast cars. Avis, their only daughter, had fair pigtails, a sunburned face, white teeth, and a snub nose. Bill felt shy with girls, having no sisters. But something about Avis

155

•••

had struck him at once. It seemed as though he had known her for years and years, and as though they shared a big secret. And he guessed that she felt the same about him because her smile wasn't just a polite smile of welcome, but one that meant, "Oh, there you are at last!" Avis was eight, and Bill two years older!

The day before, when Bill had awakened from a bad dream, he remembered that Avis had come into it, and that he had dreamed the same thing two or three times since Christmas. He couldn't say exactly what had happened in the dream, except that he was being watched by a huge, jeering crowd while some big black animal tried to kill him, and that suddenly Avis flew down from a tree and said, "It's all right, Bill. The bandages are in father's medicine chest." He thought to himself, "What a crazy dream!" Yet it still seemed real to him in a way, and he couldn't laugh it off. He couldn't even bring himself to tell his mother and father about it at breakfast.

Well, now it was Tuesday morning. And as he passed the Deeds's big house with the blueberry can slung around his neck, he suddenly said to himself, "How could I have dreamed about Avis

156

jeering: saying mean things to someone in a rude way

long before I met her? Or did I just dream that I had already dreamed the same thing two or three times before?" Bill could see nobody in the Deeds's garden, and he didn't like to shout "Avis, are you there?" So he went on towards Robson's farm, which lay hidden behind a wood. The best blueberry bushes grew on a small rocky hill nearby and he went up it, picking fast into the can, which was already half full. A few minutes later he reached the top and saw something very curious on the other side.

LEADER'S NOTES AND QUESTIONS

There stood Avis
on the back of Robson's white horse,
with one foot lifted like a dancer's, her arms
spread out, and a hay rake balanced upright on
her chin, while the horse galloped around
the field!

"That girl must have worked in a circus," he
thought. But in case she might not like being
watched, he went back behind the hilltop, picked
blueberries for another five minutes or so, and
then came up again whistling loudly. Avis had got
down from the white horse and now sat on a
rock with her head bent over some work or other.

158

...

She heard Bill's whistle.

"There you are at last," she said. "I expected you five minutes ago. Where have you been?"

But Bill was looking at a small square of white linen which she held crumpled in her hand.

"Is that what you have been sewing?" he asked. "Let me look!"

"Oh, it's not worth anything," Avis said. "This is the first time I've done needlework. I borrowed mother's colored silks. It's taken me most of the morning."

"What else have you done?"

"Oh, eaten a few blueberries and tried riding Farmer Robson's horse."

"I suppose that was the first time you ever rode a horse?" Bill asked, to tease her.

But Avis said seriously, "Yes, the first time ever, but I got along quite well."

Bill took the crumpled square of linen from her hand, and found on it the most wonderful needlework he had ever seen. It was a silk picture of flowers and butterflies sewn in about thirty different colors with hundreds of tiny stitches.

159

···

Only one flower and half a butterfly were not yet finished.

"Did you copy a pattern?" Bill asked.

"No," said Avis.

Bill looked her straight in the eyes. He said, "I saw you riding the horse. I hope you don't mind. And now there's this ==marvelous== needlework. Explain, please. . . ."

"Oh, I didn't mind being watched by *you*," said Avis. "And there's nothing much to explain, really. I wanted to do a circus act, so I just did it, because I knew how. And I wanted to make this needlework picture in colored silks, so I just did it because I knew how."

"Oh, I *see*!" said Bill.

"What do you see?" asked Avis.

"I see what's happened to you. It's like what happened to me last spring in a field near our house. I was alone, and the dogwoods had just begun to flower, and hundreds of birds sang, and the world seemed changed and *right*."

"Yes," said Avis. "That's just how I felt when I first came to this field. Go on!"

Bill went on, "Suddenly I found that I knew everything. I had only to tilt my head a little and

160

marvelous: causing wonder or amazement; excellent

...

ask myself any question I pleased, and the answer came at once."

"What *sort* of things?"

"Well, I had often wondered who first built our house and when he built it. So I tilted my head and knew that a Scotch blacksmith called Sawney Todd and his son Robb had built it in 1656. And somehow I knew that if I dug down four or five inches under my left heel, I'd find an old gold brooch belonging to Ruth Todd, Sawney's wife. So I cut out a piece of turf with my knife and found the brooch. It had 'R.T. 1654' scratched on the back."

161

brooch: a large, fancy pin

...

"Did that scare you? *I* got a scare at first by things going marvelously right like that. I'm used to them now."

"It did scare me a little. Then I went home and there was my Uncle Tim arguing with Father about some law business. They had a lot of papers spread on the table, written in very difficult English. Uncle Tim was being rather rude to my father, so I said, 'You're wrong, I'm afraid, Uncle Tim.' And I picked the papers up, read out one of the most difficult ones to him, and showed him just where he had made his mistake. They both looked at me in such surprise that I got all red and explained, 'You see, I know everything today.' Father frowned at me for boasting, but Uncle Tim laughed and asked, 'All right, Bill, if you know everything, what horse will win the big race on Saturday?' I tilted my head, and then told him, 'A big black horse called Gladiator will win. It's ridden by Sam Smile.'"

Avis interrupted. "I don't *know* everything, Bill; it's just that I can *do* everything. It's a bit different. Do you still know everything?"

Bill sighed. "No, I don't, Avis. That's what I want to warn you about, if you don't mind.

162

LEADER'S NOTES AND QUESTIONS

boasting: talking about yourself with too much pride

...

Take care not to let anyone but me into your new secret. I made a terrible mistake over mine."

"What sort of a mistake?" Avis asked.

"It had to do with money. My Uncle Tim went off to town and bet a hundred dollars that Gladiator would win the race, and it did. He made a thousand dollars from the bet, and gave me a ten-dollar bill for myself, and told all his friends about my knowing everything. One of them asked me what horse would win the next big race. I tried to tell him, but somehow no answer came. Then I hoped that I'd know if I saw a list of all the horses that were going to run.

163

Think-Aloud

"Bill had special powers, too. Avis can *do* everything but Bill *knows* everything . . . like the history of his house and where the brooch is hidden. He warns her to keep her powers a secret. What mistake did he make?"

LEADER'S NOTES AND QUESTIONS

...

The man showed me a list, but still I couldn't tell him the winner, so I guessed a horse called Clever Bill—and it came in last! That was in May, and I have never since felt that I know everything. I'm sure I lost my magic by taking the ten dollars. Magic and money don't mix."

Avis said, "You mean, Bill, that I oughtn't to tell anyone, even my mother, that I can do whatever I like? Just in case her friends try to make money out of me?"

Bill nodded. "I'm sure that's how it is."

Avis looked a little sad as she said, "Thank you, Bill. I'll have to change my plans. I'd thought of winning the hundred-dollar skating competition at the New Year Ice Carnival—I haven't ever skated, but it looks fun. And I'd thought of teaching my dog to sing real songs while I played the guitar.

164

LEADER'S NOTES
AND QUESTIONS

...

And I'd thought of growing a new red flower
with my name written in white on its petals,
which would come out only on June tenth—
that's my birthday."

"Mine too," said Bill.

"And flying round and round the White
House at Washington, just to amuse the
President. Like this . . ."

Avis suddenly jumped
into the air, glided around
a big maple tree,

165

...

picking a leaf from the top branch as she went by, and then lay down in the air about three feet from the ground as if she were on a sofa. She said, "I'm not showing off, Bill, I promise. I'm just telling you how easy it is for me to do things."

"*Please* be careful, Avis," said Bill. "If your magic went away, you'd feel so lost and empty inside."

"But it's far more fun to do things like this if someone is watching and knows that I really can do them. I'm lucky to have *you*, Bill. I trust you."

"Oh, I wish, I wish, I wish I hadn't taken Uncle Tim's money," said Bill. "I wish I knew everything again. It would make life so much easier, especially school."

"Maybe you'll get the magic back one day," said Avis.

"I doubt it," said Bill. "Anyhow don't lose yours! Don't let your father and mother find out that you aren't just an ordinary little girl. Don't fly up to your bedroom through the window when they may be looking. Use the stairs! And I'd better keep this bit of needlework hidden. Your mother might ask questions about it."

166

...

Avis gave Bill a hug and said, "I *do* like you, Bill. You're my favorite friend of all. Thank you, thank you!"

Bill said, "By the way, Avis, did you dream of me before we met?"

"Oh, yes, ever since I can remember. I guess that's because we have the same birthday."

She ran off, and Bill thought, "I'm glad she didn't fly home. Farmer Robson's in the next field and might have seen her."

Avis kept Bill's advice all that summer. They saw a lot of each other. Since she didn't really care about making money, or showing off to strangers, she might never have lost her magic but for another stupid mistake of Bill's.

167

LEADER'S NOTES AND QUESTIONS

Think-Aloud

"Bill warns Avis to keep her power secret or she will lose it. Avis takes his advice, but it sounds like she is going to lose her powers because of Bill. I wonder what he will do? Maybe he will accidentally tell someone."

...

That would have been the end of Bill, if his dream hadn't come true. Avis suddenly appeared when he had been horned three times. Somehow she tamed the bull, laid Bill (who had fainted) across the bull's shoulders, jumped up behind, and made the bull gallop back to her home!

When they got there, she called to Colonel Deeds for help. But he was bird-watching somewhere, and Mrs. Deeds had gone shopping in the station wagon. So Avis grabbed bandages and all sorts of first-aid stuff from the family medicine chest. Then she bandaged Bill's wounds, stopped the bleeding, and put Bill into the back of her mother's sports car.

LEADER'S NOTES AND QUESTIONS

170

In spite of the state police who tried to stop her at the crossroads, she drove ten miles at full speed to the nearest hospital, where the doctors took charge of Bill. She had forgotten about the bull, which ate most of the roses in the garden and made holes in the lawn with its hooves.

Avis had no chance of keeping the news quiet. The police wanted to know how she had managed to drive her mother's car so fast and well, and the doctors wanted to know who had bandaged Bill's leg in such a clever way, and Farmer Robson wanted to know how his bull had gotten over a locked gate! Reporters came from all the

LEADER'S NOTES AND QUESTIONS

...

newspapers and asked her more questions and more questions, and she kept on saying "I don't know . . . I don't know," because she had promised Bill to be careful, and it was true that she didn't know *how* she had done it all without learning. They took photographs of her and put her name in the papers as EIGHT-YEAR-OLD GIRL WONDER.

Soon the Governor called at the Deeds's house and asked to see Avis. Mrs. Deeds was very proud of the visit and let the Governor pester Avis with more questions until she got tired of answering "I don't know, I don't know." At last she burst into tears and said, "Oh, *please* go away, or you'll spoil everything! Can't you leave me and my magic alone?"

"Oh, so you do it by magic?" said the Governor, giving her a huge box of candy. "How very interesting! You mustn't cry! Will you come and show us some magic at my little girl's birthday party next Saturday?"

And before Avis could say "No, I won't! It's a secret," Mrs. Deeds answered for her. "Of course, Mr. Governor, my daughter will be *delighted*." This was how Avis lost her magic.

172

•••

When Bill got out of the hospital, none the worse, she blamed him for having spoiled her fun. But she *had* saved his life, which was the important thing; and he would always be her favorite friend.

Besides, in some ways it was a relief to be ordinary again, like Bill.

173

STUDENT LEARNING OBJECTIVES IN STAGE 6

The following list is a collection of the student learning objectives from all activities in units 7 through 10 (Stage 6).

READING COMPREHENSION

◆ To become familiar with a concept in the story

◆ To recall experience with and knowledge about a concept in the story

◆ To begin to synthesize by summarizing and responding to parts of the story

◆ To explore interpretive questions about the story

◆ To reread with a purpose and articulate ideas about the story

◆ To understand and use new words in a variety of contexts

CRITICAL THINKING

◆ To answer an interpretive question using evidence from the story and considering other students' ideas

WRITING

◆ To summarize the story with an understanding of plot as a literary element

◆ To develop an oral description and then convey it in writing

◆ To identify and explain a story's theme in an essay

◆ To write with an awareness of setting

◆ To write a narrative with a beginning, middle, and end

◆ To write an essay demonstrating a knowledge of theme and other story elements

◆ To write a vivid, persuasive narrative

STAGE 6: REFLECT AND CONNECT

Each of the activities below will give your students an opportunity to reflect on their learning process in relation to student objectives in Stage 6. Students will also review the concepts and strategies they learned in this stage and make connections between the stories. Choose any or all of the following topics: reading comprehension strategies, Shared Inquiry discussion, story-to-story comparison, and writing revision.

Reading Comprehension Strategies (45–90 minutes)

Before class, make a copy of the storyboard on pages 432 and 433 of appendix C for each student.

Briefly review with students the reading strategy of synthesizing. Tell them that during this activity, they will be putting together all of the information they have about one story to come up with their own version of it.

Tell students that their assignment is to write a big-book version of a story from Stage 6 that can be read to children in kindergarten or first grade. Show them an example, pointing out that the words are large enough that children can follow along as the story is read aloud and that each page has an illustration.

Divide your class into small groups and hand out the storyboards you photocopied earlier. Write the following procedure on the board:

- Look over the story, your notes, and your Reader's Journal pages to remember important ideas to include in your retelling of the story.

- With your group, use the storyboard pages to write what happened in the story in your own words. Make sure to put events in the order they happened. In the boxes, sketch the drawings you would like to include.

- Using large paper, copy your retelling on the bottom half of each page and draw pictures to go along with the story on the top half. Make sure to write neatly and in large print so younger children can follow along as they listen to the story.

Have student groups complete their storyboards, dividing the copying and illustrating tasks evenly among group members.

If time permits, have students visit a kindergarten or first-grade classroom and take turns reading their books aloud to groups of younger students.

Appendixes

APPENDIX A: ASSESSMENT KIT

This assessment kit provides you with various resources to track your students' learning in Junior Great Books and help you plan instruction to meet their needs. The kit contains:

STORY COMPREHENSION TESTS (PAGE 396)

Multiple-choice tests of comprehension skills, including inference, word meaning in context, and main idea. There are three tests, each based on the last story in each stage.

CRITICAL-THINKING RUBRIC (PAGE 408)

A rubric featuring the critical-thinking objectives of Shared Inquiry discussion and the Junior Great Books program as a whole. The rubric levels you might expect to see at each stage of the current series are labeled.

WRITING RUBRIC (PAGE 411)

A rubric featuring writing content and organization goals. The writing rubric, which aligns with most state rubrics and scoring guides for writing, is tailored to the expository writing assignments for this series. The writing rubric reflects rising expectations as your students progress through this series.

ACTIVITY SCORE GUIDELINES (PAGE 413)

A procedure for assigning a grade for students' class participation and informal writing activities. The activity score is based on the student learning mini-rubrics—which appear in each unit of this Leader's Edition—as well as your own sense of each student's participation.

PORTFOLIO ASSESSMENT (PAGE 414)

Suggestions for using activity pages from the Reader's Journal for portfolio assessment. Portfolio assessment enables you and your students to track the progress of their work over a semester or a school year, and to identify their special strengths and interests.

LEADER REFLECTION (PAGE 417)

A checklist to help you link your students' progress in critical thinking with your own use of Shared Inquiry questioning strategies. This reflection helps you identify your students' level of achievement and suggests Shared Inquiry problem-solving strategies for areas in which students may struggle.

These assessment tools emphasize the three key student learning strands of reading comprehension, critical thinking, and writing. You can see a broader view of these objectives in the chart of Series 3 Learning Goals (appendix B, page 421). The student learning objectives and mini-rubrics, which appear with most core activities in this Leader's Edition, are also aligned with the learning goals.

The learning goals chart includes many other language arts objectives addressed by Junior Great Books, most notably listening and speaking. Assess your students' progress toward these other goals by applying your usual methods.

PLANNING FOR ASSESSMENT

Using a variety of assessments will give you the best understanding of your students' progress, and using assessments regularly will allow you and your students to become accustomed to them and proficient at using them. The sample assessment plan below shows how a leader might use the full range of assessment options, alternating options unit by unit to ensure a thorough but manageable assessment schedule.

Sample Assessment Plan

		ACTIVITY SCORE	STORY COMPREHENSION TEST	CRITICAL-THINKING RUBRIC	WRITING REVISION AND RUBRIC	PORTFOLIO ASSESSMENT	LEADER REFLECTION
Book One	**Stage 1**	Unit 2	After Unit 3	Unit 3			After Reflect and Connect
	Stage 2	Unit 4 Unit 6			Reflect and Connect		After Reflect and Connect
	Stage 3	Unit 8	After Unit 10	Unit 7		After completing Book One	After Reflect and Connect
Book Two (this volume)	**Stage 4**	Unit 1 Unit 3			Reflect and Connect		After Reflect and Connect
	Stage 5	Unit 5	After Unit 6	Unit 5			After Reflect and Connect
	Stage 6	Unit 7 Unit 9			Reflect and Connect	After completing Book Two	After Reflect and Connect

Of course, your own assessment plan will take into account your Junior Great Books plan as well as your overall curriculum and calendar. For instance, if you target reading comprehension and critical thinking in your Junior Great Books program, you might not make use of the writing assessment tools. Whatever your goals, strive for a variety of assessments to gain a full picture of students' learning and to guide your instruction.

Story Comprehension Tests

The story comprehension tests will allow you to assess your students' basic reading comprehension skills at each stage. Basic comprehension skills are not directly taught in Junior Great Books, but they develop as a result of the reading comprehension and critical-thinking strategies emphasized by the program. (As the noted educator Benjamin Bloom observed, higher-level objectives such as critical thinking include within themselves lower-level objectives such as literal comprehension.) Used with the writing and critical-thinking assessments, the story comprehension tests will help you get the full picture of your students' learning in Junior Great Books. Story comprehension tests (one per stage) start on page 398.

These tests feature the multiple-choice format of most standardized reading tests. The questions on each test address the following skills:

◆ Explicit fact—identifying details that are stated in the story

◆ Implicit fact—identify facts that can be inferred from the story

◆ Word meaning—identifying a definition within the context of the story (vocabulary words not included on the story comprehension tests)

◆ Sequence—relating story incidents to each other in proper order

◆ Theme—identifying a valid statement of theme for the story

◆ Summary—identifying a valid statement of the main character's problem or the basic plot of the story

The answer key (page 407) shows the skills addressed by each question.

The story comprehension tests do not include interpretive questions. As with most reading comprehension multiple-choice tests, the story only supports one answer for each question; another answer may be plausible but not determinable from the story.

We recommend that you track students' comprehension skills by giving tests at intervals throughout your use of Junior Great Books. As you compare each student's test results, keep in mind that Junior Great Books stories are arranged in order of increasing difficulty throughout each series.

USING THE STORY COMPREHENSION TESTS

Give the test after completing the unit activities for the story. The test is open book, so make sure students have their books.

Review the procedures for a multiple-choice test with your students:

- Write your name clearly on your test paper.

- Read all the possible answers and review the story before marking your answer.

- Choose the *best* answer for each question.

- Mark the letter for your answer clearly.

Review the graded tests with your class, asking students to explain their answers.

Caporushes

- Write your name clearly on your test paper.
- Read all the possible answers and review the story before marking your answer.
- Choose the *best* answer for each question.
- Mark the letter for your answer clearly.

1. When the three daughters answer their father's question, how can you tell that Caporushes really cares about what she says?
   a) She answers most quickly.
   b) She thinks about her answer.
   c) She tries to make her father laugh.
   d) She wants to be like her sisters.

2. After Caporushes is turned out of the house by her father, the main thing she tries to do in the rest of the story is
   a) make the young master fall in love with her.
   b) help other people with their chores.
   c) tell others what she thinks of them.
   d) keep people from knowing who she is.

3. In the story, the word *rushes* (page 42) most likely means
   a) getting excited.
   b) hurrying.
   c) water plants.
   d) water birds.

4. Which sentence most helps you understand what Caporushes does after she is ordered to leave her house?
   a) "He will find someone else."
   b) "Hide my heart, O robe o' rushes."
   c) "Let me stir it," she said, "while you fetch a cup from the pantry room."
   d) "I should like to see her, but I don't think I ever shall."

5. In the song the fen birds sing to Caporushes, they say that she
    a) looks ugly in her cap.
    b) gave her father a good answer.
    c) will be sad to leave her father.
    d) hides her heart with her robe.

6. On page 44, which sentence helps you understand what *a night's lodging* means?
    a) "So if you will do my work you shall share my bed and have a bite of my supper."
    b) "Only mind you scrub the pots clean, or Cook will be at me."
    c) "By this time she was very, very hungry, so she wandered on, and she wandered on."
    d) "I was just wanting badly to go walking with my sweetheart."

7. After the first two balls, why does Caporushes tell herself she will not dance again?
    a) She doesn't like dancing with the young master.
    b) She is too tired from cleaning pots and scraping saucepans.
    c) It isn't right to pretend to be someone else.
    d) It isn't right for a young man to be in love with his maid.

8. What does Caporushes mean when she says that the young master "will find someone else"?
    a) He is not as much in love as he thinks.
    b) He doesn't know where to find her.
    c) He will find the beautiful stranger.
    d) He is too young and healthy to die of love.

9. What happens just before the young master finds his ring in his gruel?
    a) He asks for the cook to come to his room.
    b) He stops eating his meals.
    c) Caporushes stirs the gruel for the cook.
    d) Caporushes finds his ring in her hand.

10. Why does the young master send for the cook after he finds his ring in the gruel?

    a) He wants the cook to make something better than gruel.

    b) He wants the cook to stop putting things in his food.

    c) He thinks that the cook is the beautiful dancer.

    d) He thinks the cook has seen the beautiful dancer.

11. What is another way to say *dress every dish* (page 54)?

    a) Prepare the food.

    b) Cover the plates.

    c) Eat the meal.

    d) Use a tablecloth.

12. Why doesn't Caporushes' father recognize his daughter at her wedding?

    a) He is so sad that he can't look at others.

    b) She still wears her cap of rushes.

    c) He is blind.

    d) She has grown up.

NAME _____

The Ugly Duckling

- ◆ Write your name clearly on your test paper.
- ◆ Read all the possible answers and review the story before marking your answer.
- ◆ Choose the *best* answer for each question.
- ◆ Mark the letter for your answer clearly.

1. The mother duck decides that the ugly duckling is not a turkey because
   a) he is very big.
   b) he can swim.
   c) he can quack.
   d) he looks different.

2. On page 87, the mother duck asks her ducklings, "Do you imagine this is the whole of the world? It goes far beyond the other side of the garden, right into the Rector's field, but I've never been there yet." This lets you know that the mother duck
   a) doesn't know how big the world is.
   b) likes to travel and explore.
   c) wants her ducklings to travel.
   d) likes to scare her ducklings.

3. After seeing the gun-dog, why does the duckling "wait several hours before he looked about him"?
   a) He doesn't know where the swans were.
   b) He is thinking about going back to the barnyard.
   c) He is scared the men and the dogs might come back.
   d) He can't move because the dog hurt him.

4. The ugly duckling goes into the "wretched little hut" (page 96)
   a) to get away from the men with guns.
   b) to get out of the storm.
   c) to learn to lay eggs and give off sparks.
   d) to find friends who will accept him as he is.

5. What is the best meaning of the phrase "Don't give yourself such airs," on page 99?

   a) Don't pant when you run.

   b) Don't talk when no one is listening.

   c) Don't get upset and worried.

   d) Don't act like you're better than others.

6. You can tell that the old woman is very poor because

   a) her cat lives in the house with her.

   b) she likes to eat duck eggs.

   c) she doesn't see very well.

   d) her house is about to fall down.

7. On page 97, when the old woman says, "What a windfall!" she probably means

   a) "What a good egg!"

   b) "What good fortune!"

   c) "What a large storm!"

   d) "What a nice pet!"

8. *Snubbed* (page 100) probably means

   a) hit in the nose.

   b) allowed to swim.

   c) treated without respect.

   d) loved.

9. Which is the last group of creatures the ugly duckling meets before he meets the swans and discovers he is one?

   a) the children in the farmer's house

   b) the ducks and fowl in the barnyard

   c) the cat and hen in the old woman's house

   d) the wild ducks and geese in the marsh

10. When does the duckling find out that he is really a swan?
    a) summer
    b) winter
    c) autumn
    d) spring

11. What is a main problem in the story for the ugly duckling?
    a) He runs away from home when he is too small to take care of himself.
    b) He doesn't find other animals who accept him the way he is.
    c) He goes out in the wide world when he doesn't know what he wants to do.
    d) He isn't friendly toward the other animals he meets.

12. Which statement from the story tells you an important lesson in the story?
    a) "He bowed his head down on the surface of the stream, expecting death."
    b) "The duckling recognized the glorious creatures and felt a strange sadness come over him."
    c) "It does not matter being born in a duckyard, if only one has lain in a swan's egg."
    d) "The great swans swam round him and stroked him with their beaks."

NAME _____

Two Wise Children

◆ Write your name clearly on your test paper.

◆ Read all the possible answers and review the story before marking your answer.

◆ Choose the *best* answer for each question.

◆ Mark the letter for your answer clearly.

1. *Struck him* on page 156 most likely means
   a) hurt him.
   b) scared him.
   c) interested him.
   d) made him shy.

2. Why doesn't Avis mind that Bill watches her ride the horse?
   a) She knows he won't tell Farmer Robson.
   b) She recognizes Bill from her dreams.
   c) She likes to show off how well she can do things.
   d) She knows she will lose her magic powers.

3. Which phrase most helps the reader understand what *needlework* means?
   a) "she held crumpled in her hand"
   b) "flowers and butterflies"
   c) "thirty different colors"
   d) "hundreds of tiny stitches"

4. *Tilt* on page 160 most likely means
   a) turn slightly.
   b) whirl around.
   c) scratch gently.
   d) use intelligently.

5. Avis tells Bill that when she first found that she could do anything she wanted she felt

    a) scared.

    b) surprised.

    c) happy.

    d) relieved.

6. How does Bill convince Avis not to show people she can do anything she wants?

    a) He reminds her that her parents will be upset if she flies.

    b) He explains how he got his magic.

    c) He warns her that the Governor will want to know about it.

    d) He tells her how he lost his magic.

7. Which of the following sentences most helps you understand why Bill tries to learn Avis's magic?

    a) "Maybe you'll get your magic back one day."

    b) "If your magic went away, you'd feel so lost and empty inside."

    c) "It would make life so much easier, especially school."

    d) "You're my favorite friend of all."

8. Which of the following does Bill do just after he learns about Avis's magic?

    a) He tells his Uncle Tim which horse will win the race.

    b) He dreams that a big black animal tries to kill him.

    c) He tries to have a bullfight with Farmer Robson's bull.

    d) He sees Avis standing on a horse's back and balancing a rake.

9. Which of the following most helps you understand why Mrs. Deeds accepts the Governor's invitation to his daughter's party without asking Avis?

    a) "Mrs. Deeds was very proud of the visit."

    b) "Oh, *please* go away, or you'll spoil everything!"

    c) "Of course, Mr. Governor, my daughter will be *delighted*."

    d) "How very interesting! You mustn't cry!"

10. Why doesn't Avis answer the reporters' questions?
    a) She can't know everything the way Bill used to.
    b) She doesn't want her mother to be mad at her.
    c) She doesn't want to tell them about her magic.
    d) She can't explain how to drive a car.

11. The best summary for this story is
    a) a boy meets a girl who pretends she can do anything.
    b) a boy and a girl dream about each other.
    c) a girl rescues a boy when he makes a mistake.
    d) a boy and a girl get magic powers and lose them.

12. According to the story, what is a good part of having the magic Bill and Avis have?
    a) It makes other people do whatever you say.
    b) It lets you explore things you find interesting or fun.
    c) It changes you into a nicer person that others will like.
    d) It gives you the money and things you want.

Answer Key

CAPORUSHES

1. b Implicit
2. d Summary
3. c Word meaning
4. b Theme
5. b Implicit
6. a Word meaning
7. d Explicit
8. a Implicit
9. c Sequence
10. d Implicit
11. a Word meaning
12. c Explicit

TWO WISE CHILDREN

1. c Word meaning
2. b Implicit
3. d Word meaning
4. a Word meaning
5. a Explicit
6. d Implicit
7. b Implicit
8. c Sequence
9. a Implicit
10. c Explicit
11. d Summary
12. b Theme

THE UGLY DUCKLING

1. b Explicit
2. a Implicit
3. c Implicit
4. b Implicit
5. d Word meaning
6. d Implicit
7. b Word meaning
8. c Word meaning
9. a Sequence
10. d Explicit
11. b Summary
12. c Theme

Critical-Thinking Rubric

The critical-thinking rubric on page 410 gives you a detailed view of the critical-thinking skills developed through Shared Inquiry discussion and the Junior Great Books program as a whole. It will alert you to the performance levels you can expect to see as your students gradually improve their thinking skills, and it will enable you to assess the skills of individual students.

Your consistent interpretive questioning is the most important factor in improving your students' critical-thinking skills. After you assess students' work, reflect on how you might improve your questioning skills to give students more opportunities and support for growth.

This rubric focuses on three areas of critical thinking:

- Idea—generating and clarifying ideas of what the story might mean

- Evidence—supporting and checking these ideas, based on what is in the story

- Response—considering alternative ideas and adjusting thinking

The rubric is labeled to show the levels you can expect for most of your students at stages 1 through 6 of this Junior Great Books series. The student learning mini-rubrics for the second reading and for Shared Inquiry discussion in each unit are derived from these levels of the critical-thinking rubric. (See also the activity score assessment on page 413.)

USING THE CRITICAL-THINKING RUBRIC FOR ASSESSMENT

The critical-thinking rubric can be used to assess students' critical thinking in both discussion and writing. Using these methods together at regular intervals will give you more complete and dependable information.

GRADING CRITICAL THINKING IN WRITTEN RESPONSES. The Building Your Answer pages of the Reader's Journal can show you students' thinking about a discussion question in a form that is convenient for you to grade.

Each student has the same opportunity to respond to the focus question in writing, so quiet or shy students can say as much as their more verbal classmates. Also, modifying their answers after discussion encourages students to feel more accountable for learning during the discussion. On the other hand, students who struggle with writing, and even more proficient writers, may express their thinking better in discussion.

To use the Building Your Answer pages to grade students' written responses:

1. Review with your students the relevant levels of the critical-thinking rubric on page 410. Try to recall specific examples from class of the thinking described.

2. Plan to allow enough time in Shared Inquiry discussion for all students to participate fully, including time after discussion for students to change or add to their answers.

3. Read students' work carefully and assign separate grades for idea, evidence, and response, or grade for just one objective. (Written examples of response will usually not appear unless the Building Your Answer prompt calls for it.)

4. Comment briefly on each student's paper, in addition to assigning a grade.

GRADING CRITICAL THINKING IN DISCUSSION. Discussion responses may display the strengths of students who may not write well, but students' responses will be affected by other factors such as time limitations, group size, shyness, and group dynamics. Also, it is unavoidable that your follow-up questions will give different students varying opportunities to develop their responses.

Your seating chart will help you recall students' discussion responses. If you also review students' Building Your Answer pages, you can further bolster your memory. Better still, record the discussion you wish to assess, either with a video or audio recorder, or have a colleague keep a seating chart for you.

To use the seating chart to grade students' discussion responses:

1. Allow enough time in Shared Inquiry discussion for all students to participate fully. This will be easier if you keep the size of the discussion group manageable.

2. Immediately after discussion, review your seating chart and take fuller notes on students' responses.

3. Assess students' contributions, as you recall them, in the areas of idea, evidence, and response. Often individual responses and even a student's entire contribution to a discussion will pertain only to one area.

Confer with your students individually while their recollections of the discussion are still fresh. Encourage them to add to and explain their comments. Then, describe the strengths you saw and your suggestions for improvement.

Critical-Thinking Rubric

This rubric shows three major critical-thinking areas—idea, evidence, and response—at five performance levels. The first column indicates probable performance levels for students at stages in this Junior Great Books series.

PERFORMANCE LEVELS		IDEA: GENERATING AN INTERPRETATION	EVIDENCE: USING SUPPORT FROM THE STORY	RESPONSE: LEARNING WITH AND FROM OTHER STUDENTS
5	**Explains answers (Stages 5 and 6)**	Explains how an idea answers the question • Relates actions, characters to each other • To clarify, spells out assumptions and relates them to the question	Explains how a passage supports an idea • Explores meanings, connotations for relevant words, phrases • Sees when evidence works against own idea	Explains and gives reasons for agreement and disagreement • Critiques or supports other students' ideas • Asks other students simple questions
4	**Understands issues (Stages 3 and 4)**	Fully understands the interpretive issue • Infers motives and causes; addresses the question directly • To clarify, tells more about the answer	Understands the need for evidence • Spontaneously goes back to the story • Focuses on relevant sentences	Understands and roughly summarizes other students' ideas • May be convinced by others • Follows other students' counterarguments
3	**Recognizes alternatives (Stage 2)**	Asserts a considered answer, aware of alternative ideas • May hesitate between answers • To clarify, paraphrases answer	Supports answer against alternative answer • Locates relevant major passages • Reads or recounts whole passages	Recognizes alternative answers and agrees or disagrees simply
2	**Offers simple, quick answers (Stage 1)**	Gives quick, simple answer to the question • All-or-nothing, snap judgment • To clarify, repeats answer	Tends not to volunteer support; offers support only when asked • Recalls major story facts • Considers answer self-evident	Reacts briefly/quickly to other students' answers without talking about them
1	**Begins to answer**	Talks about the story without addressing the question	Mentions characters and events; may retell the story	Allows other students to speak without interruption

The Writing Rubric

The writing rubric on page 412 will help you assess students' expository writing. Because the expository writing assignments focus on the interpretation of stories, the rubric will also reflect students' growth in this area.

This writing rubric focuses on two traits addressed by expository writing assignments in Junior Great Books—content (ideas and evidence) and organization. The writing rubric aligns with most state rubrics and scoring guides that deal with content and organization for expository writing.

Since Junior Great Books strongly emphasizes content and organization, the writing rubric does not include such elements of writing as voice, sentence structure, word choice, and conventions or mechanics. If you wish to assess these elements as well, apply your usual rubric or standards.

USING THE WRITING RUBRIC TO GRADE PAPERS

Students can revise their work during Reflect and Connect. Revised student papers will give you the fairest assessment of what your students can do. Follow the suggestions for revision in the Writing Notebook section of the Reader's Journal (page 139). Also, review the writing rubric with your students each time they revise, so they have a clear notion of what to aim for.

As you grade the papers, read through the rubric and keep it in view. Give each paper a score for content and a score for organization, since students might do better with one element than with the other. If you wish, add the two for a total grade.

To use the writing rubric:

◆ Orient yourself by quickly reading through all your students' papers and sorting them into three piles: strong, average, and struggling. Compare each pile to the rubric levels before you grade the papers individually.

◆ Hold grading sessions with colleagues: share copies of papers, grade them independently, and then meet to compare and discuss your grading.

◆ As you grade, add your own descriptive notes to the rubric to reflect your students' work.

In addition to the number grade from the rubric, give each student's paper two comments—a positive comment and a gentle suggestion for the next paper. The most effective comments are specific responses to students' ideas, such as, "I was really interested in your idea about Rogelia," or "Your quotation from page 29 seemed very convincing." Such comments encourage students to value and develop their ideas in writing.

Writing Rubric

This rubric shows two major elements of writing, content (idea and evidence) and organization. The five performance levels that are defined are appropriate for this series of Junior Great Books.

PERFORMANCE LEVELS	CONTENT: IDEAS AND EVIDENCE	ORGANIZATION
5	**The writing offers interesting, convincing ideas.** • The main idea is worthwhile; it makes the reader think. • The evidence clearly supports the main idea and there is enough of it; the reader is convinced or at least impressed.	**The writing is thorough and easy to follow.** • The introduction leads directly to the main idea; the reader grasps quickly where the piece is going. • The piece keeps focused on the main idea and lays out evidence logically; the reader sees clearly how all evidence relates to the main idea.
4	**The writing makes a point that is partially developed and supported.** • The main idea is strong and clear; it interests the reader. • Evidence supports several aspects of the main idea; the reader can see that the idea is logical and probable.	**The writing is easy to follow and fairly complete.** • There is an introduction; the reader can connect it with the main idea. • Most of the piece deals with the main idea and evidence for it; the reader can see how parts are connected.
3	**The writing makes a clear point about the topic with some support.** • The main idea makes sense; the reader can understand it. • Some evidence is given; the reader can see that the main idea fits some of the story facts.	**The writing is not always easy to follow.** • The piece starts without an introduction; the reader sees what the main idea is. • In places, the writing jumps from one idea or piece of evidence to another; the reader can follow but sometimes gets a little lost.
2	**The writing addresses the topic question or issue.** • There is an answer to the question; the reader can tell what the general opinion is. • A few specific parts of the story are referred to; the reader can see that the opinion is based partially on the story.	**The writing has a very simple organization or is very short.** • The piece stresses one or two important ideas; the reader can see what they are. • The piece is short or breaks off.
1	**The writing is related to the general subject or story.** • There is no clear answer to the question; the reader is not sure what the paper is trying to say. • The story is barely mentioned, or parts are simply retold; the reader can see that the piece is about the story.	**The writing is hard to follow or is incomplete.** • The piece has no separate parts; the reader has to try to figure out how sentences are connected. • The piece is very short; the reader doesn't have enough to see the point.

Activity Score Guidelines

The activity score is a simple and flexible way to track your students' work in reading comprehension and critical thinking, as well as their language arts skills and class participation.

You may choose any of the activities in a unit for an activity score. It is especially easy to use the core activities that have a student learning mini-rubric with ready-made criteria for scoring. The mini-rubric for the sharing questions activity focuses on reading comprehension behaviors, while the mini-rubrics for the second reading and Shared Inquiry discussion are aligned with the critical-thinking rubric on page 410. If you wish to score another activity, use the student learning objective and your usual standards for class participation.

The activity score is a rough, rule-of-thumb assessment, but as you tally scores over time they will result in an accurate picture of each student's individual achievement.

USING ACTIVITY SCORES

After each Junior Great Books session, mentally review students' participation and record a plus (+), check (✔), or minus (−) for each student:

1. Plan to take a few minutes after each Junior Great Books session to record the scores.

2. Decide which activity or activities to score, and review the student learning objectives and the mini-rubrics. Label your grade book column with the activity name.

3. Working in your grade book, quickly review each student's participation, asking yourself the following questions:

   Was the student . . .

   ◆ High on the rubric, on target for the objective, or especially helpful to the class? Mark a plus.

   ◆ Satisfactory on the rubric, approaching the objective, or participating but not in a way that stands out? Mark a check.

   ◆ Low on the rubric, struggling with the objective, distracting the class, or not participating? Mark a minus.

4. Later, when you calculate grades, assign values to the scores in accordance with your overall grading system.

5. Share students' scores with them from time to time. After several weeks of scoring you will be able to tell students which Junior Great Books activities and critical-thinking objectives are their strongest and weakest, and to address their needs with small-group instruction and targeted follow-up questions.

USING THE STUDENT LEARNING MINI-RUBRICS

In each unit of stages 4 and 5, the student learning mini-rubrics (labeled Look For Students To) for the second reading and Shared Inquiry discussion focus on one element of critical thinking—idea, evidence, or response. If you designate these as I, E, and R in your grade book, you will be able to track your students' performance in specific areas of critical thinking. (Idea units are units 1 and 4; evidence units are units 2 and 5; and response units are units 3 and 6. For Stage 6 units, track performance in the area that you choose to pursue.)

Portfolio Assessment

Junior Great Books is well suited to portfolio assessment. The Reader's Journal comprises a complete collection of students' drafts, works in progress, and revisions. This will make it easy for students to review their work over a semester, identify the most significant pieces, and reflect on their growth as writers.

USING THE PORTFOLIO ASSESSMENT

To perform a portfolio assessment at the end of each semester:

1. Before class, prepare six copies of the portfolio comment sheet (see following page) for each student.

2. Explain to students the purpose of a portfolio—to show the best examples of the many kinds of work they have done, and to show how their work has improved over time. Share with them the portfolio assessment rubric on page 416.

3. Review the portfolio comment sheet with students. Discuss aspects of their work they might feel proud of.

4. Ask students to choose the Reader's Journal pages for assessment and write a comment sheet about each page.

5. Review your students' Reader's Journals, writing your comments on the comment sheets.

6. Complete a portfolio assessment rubric for each student's portfolio. Arrange to confer with each student about his or her portfolio.

Portfolio Comment Sheet

Choose six pieces of work from your Reader's Journal that you are especially proud of. Include several different kinds of work. Attach one comment sheet to each, with your comment. After I collect your Reader's Journal, I will also write a comment.

STUDENT: I'M PROUD OF THIS PAGE BECAUSE _____

_____

_____

_____

LEADER: THIS PAGE SHOWS ME THAT YOU _____

_____

_____

_____

Portfolio Comment Sheet

Choose six pieces of work from your Reader's Journal that you are especially proud of. Include several different kinds of work. Attach one comment sheet to each, with your comment. After I collect your Reader's Journal, I will also write a comment.

STUDENT: I'M PROUD OF THIS PAGE BECAUSE _____

_____

_____

_____

LEADER: THIS PAGE SHOWS ME THAT YOU _____

_____

_____

_____

Portfolio Assessment Rubric

STUDENT _____

LEADER _____ DATE _____

SCORES	5	4	3	2	1
	SUPERIOR	EXCELLENT	GOOD	SATISFACTORY	NEEDS IMPROVEMENT

YOUR PORTFOLIO	COMMENTS	SCORE
SHOWS INTERESTING IDEAS ABOUT THE STORIES YOU READ		
INCLUDES SEVERAL DIFFERENT KINDS OF WORK		
WAS DONE CAREFULLY AND COMPLETELY		
SHOWS THAT YOU KEPT TRYING AND IMPROVING		

Leader Reflection

Your students' progress is closely tied to your own development as a leader of Shared Inquiry discussion. The leader reflection form is designed to help you recognize your own strengths and challenges and identify needed changes as you incorporate the Shared Inquiry method into your teaching.

This form focuses on the key critical-thinking elements—idea, evidence, and response—as well as on classroom culture. This aligns with the critical-thinking rubric and the content (idea and evidence) area of the writing rubric. Because your students' critical-thinking skills are supported by your questions, thinking about your students' achievement will enable you to see areas in which you can improve your questioning strategies to help them.

The classroom culture section refers to the level of energy, enthusiasm, and confidence your students exhibit in Junior Great Books. This, too, is an important indicator of your students' learning, and one you can address with questioning strategies.

USING THE LEADER REFLECTION FORM

To use this form after you have graded your students' work for each stage:

1. Make a copy of the form to write on, so you can compare your progress from stage to stage.

2. Referring to the left-hand column, consider your students' overall levels of achievement as a class for each of the four critical thinking elements. Note your own observations of their breakthroughs and struggles.

3. Set a priority—an area for faster progress, or a problem to solve.

4. Consider the strategies in the right-hand column: How could you use them to achieve your priority? How might your students respond?

5. Decide on a few strategies to use, or let the examples help you think of your own strategies.

6. If possible, meet with teachers and other discussion leaders to fill out your forms. As you discuss your students' work and your own use of the questioning strategies, you and your colleagues can give one another insight and professional support. If you are working with a Great Books consultant, he or she will also be able to help you set and meet your goals as a discussion leader.

SETTING PRIORITIES

As a conscientious leader committed to achieving all objectives, you might find it hard to set priorities. However, the Junior Great Books learning objectives complement one another, so as you work on one, your students will make some gains in the others. For instance, as you encourage students to use more evidence, they will generate more ideas and explain them better, improving their reading comprehension skills. If you continue to track priorities and reflect regularly, you will quickly spot areas of improvement and can turn your attention from objectives you have reached to those that still require work.

Leader Reflection

The left-hand column shows likely student behaviors in four areas of Junior Great Books: idea, evidence, response, and classroom culture. For each, likely student behaviors are shown in order, from simple beginning behaviors to more complex ones.

The right-hand column lists strategies that address each area as a whole. The strategies are arranged in two groups, based on their likely difficulty for you as a leader.

STAGE: _____ DATE: _____

	I SEE THAT MY STUDENTS:	MY FOCUS FOR THE NEXT STAGE WILL BE TO:
IDEA	• Talk about the story in general terms • Give short, superficial answers • Give thoughtful answers • Give answers based on motives and causes • Explain answers **Observations:**	☐ **Ask follow-up questions to help students clarify ideas** **Simpler strategies:** ☐ Pause to think about each student's comment before asking a question ☐ Ask students to tell you more about their idea ☐ Invite students to ask questions when they do not understand one another's ideas **Advanced strategies:** ☐ Ask questions about specific words and phrases ☐ Set a relaxed pace in discussion, giving students sufficient time to explore ideas ☐ Return to students later to ask if they wish to add to earlier comments **Further strategies:** ☐ ☐
EVIDENCE	• Retell parts of the story • Point to relevant passages • Offer simple explanations for pointing to certain passages • Offer an idea based on evidence from the story • Explain how evidence supports an idea **Observations:**	☐ **Ask follow-up questions for evidence and support** **Simpler strategies:** ☐ Ask students to hold up their books to point out a passage so everyone can find it ☐ Ask the group to help a student find a passage ☐ Invite students to read passages aloud as evidence **Advanced strategies:** ☐ Ask for evidence consistently ☐ Suggest a passage, and ask if it supports the idea ☐ Ask students to comment on evidence cited by another student **Further strategies:** ☐ ☐

I SEE THAT MY STUDENTS:	MY FOCUS FOR THE NEXT STAGE WILL BE TO:

RESPONSE

- Allow others to speak
- React quickly and briefly to other students' answers
- Hear and consider other students' answers before speaking
- Agree or disagree with other students' ideas
- Explain why they agree or disagree

Observations:

☐ **Ask follow-up questions for listening and responding**

Simpler strategies:
☐ Coach students in listening and discussion manners
☐ Avoid paraphrasing or repeating comments myself
☐ Focus on one idea at a time, letting the group discuss it thoroughly before moving on to another idea

Advanced strategies:
☐ Refer to the seating chart to ask students specifically about other students' ideas
☐ Invite students to repeat comments so others can hear them
☐ Encourage students to speak directly to each other

Further strategies:
☐
☐

CLASSROOM CULTURE

- Phase in and out
- Hang back from participating
- Direct comments to the leader
- Direct comments to the group
- Think through ideas spontaneously and without apparent self-consciousness

Observations:

☐ **Show openness to students' ideas (no single right answer in mind)**

Simpler strategies:
☐ Discuss the story with a colleague to get another perspective
☐ Anticipate better comprehension over time rather than immediate mastery
☐ Circulate while students complete the Building Your Answer page to see the variety of ideas, so you know what to expect during discussion

Advanced strategies:
☐ Give shy students other ways to participate, such as reading aloud their Building Your Answer responses or commenting on another student's idea
☐ Prepare for each story by thinking through several different answers to the discussion questions (alone or with colleagues)
☐ Avoid unintentionally favoring some students (calling on or questioning them more)
☐ Be patient as students read longer, more difficult stories

Further strategies:
☐
☐

APPENDIX B:
JUNIOR GREAT BOOKS
SERIES 3 LEARNING GOALS

Below are the educational goals that the Series 3 Junior Great Books program meets. These goals represent standard criteria for a mid- to upper-elementary language arts program. Check marks indicate in which book a goal is addressed.

READING	BOOK ONE	BOOK TWO
Reading process: Incorporated into program activities		
Use prereading strategies	✓	✓
Read with fluency	✓	✓
Use reference materials for unknown words	✓	✓
Ask questions to set a purpose for reading	✓	✓
Reread, take notes, and read with a purpose to monitor comprehension	✓	✓
Make generalizations and draw conclusions	✓	✓
Answer questions about the story's meaning	✓	✓
Paraphrase passages	✓	✓
Summarize passages		✓
Discuss interpretations of the story	✓	✓
Extend ideas about the story after discussion	✓	✓
Write responses to the story	✓	✓
Write to connect story ideas to the real world	✓	✓
Compare and contrast stories	✓	✓
Read stories from a variety of cultures	✓	✓

Comprehension strategies: Explained, modeled, and developed with guided practice		
Ask questions to comprehend the story	✓	
Make connections to the story	✓	
Visualize textual information	✓	
Make inferences and predictions based on the story		✓
Determine important ideas in the story		✓
Synthesize textual information		✓
Skills: Incorporated into program activities		
Recognize a story's purpose or perspective	✓	✓
Explain how a story's language conveys a message	✓	✓
Modify interpretation to incorporate new ideas and textual evidence	✓	✓
Cite passages to support questions and ideas	✓	✓
Understand the sequence of story events	✓	✓
Use context clues to figure out word meaning	✓	✓
Identify character motivation	✓	✓
Understand figurative language		✓

CRITICAL THINKING	BOOK ONE	BOOK TWO
Processes: Incorporated into program activities		
Ask interpretive questions	✓	✓
Generate ideas with a clear focus in response to questions	✓	✓
Support ideas with relevant evidence	✓	✓
Respond to other students' ideas, questions, and arguments	✓	✓
Skills: Incorporated into activities, questions, and discussion		
Revise ideas and evidence based on Shared Inquiry discussion	✓	✓

WRITING	BOOK ONE	BOOK TWO
Writing to learn: Explained and developed with guided practice		
Take notes about a story	✓	✓
Record personal responses to reading	✓	✓
Write interpretive questions about the story		✓
Write responses to questions before discussion	✓	✓
Revise responses after discussion	✓	✓
Write for various audiences and purposes	✓	✓
Expand on ideas raised in discussion	✓	✓
Write about story themes		✓
Write about literary elements such as character, plot, and setting		✓
Products: Explained and developed with guided practice		
Reflections and responses to reading	✓	✓
Descriptive paragraph	✓	✓
Story	✓	✓
Expository text	✓	✓
Personal narrative	✓	✓
Letter	✓	✓
Directions for how to do or make something		✓
Persuasive piece	✓	✓
Poem	✓	✓
Processes: Explained and developed with guided practice		
Generate and note original ideas for writing	✓	✓
Use discussion to generate and develop ideas	✓	✓
Brainstorm ideas as a class	✓	✓
Use graphic organizers to plan writing	✓	✓
Plan and organize ideas before writing	✓	✓

	BOOK ONE	BOOK TWO
Develop ideas before writing	✓	✓
Write a first draft	✓	✓
Revise writing in response to feedback	✓	✓

SPEAKING AND LISTENING	BOOK ONE	BOOK TWO
Listening: Incorporated into program activities		
Listen to comprehend stories read aloud	✓	✓
Set a purpose for listening (e.g., answer a question, consider new arguments)	✓	✓
Listen actively in discussion (e.g., sustain eye contact, listen without interruption)	✓	✓
Listen carefully to other students	✓	✓
Ask a speaker questions for clarification	✓	✓
Respond to other students' questions	✓	✓
Paraphrase what other students have said	✓	✓
Listen for differing ideas	✓	✓
Speaking: Incorporated into program activities		
Speak clearly	✓	✓
Participate in discussion	✓	✓
Identify ways to improve group participation	✓	✓
Ask questions to learn more about other students' ideas	✓	✓
Maintain a clear focus	✓	✓
Respond to other students	✓	✓
Rephrase or explain to help listeners understand	✓	✓
Speak directly to individuals within the group	✓	✓
Agree and disagree constructively	✓	✓

APPENDIX C: LEADER AIDS (REPRODUCIBLE MASTERS)

The following leader aids were developed to enrich your Junior Great Books experience:

THE FIVE GUIDELINES FOR SHARED INQUIRY DISCUSSION (PAGE 426)

Guidelines for you to review with your class from time to time.

OUR COLLABORATION (PAGE 427)

A form you can use to help your class consider what makes a good Shared Inquiry discussion.

STAGE 4: REFLECT AND CONNECT (PAGE 428)

Pages to distribute to students for the reading comprehension activity.

STAGE 5: REFLECT AND CONNECT (PAGE 430)

Pages to distribute to students for the Shared Inquiry discussion and story-to-story comparison activities.

STAGE 6: REFLECT AND CONNECT (PAGE 432)

Pages to distribute to students for the reading comprehension activity.

FOLLOW-UP QUESTIONS (PAGE 434)

A list of follow-up questions from units 1 through 7.

LETTER TO PARENTS AND GUARDIANS (PAGE 435)

A letter you can personalize and send home, to let your students' families know how to support their children in Junior Great Books.

THE FIVE GUIDELINES
FOR
SHARED INQUIRY DISCUSSION

1. Read the story carefully before participating in the discussion.

2. Discuss only the story everyone has read.

3. Support your ideas with evidence from the story.

4. Listen to other participants and respond to them directly.

5. Expect the leader to only ask questions.

NAME _____ DATE _____

Our Collaboration

For each pair of statements, rate our whole group in Shared Inquiry discussion by circling one of the numbers. A ⑤ means you agree strongly with the statement to the left of the row of numbers. A ① means you agree strongly with the statement to the right. We will discuss our responses together so that you can offer examples and suggestions for ways we can all improve.

Almost all of us contribute.	5 4 3 2 1	A few people do most of the talking.
We come up with many different ideas about the story.	5 4 3 2 1	We all tend to say the same thing.
We try to back up our ideas with details from the story.	5 4 3 2 1	We just state our ideas and don't explain where they come from.
We listen and comment on one another's ideas.	5 4 3 2 1	We don't pay much attention to what others say.
When asked, we try to explain our ideas and make them clearer to others.	5 4 3 2 1	It's hard for us to say more about our ideas.
We're interested and learn a lot.	5 4 3 2 1	We aren't interested and don't learn much.

Our goals for next time:

_____

_____

_____

YOUR NAME _____

YOUR PARTNER'S NAME _____

Stage 4: Reflect and Connect

Write two inferences you make as you read the story you chose. Then switch stories with your partner and write two inferences you make about that story.

> **Inferences** can help you figure out things that are not directly stated in the story. To make an inference, you combine clues in the story with your own ideas.

FIRST STORY TITLE: _____

An inference you made: _____

_____

_____ page _____, paragraph _____

If your partner made an inference about this passage, how was it similar and how was it different?

_____

_____

_____

An inference you made: _____

_____

_____ page _____, paragraph _____

CONTINUE ⟶

If your partner made an inference about this passage, how was it similar and how was it different?

_____

_____

_____

SECOND STORY TITLE: _____

An inference you made: _____

_____

_____ **page** _____, **paragraph** _____

If your partner made an inference about this passage, how was it similar and how was it different?

_____

_____

_____

An inference you made: _____

_____

_____ **page** _____, **paragraph** _____

If your partner made an inference about this passage, how was it similar and how was it different?

_____

_____

_____

YOUR NAME _____

YOUR PARTNER'S NAME _____

Stage 5: Reflect and Connect

Our focus question is from the story (*circle one*):

THE UPSIDE-DOWN BOY　　　**THE GREEN MAN**　　　**THE UGLY DUCKLING**

Complete the diagram below with a partner. Look through the story and your Reader's Journal pages to help you.

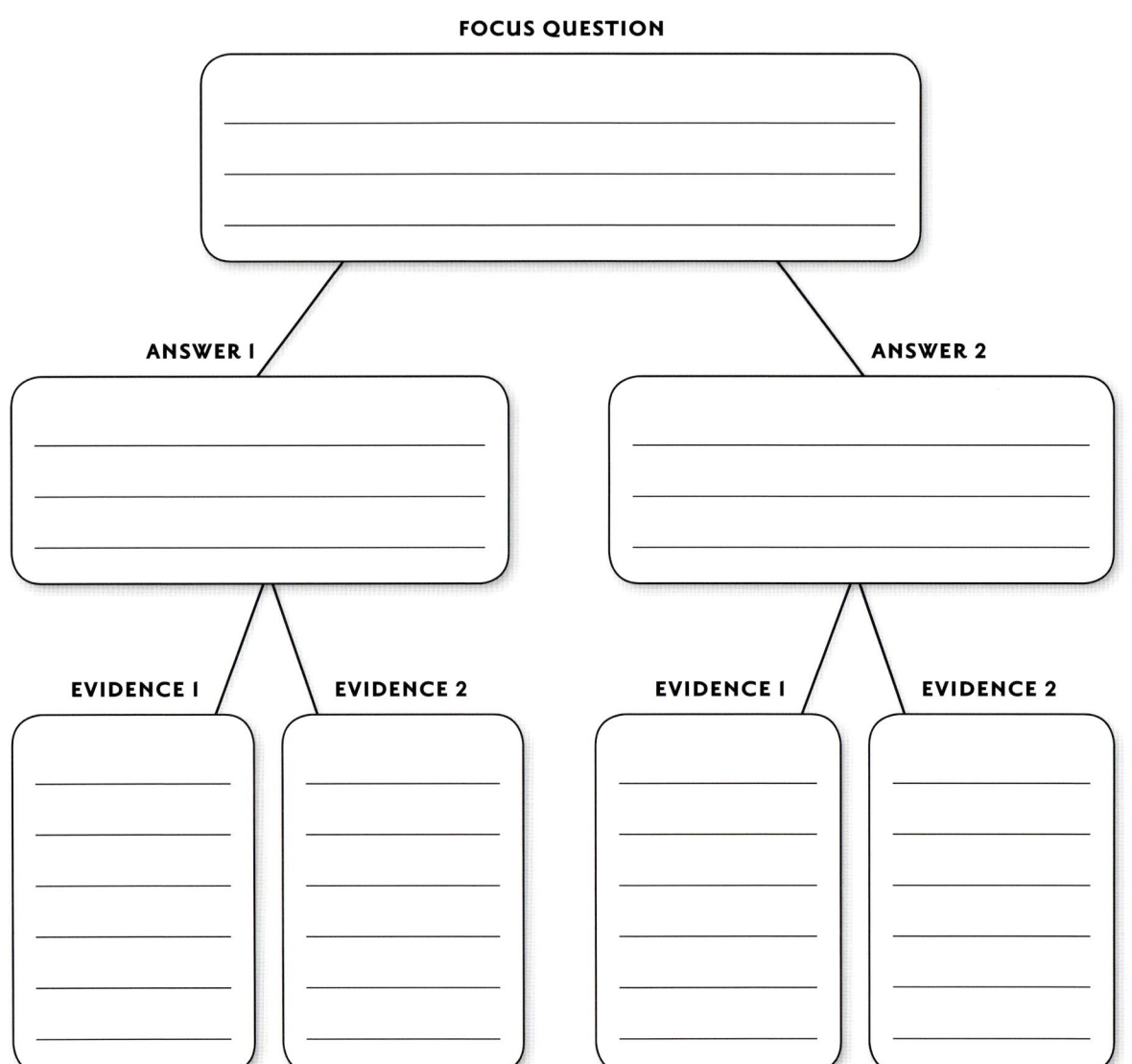

REPRODUCIBLE MASTER © 2006 by The Great Books Foundation

NAME _____ DATE _____

Stage 5: Reflect and Connect

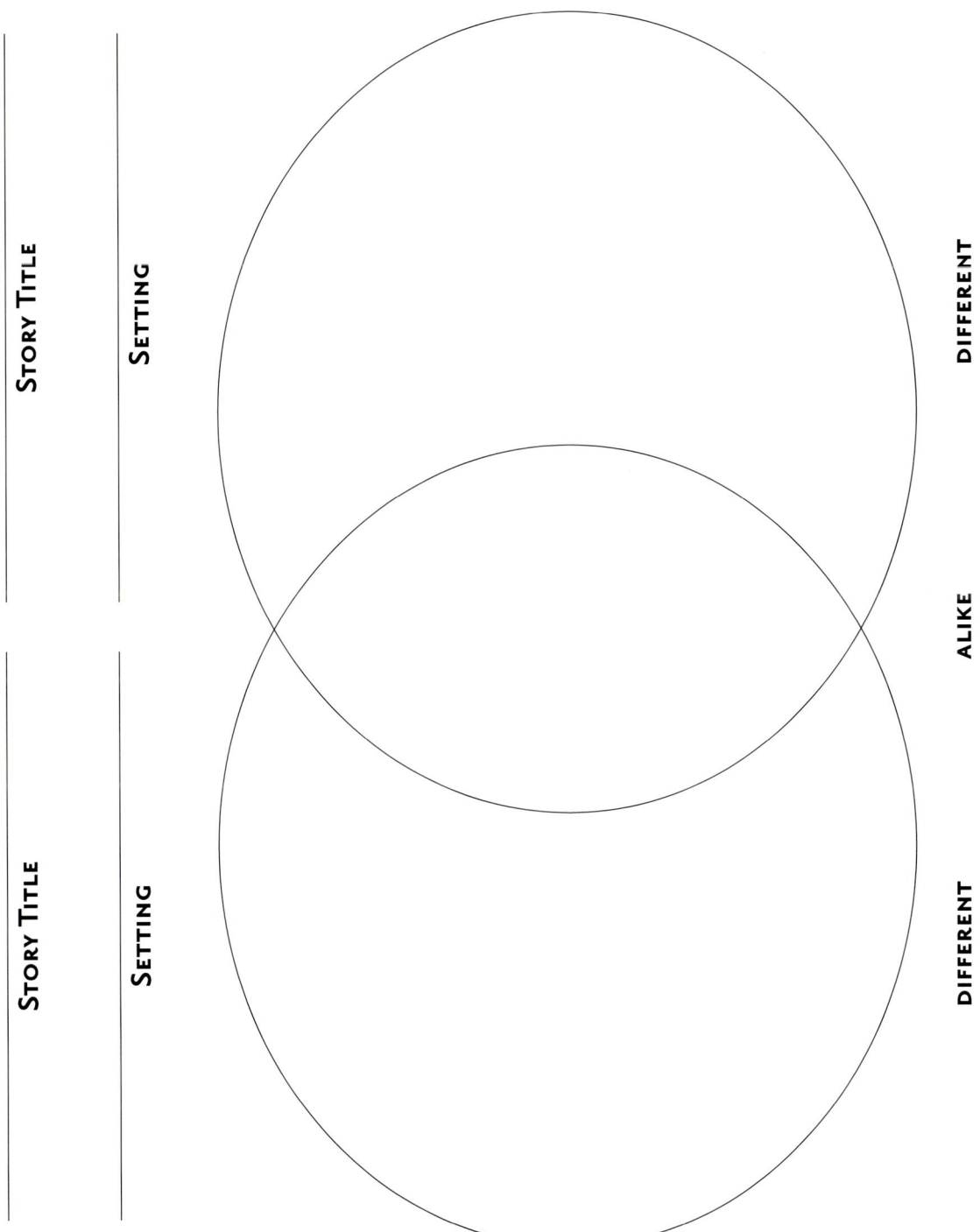

STORY TITLE

SETTING

STORY TITLE

SETTING

DIFFERENT

ALIKE

DIFFERENT

GROUP MEMBERS' NAMES _____

_____

Stage 6: Reflect and Connect

Circle the story you wish to retell in a big book:

WHITE WAVE	THE MOUSEWIFE
HOW THE TORTOISE BECAME	TWO WISE CHILDREN

Retell important parts of the story on the lines below the boxes. In the boxes, sketch an idea for a picture to go along with the words you write.

_____   _____

_____   _____

_____   _____

CONTINUE ⟶

Follow-up Questions

While students are sharing their notes after the second reading it is an ideal time for you to practice asking different kinds of follow-up questions. Sample questions in each unit of stages 4 and 5 are targeted to a particular area of critical thinking: developing meaningful **ideas**, supporting ideas with **evidence**, or **responding** to the ideas of others. Unit 7 offers questions targeted to helping students add depth to their reasoning. Below is a chart of follow-up questions, collected under the three key areas of critical thinking. Use this chart to plan your strategy for follow-up questioning during the second reading as well as Shared Inquiry discussion, particularly in units 8, 9, and 10.

IDEA	EVIDENCE	RESPONSE
Clarifying Ideas • How does this passage show that? • Who has a different idea about the passage? • When you say that character is being bad, what do you mean by "bad"?	**Seeing Evidence in Different Ways** • Is there a particular word or phrase that supports your opinion? • How does that word or phrase support your opinion? • Does anyone see this passage differently?	**Commenting on Classmates' Ideas** • Why did you mark this place with a different note than Amir did? • Do you have a question for Kwan about the way he marked that passage? • Did you mark this place for the same reason Joan did?
Explaining Ideas • What part of that passage made you mark it with a note? • What makes that phrase interesting to you? • What is another way for you to say that?	**Providing Precise Evidence** • Which words or phrases in this passage help you understand that about the character? • Are there certain words or phrases that tell you how the character is changing? • What else does the character do or say to lead you to think that?	**Connecting Students' Ideas** • Why do you agree with the way Jason marked that passage? • Did you mark it that way for the same reason Deborah did? • Can you ask Cai to explain the part of her idea that you don't understand?

ADDING DEPTH TO REASONING
• How does the passage that Teddy just read fit in with what you just said, Kwan? • In that case, what do you think of the point that Tasha made? • Since you think the passage you marked means that, how would you mark this passage over here?

Dear Parent or Guardian:

Our class is using Junior Great Books in our reading program. In Junior Great Books, I guide students through reading a story carefully, asking questions about the story, taking notes about ideas in the story, discussing the story together, and writing about some of the things we discussed. Junior Great Books has been an active part of language arts programs in schools across the country for about fifty years. The program fosters a love and appreciation of literature, encouraging young learners to become lifelong readers. It also closely aligns with our core language arts standards.

Our story this week is _____ .

You can help your child excel with Junior Great Books in three ways:

1. Spend time at home reading together, or have your child read out loud to you. Your child can read aloud while you drive, make dinner, or shop for groceries. If your child finds some words hard to read, encourage him or her to try to figure them out and keep reading.

2. Ask your child to tell you about the story. Here are some questions you can ask:

   ◆ Can you tell me more about the story? And what happened then?

   ◆ Who is your favorite character? Why?

   ◆ What do you like about the story? What don't you like about it?

   ◆ Does the story remind you of anything you've done or seen? Does it remind you of another story you've heard or read?

3. Listen to and enjoy what your child has to tell you!

Please let me know if you have any questions, or if you have suggestions or information that I can use to help your child with Junior Great Books.

Sincerely,